MW01676235

剑桥雅思最新真题题源详解

——写作（学术类）

（第二版）

刘民　编著

中国人民大学出版社
·北京·

编　委　会

（排名不分先后）

IELTS 第二版前言

在 2011 年第一季度的 12 次雅思考试中，有 7 次考试的议论文写作题目是以前年度考题的“原题重现”或以“类似考题”的形式重现。具体日期如下(考题回顾及范文见本书内文部分)：

考试日期	原题日期	考试日期	原题日期
2011 年 1 月 8 日	2010 年 3 月 20 日	2011 年 2 月 19 日	2010 年 4 月 15 日
2011 年 1 月 22 日	2010 年 8 月 5 日	2011 年 2 月 26 日	2008 年 2 月 23 日
	2010 年 1 月 30 日		2007 年 6 月 16 日
	2009 年 12 月 9 日	2011 年 3 月 19 日	2009 年 12 月 12 日
	2005 年 1 月 22 日		2008 年 11 月 15 日
2011 年 2 月 12 日	2008 年 11 月 20 日		2008 年 10 月 23 日
	2007 年 6 月 2 日		
2011 年 2 月 17 日	2010 年 1 月 14 日		
	2006 年 4 月 29 日		

这就再次提示我们要特别注意以下两点：

第一，对于 2008 年到 2011 年曾经考过的题目要格外重视；

第二，掌握历年考题的范文和句型对提高雅思写作成绩至关重要。

本书出版后，其中的很多题目在后来的考试中“重现”，被广大考生誉为“雅思写作真题押题宝典”。具体重现日期统计如下（考题回顾及范文见本书内文部分）：

考试日期	重现日期	考试日期	重现日期
2008 年 4 月 24 日	2009 年 1 月 15 日	2008 年 6 月 21 日	2010 年 5 月 20 日
2008 年 9 月 6 日	2009 年 10 月 8 日	2008 年 9 月 27 日	2010 年 6 月 5 日
2009 年 2 月 21 日	2009 年 10 月 31 日	2008 年 10 月 23 日	2010 年 5 月 15 日
2008 年 1 月 12 日	2009 年 9 月 17 日	2008 年 8 月 21 日	2010 年 6 月 26 日
2009 年 3 月 5 日	2009 年 8 月 22 日	2008 年 12 月 20 日	2010 年 8 月 21 日
2008 年 1 月 10 日	2010 年 3 月 27 日	2008 年 10 月 11 日	2010 年 9 月 16 日
	2010 年 9 月 25 日	2009 年 1 月 10 日	2010 年 1 月 23 日
	2010 年 11 月 4 日		2010 年 2 月 27 日

本书自出版以来，受到了广大考生的热烈欢迎，此次再版，又加入了 22 篇真题，并标明了具体考试日期。这些题目都是当前考试的热点，在

以后的考试中还会不断重复出现。提前演练这些题目并掌握书中的范文和句型，可使备考更有针对性，对于提高写作水平和成绩起到事半功倍的作用。

编著者

于 2011 年 6 月

IELTS

第一版前言

透视雅思写作重题

近年来，雅思考试学术类写作 TASK 2 部分多次原题重现。以 2008 年为例，在 2008 年第一季度的前 11 次雅思考试中，我们发现绝大多数的考题还是属于“中规中矩”的常规话题，属于历年雅思考试中常见的几大类话题，如教育类、犯罪类、文化类和政府责任类等。甚至有几道考题几乎是过去考题的翻版，其中有三次比较明显，那就是：2008 年 1 月 12 日考题是 2007 年 10 月 25 日考题的重现；2008 年 2 月 2 日考题是 2005 年 9 月 17 和 2006 年 5 月 27 日考题的重现；尤其是 2008 年 2 月 23 日考题，分别在 2005 年 11 月 12 日、2007 年 4 月 28 日和 2007 年 6 月 16 日以原题或类似考题的形式多次重复出现。

这就给我们以下三个提示：第一，以后的雅思考试写作出题会趋于稳定；第二，对于 2008 年所有曾经考过的题目要格外重视，尤其是 TASK 2 中的题目；第三，许多所谓的新题很可能就是 2008 年及以前老题的翻版甚至是原题重现。因此，熟练掌握 2008 年及以前年度重点考题的试题、范文、重点词汇、实用题型及历年曾经出现的原题或类似考题，是考生快速取得高分的关键。

本书的几大特点

1. 原题重现

本书囊括了 2009 年部分题目、2008 年的全部考题及以前年度的部分重点题目，每道题目都是真实考试题目的回顾，大部分还注明了考试日期，这些题目在以后的考试中重复出现的频率极高，有很多题目甚至会原题重现，并且这些题目与《剑桥雅思全真试题 3—6》中的题目完全属于同等级别，具有最高的权威性。

2. 高分范文

针对考试原题，书中所给范文字字斟酌，用词丰富；句句推敲，句式多样；框架清晰，供考生临摹。这些范文都配有相应的译文，方便考生快速理解和模仿。

3. 实用句型

这些句型结构具有广泛的应用价值，除了在范文中使用，在很多其他的文章中也可以用到，因此又称万能句型。熟练掌握这些句型结构，就可以举一反三，以不变应万变。

4. 闪光词汇

所列出的词汇不一定是最有难度的词汇，但一定是最恰当、最丰富的词汇，并且都配有例句，帮助考生理解、记忆并熟练应用。因此，闪光的不仅仅是词汇，更是分数。

5. 类似考题

类似的考题，是指以前曾经出过的原题或者是类似的题目。下次考试，题目很可能是以前出现过的。写作其实绝大部分是“老题”的翻版甚至“原题重现”。

总之，本书以历次考试信息为核心资源，资料来源精准权威，直击考试得分点，结合名师多年高分辅导实用技能，帮助考生真正达到事半功倍的效果。

刘　民

第一篇 2011—2008年议论文

第二篇　历年高频话题

第三篇 图表作文

第一篇

2011—2008 年议论文

Unit 1

Education and Learning

教育与学习

2011 年 3 月 10 日考题回顾

孩子应该几岁入学

WRITING TASK 2

You should spend about 40 minutes on this task.

Write about the following topic:

> ***In some countries, children start school at the age of seven, so they could have more time to build relationship with their parents. In other countries, some people think that children should start school as young as possible. Discuss both views and give your own opinion.***

Give reasons for your answer and include any relevant examples from your own knowledge or experience.

Write at least 250 words.

题目解释

在一些国家，孩子 7 岁入学，因此他们有更多的时间建立与父母的关系。而在其他国家，有些人却认为孩子要尽早入学。讨论这两种观点并给出你自己的意见。

高分范文

Nowadays, there have always been some heated debates as to whether we should let our children go to school at the age of seven or earlier. Some take the view that the earlier the kids receive their education, the better it will be. However, when it comes to my personal perspective, the issue discussed here is such a delicate one that I am confident with kids' initiating their education at the age of seven for the following two reasons.

To start with, the first point that we have to make it clear is that the involvement in gaining education for our kids in a quite early age does not mean being efficient in knowledge. Namely, starting schooling earlier does not imply children can learn more. Having our children receive formal education as early as possible is exerting a negative impact on their academic performance and frustrating their studying passion. Because, to some degree, the development of children's intelligence cannot match with their learning abilities, which, in turn, can be a curse rather than blessing. As the universally-known adage goes, "Rome was not built in a day," which exhorts us to obey the appropriate principle of small children's development, both physically and psychologically.

The second factor is in relation with the status quo of the financial conditions of families and society. Apparently, starting schooling at 7 saves educational budget, facility costs as well as resources payment.

Admittedly, to those who are outstanding and extremely talented, it is advisable to show some respect to their personal development; however, so seldom do we witness this kind of children. In contrast, it is desirable for us to get children cultivated at the age of seven. As a satisfying result, the educational effect will be doubled instead of bringing them some obstacles and frustration to the development of their future.

范文翻译

如今，对于是否应该让孩子7岁或在更小的时候入学一直存在着一些激烈的争论。有些人认为孩子越早接受教育越好。然而，从个人的观点来看，这个议题非常微妙，基于以下两个原因，我对孩子7岁开始接受教育非常有信心。

首先，我们必须明确的一点是，让我们的孩子在较早的年龄就开始接受教育并不意味着在学习知识方面就有效率。也就是说，早点开始教育并不意味着孩子可以学到更多知识。让孩子尽早接受正规教育对他们的学术表现会产生负面影响，使他们丧失学习的热情。因为，在一定程度上，孩子的智力发育不能与他们的学习能力相匹配，这反过来可能是祸而不是福。正如著名的谚语所说，“罗马并非一日之功”，这告诫我们要遵循儿童的发展规律，不管是生理上的还是心理上的。

第二个原因与家庭和社会的现实经济条件有关。显然，7岁开始上学可以节省教育经费、设施成本以及资源成本。

诚然，对于那些与众不同、智商极高的小孩，我提倡尊重他们的个人发展；然而，我们所见的这样的孩子太少了。相反，让大多数小孩7岁开始受教育更值得我们赞同，教育的结果将会事半功倍，而并非给他们的未来发展带来障碍和挫折。

闪光词汇

★ **delicate** ['delikit] *adj*. 微妙的
This is a **delicate** diplomatic question. 这是一个微妙的外交问题。

★ **frustrate** [frʌs'treit] *v*. 挫败
The police **frustrated** the bandit's attempt to rob the bank. 警方挫败了匪徒抢劫银行的企图。

★ **adage** ['ædidʒ] *n*. 谚语
Remember the old **adage**—buy cheap, buy twice! 记住那句俗语：便宜无好货。

★ **cultivate** ['kʌltiveit] *vt*. 培养
One should **cultivate** good manners from childhood. 一个人应该从小就要学习讲礼貌。

实用句型

1. **Nowadays, there have always been some heated debates as to whether**... 如今，对于是否……一直存在着一些激烈的争论。这种句型一般用于第一段开头，介绍背景，同时引出话题。
请看范文中的这句话：
Nowadays, there have always been some heated debates as to whether we should let our children go to school at the age of seven or earlier. 如今，对于是否应该让孩子7岁或在更小的时候入学一直存在着一些激烈的争论。
2. **However, when it comes to my personal perspective, the issue discussed here is such a delicate one that I am... for the following two reasons.** 然而，从个人的观点来看，这个议题非常微妙，基于以下两个原因，我……。这种句型一般用于第一段，用来表明作者的观点，同时引出下文。
请看范文中的这句话：
However, when it comes to my personal perspective, the issue discussed here is such a delicate one that I am confident with kids, initiating their education at the age of seven for the following two reasons. 然而，从个人的观点来看，这个议题非常微妙，基于以下两个原因，我对孩子7岁开始接受教育非常有信心。
3. **To start with, the first point that we have to make it clear is that**... 首先，我们必须明确的一点是，……。这种句型一般用做第二段的中心句，表示开始分析支持作者观点的第一个理由。
请看范文中的这句话：
To start with, the first point that we have to make it clear is that the involvement in gaining education for our kids in a quite early age does not mean being efficient in knowledge. 首先，我们必须明确的一点是，让我们的孩子在较早的年龄就开始接受教育并不意味着在学

习知识方面就有效率。

4. **The second factor is in relation with** ... 第二个原因与……有关。这种句型一般用做第三段的中心句，表示开始分析支持作者观点的第二个理由。

请看范文中的这句话：

The second factor is in relation with the status quo of the financial conditions of families and society. 第二个原因与家庭和社会的现实经济条件有关。

2010年5月8日考题回顾

各种课程对职业的重要性

WRITING TASK 2

You should spend about 40 minutes on this task.

Write about the following topic：

> ***Schools should teach students some academic subjects which will be beneficial to their future careers. Therefore，other subjects such as music and sports are not important.***
>
> ***To what extent do you agree or disagree with this opinion?***

Give reasons for your answer and include any relevant examples from your own knowledge or experience.

Write at least 250 words.

题目解释

学校应该教学生一些对他们未来的职业有帮助的学术课程。因此，其他的科目，例如音乐课和体育课是不重要的。你在多大程度上同意或不同意这种观点？

高分范文

Recently, whether schools should concentrate on academic classes has triggered a heated discussion. Some people contend that career-oriented education for students should be encouraged and schools should mainly provide academic classes. But there are also a majority of people who suggest that personality-oriented education is necessary and music and sports classes should also be offered. Personally, I am inclined to be on the side of the latter for the following reasons.

On the one hand, if schools only taught academic classes, the school life would definitely be monotonous and boring. No one can tolerate such tough days. Most students treasure their happy years in school because they are colorful and diversified.

On the other hand, music and sports lessons are extremely important to students. To start with, sports and music can accompany one throughout his life. Some students may forget the academic knowledge learned at school, but they will not forget how to do sports and appreciate music. Furthermore, music classes can cultivate one's mind and temperament, which are helpful in building one's optimistic personality. Sports can help students keep fit and build up strong character. Last but not least, sports and music can raise one's taste. People with good taste of music and sports usually keep away from bad behaviors.

Based on the above discussion and analysis, we can see that academic classes are not as important as some people think, and music and sports classes are not useless, either. Academic classes develop one's ability; music and sports classes improve one's personality charm. In contemporary society, only able persons with fine character and moral win the career game.

范文翻译

最近，是否学校应该致力于学术课程引起了热烈的讨论。一些人主张，对学生进行以职业为导向的教育应该受到鼓励，学校应该主要提供学术课程。但是也有很多人建议以人格为导向的教育是必要的，音乐和体育课程也应该开设。就我个人而言，我倾向于后者，理由如下。

一方面，如果学校只教学术课程，那么学校生活必定单调和无聊。没有人能忍受那样枯燥的日子。大多数学生珍惜他们在学校的美好岁月，是因为学校生活丰富多彩。

另一方面，音乐和体育课程对学生来说极为重要。首先，体育和音乐将陪伴一个人的一生。一些学生可能会忘记在学校所学的学术知识，但他们不会忘记如何参加体育活动以及如何欣赏音乐。而且，音乐课能够培养一个人的精神和气质，这有助于他们形成乐观的人格。体育能帮助学生保持健康，形成坚强的性格。最后但不是最不重要的是，体育和音乐可以提高一个人的品味。对音乐和运动有较高品味的人一般会远离不良行为。

基于上述讨论和分析，我们能够明白学术课不像某些人认为的那样重要，而音乐和体育也不是毫无用处。学术课程发展一个人的能力；音乐课和体育课增强一个人的人格魅力。在当代社会，只有有能力又有良好的性格和道德的人才会取得职业生涯的成功。

闪光词汇

★ **concentrate on** 专心，把思想集中于

Many firms are **concentrating on** increasing their markets overseas. 许多公司正在集中精力开拓它们的海外市场。

★ **monotonous** [mə'nɔtənəs] *adj*. 单调的，无变化的

She thought life in the small town was **monotonous**. 她觉得小镇上的生活单调而乏味。

★ **tolerate** ['tɔləreit] *vt*. 忍受，容忍

She cannot **tolerate** that rude fellow. 她不能容忍那个粗鲁的家伙。

★ **treasure** ['treʒə] *vt*. 珍爱，珍惜

I certainly **treasure** the friendship between us very much. 我当然非常珍视我们之间的友谊。

★ **temperament** ['tempərəmənt] *n*. 气质，性情

Success often depends on **temperament**. 成功常常取决于一个人的性格。

★ **keep fit** 保持健康

We work out regularly to **keep fit**. 我们坚持锻炼以保持健康。

实用句型

1. **Some people contend that**...**But there are also a majority of people who suggest that**... 一些人主张……，但是也有很多人建议……。这种句型常用于第一段，介绍双方观点。

请看范文中的这句话：

Some people contend that career-oriented education for students should be encouraged and schools should mainly provide academic classes. **But there are also a majority of people who suggest that** personality-oriented education is necessary and music and sports classes should also be offered. 一些人主张，对学生进行以职业为导向的教育应该受到鼓励，学校应该主要提供理论课程。但是也有很多人建议以人格为导向的教育是必要的，音乐和体育课程也应该开设。

2. **Personally, I am inclined to be on the side of the latter one in the following reasons.** 个人而言，我倾向于后者，理由如下。这个句型一般用于开头段最后一句，表明作者赞成哪一方的观点，同时引出下文。

类似考题

2005年3月5日

Some academic subjects are useful for children's future careers, while some subjects such as music and sports are not useful. What's your opinion?

2007年7月7日

In some countries, schools aim to provide a general education across a range of subjects. In other countries, children focus on a narrow range of subjects related to a particular career. For today's world, which of these systems is more appropriate?

2008年3月1日

Schools offer a wide range of courses such as physical education, music, economics, philosophy, math, English, geography, physics and history. Among all these subjects, which one do you think is the most important and which one is the least important?

2008年5月22日

Some people think that schools should concentrate on academic classes, because they are helpful for future career. But they think music and sports classes are not useful. To what extent do you agree or disagree?

2008年6月5日

Some people think that university students should specialize in one subject, while others think universities should encourage students to learn a range of subjects. Discuss both views and give your opinion.

2008年7月5日

Nowadays, more university students choose to study some practical subjects (such as marketing, computer programming, etc.) instead of theoretical subjects (such as economy, math, chemistry, etc.). Some people suggest that universities should focus on practical subjects, but not theoretical subjects. Do you agree or disagree?

2010 年 5 月 15 日考题回顾

远程学习和上大学的利弊

WRITING TASK 2

You should spend about 40 minutes on this task.

Write about the following topic:

> ***Many people use distance-learning programs to study at home, but some people think that it cannot bring the benefit as much as attending college or university. To what extent do you agree or disagree?***

Give reasons for your answer and include any relevant examples from your own knowledge or experience.

Write at least 250 words.

题目解释

许多人利用远程教育课程在家学习，但是一些人认为这不如上大学好。你是否同意这种观点？

高分范文

With the development of distance education，a large number of students choose distance-learning programmes which enable them to study at home. But some people think that studying in college or university is better than using distance-learning programmes. As for me，benefits and disadvantages of each side should be carefully examined.

The main advantage of using distance-learning programmes to study is convenience. The students just stay at home instead of going to school by any means of transportation. And then，I think using distance-learning programmes can improve their ability to study independently. The disadvantage is that they cannot find and correct their mistakes timely which may lead the students to indolence. And credibility is another crucial issue. There are more and more private and public，non-profit and profit-oriented institutions offering courses and degree programs through distance education. However，some of them have received little outside supervision，and some of them may be fraudulent diploma mills. In this case，students need to be very careful while making choices.

If studying in college or university，the students can communicate with the teachers face to face. And the teachers can work out plans which are suitable for students. Moreover，the surroundings of the college or university enable the students to relax when they feel very tense and they can discuss problems with their classmates. But some students must spend much time going to school since they live far away.

To sum up，there are more advantages in learning in college or university than taking a distance-learning programme，and the disadvantages of distance education mentioned above can also be properly avoided by universities and colleges.

范文翻译

随着远程教育的发展，大量学生选择远程学习课程，这样他们就可以待在家里学习。但是，有些人认为在大学学习比利用远程教育课程学习更好。在我看来，应该仔细衡量两者的优点和缺点。

利用远程教育课程学习的主要优点就是方便。学生只需要待在家里，不用乘任何交通工具去学校。而且，我认为，利用远程教育课程学习能够提高学生独立学习的能力。缺点是不能及时发现和纠正错误，这可能导致学生的懒惰。可信度是另外一个非常重要的因素。通过远程教育提供课程和授予学位的私人的、公共的、非盈利的和盈利的机构变得越来越多。然而，其中的一些机构很少受到外界的监督，还有一些可能是欺诈性的学位加工厂。在这种情况下，学生们在做选择的时候应该非常小心。

在大学里学习，学生可以和老师进行面对面的交流。老师可以给学生制定出适合他们的计划。而且，大学的环境能使学生们在感到紧张的时候放松，还可以和同学讨论问题。但是一些住得远的学生必须花费时间去学校。

总之，在大学学习比利用远程教育课程学习有更多的优点。上面提到的远程教育的缺点在大学里也可以很好地避免。

闪光词汇

★ **convenient** [kən'viːnjənt] *adj.* 便利的，方便的

We must arrange a **convenient** time and place for the meeting. 我们必须安排一个合适的时间和地点开会。

★ **fraudulent** ['frɔːdjulənt] *adj.* 欺诈的

He got the job of science teacher by **fraudulent** means. 他用欺骗手法取得了理科教员的职位。

★ **suitable for** 适合……的

The weather is **suitable for** outdoor activities. 天气适合户外活动。

实用句型

To sum up, there are more advantages in...**and the disadvantages of**...**can also be probably avoided by**... 总之，……有很多的优点，缺点也可能通过……避免。

雅思写作中，题目经常要求对某种社会话题进行讨论，讨论的过程就是分析优点和缺点的过程。分析完毕，就需要在最后一段对所有分析的内容进行总结，上面的这个句型就是用来做这种总结的很好的结构。

请看范文中的这句话：

To sum up, there are more advantages in learning in college or university than taking a distance-learning programme, **and the disadvantages of** distance education mentioned above **can also be properly avoided by** universities and colleges. 总之，在大学学习比利用远程教育课程学习有更多的优点。上面提到的远程教育的缺点在大学里也可以很好地避免。

类似考题

2004 年 11 月 13 日

Many people use distance-learning programmes (study material post, TV, Internet...) to study at home, but some people think that it can not bring the benefit as much as attending college or university. Do you agree or disagree?

2008 年 10 月 23 日

Many people use distance-learning programs to study at home, but some people think that it cannot bring the benefit as much as attending college or university. To what extent do you agree or disagree?

2008 年 11 月 15 日

More and more people work or study at home with the development of computer technology. Do you think it is a positive or negative development?

2010 年 5 月 20 日考题回顾

孩子应该遵守规则还是应该少受控制

WRITING TASK 2

You should spend about 40 minutes on this task.

Write about the following topic：

> ***Some people think that children should obey rules or do what their parents and teachers want them to do. But others think that children controlled too much cannot deal with problems well by themselves. Discuss both views and give your own opinion.***

Give reasons for your answer and include any relevant examples from your own knowledge or experience.

Write at least 250 words.

题目解释

一些人认为，孩子应该遵守规则，或者去做父母和老师希望他们做的事情，但是另一些人认为，受到控制太多的孩子不能够很好地自己处理问题。讨论这两种观点并表明你的看法。

高分范文

As we know，the process of growing up is very complex for every child. So a sizable percent of people assert that children should observe rules or that parents and teachers should plan their children's action carefully. However，quite a few people hold the view that children who are controlled too much cannot deal with problems well by themselves. Actually，the two viewpoints stand with reasons to some extent.

Children are different from adults. They do not know how to distinguish between right and wrong. In order to protect them，schools establish rules and daily action criteria. Children must learn to discipline themselves，and observe rules and regulations. Meanwhile，parents should influence their children by example and force of character and teachers should also maintain discipline in the classroom；otherwise，children will be uncontrollable and may do harm to others and society. This may result in the sharp rise in the rate of juvenile delinquency.

On the other hand，children disciplined strictly may rely on their parents and teachers for everything and cannot deal with problems properly by themselves. So adults should give children some freedom and be the children's guides，partners，or competitors. They should encourage them to "try，and try again" when children do their best to deal with problems.

Generally speaking，the growth of children should not be overlooked. They need care，protection and discipline. When children are young and raw，more control will help them to accumulate knowledge. When they are older and knowledgeable，timely and proper advice and directions help them to improve ability. That is to say，parents and teachers should control the children properly but not poorly.

范文翻译

我们知道，每个孩子的成长过程都是非常复杂的。因此，有相当大的一部分人声称，孩子应该遵守规则，或者父母和老师应该严格规范孩子们的行为。但是，相当的一部分人持有这样的观点，那就是受到控制太多的孩子不能够很好地自己处理问题。实际上，这两种观点在某种程度上都有一定的道理。

孩子不同于成年人，他们不懂得辨别是非。为了保护孩子，学校制定了纪律和日常行为规范。孩子必须学会约束自己，遵守规章制度。同时，父母应该以身作则，通过人格力量影响孩子，老师也应该在课堂上维持纪律，否则，孩子就会无法无天而且可能做出对别人和社会有害的事情。这可能会导致青少年犯罪的急剧增加。

另一方面，受到控制太多的孩子可能事事都依赖父母和老师，不能够很好地自己处理问题。因此，大人应该给孩子一些自由并且成为孩子的向导、伙伴甚至竞争者。他们应该在孩子尽自己最大努力处理问题的时候鼓励他们“努力，再努力”。

总的说来，孩子的成长不应该被忽视，他们需要关心、爱护和约束。孩子年轻稚嫩的时候，更多的控制可以帮助他们积累知识。当孩子长大且具备知识的时候，及时正确的建议和指导可以帮助他们增长能力。父母和老师应该恰当控制孩子而不是过分控制。

闪光词汇

★ **deal with** 处理

Deal with a man as he deals with you. 以其人之道，还治其人之身。

★ **viewpoint** ['vjuːˌpɔint] *n.* 观点

It fits completely my **viewpoint**. 它完全符合我的观点。

★ **extent** [iks'tent] *n.* 范围，程度

To some **extent** you are correct. 在某种程度上你是正确的。

★ **different from** 异于

My idea is **different from** yours. 我的想法跟你的不同。

★ **distinguish between** 区别

We should **distinguish between** right and wrong. 我们应该明辨是非。

★ **juvenile delinquency** 少年犯罪

Now she returned to the subject of **juvenile delinquency** in that country. 现在她又回过来讲那个国家少年犯罪的问题。

实用句型

Actually, the two viewpoints stand with reasons to some extent. 实际上，这两种观点在某种程度上都有一定的道理。

雅思写作中，很多大作文考题都要求考生针对题目中给出的两种对立的观点进行讨论。其实，两种观点无非是见仁见智，并没有标准答案，其实说的无非是同意事物的两个不同的方面，所以都会有一定的道理。上面的句子可用于第一段的末尾，起承上启下的作用。

类似考题

2008 年 6 月 21 日

Some people think that children should obey rules or do what their parents and teachers want them to do. But others think that children controlled too much cannot deal with problems well by themselves. Discuss both views and give your own opinion.

2008 年 10 月 11 日

Society is based on rules and laws. It could not function if individuals were free to do whatever they want. To what extent do you agree or disagree?

2010 年 6 月 5 日考题回顾

农村学生上大学问题

WRITING TASK 2

You should spend about 40 minutes on this task.

Write about the following topic：

> ***Students from poor background such as rural areas often find it difficult to have access to university education，so some people think universities should make it especially easy for them to study at. To what extent do you agree or disagree?***

Give reasons for your answer and include any relevant examples from your own knowledge or experience.

Write at least 250 words.

题目解释

背景贫穷的学生例如农村地区的学生经常感到很难有接受大学教育的机会，因此，一些人认为，大学应该给这些学生提供特别容易的学习机会。你在多大程度上同意或不同意这一观点？

高分范文

Nowadays, an increasing number of students from rural areas have no access to university education, so some people contend that universities should offer especially easy opportunities for them to study at. I disagree with this opinion.

For every student, the opportunity should be equal. Privileges should not exist either for the poor or for the rich. I do not deny the fact that it is difficulty for the students from poor background to have access to university education, but it cannot be the reason to sacrifice fairness at the expense of millions of other students.

Actually, we can find some other approaches to fill the gap between the students from rural areas and students in cities. Firstly, the government should allocate more money for the education infrastructure constructions and facilities there. That will solve the problem from the roots. Secondly, we may send some excellent teachers to work in rural areas for one year or two. These teachers will bring the best learning methods to students from poor background. At the same time, the government should also take out some capital for the training of those teachers in rural areas. Only when the levels of teachers are improved, can the good achievements of the students there be a reality. And they will not feel it difficult to get access to university education.

So after pondering this question on many occasions, I have finally reached the conclusion that we should try our best to improve the study condition of rural areas. Privileges will not be good for those poor students' future development. Just as buildings will collapse soon if based on sand so without a solid foundation, students will lag behind even if they are allowed to study further.

范文翻译

如今，越来越多的农村地区的学生没有机会接受大学教育，因此一些人认为大学应该给这些学生提供特别容易的学习机会。我不同意这个观点。

对于每个学生来说，机会应该是均等的。特别待遇不应该存在，不管是对贫穷的还是富有的。我不否认贫困学生确实很难有机会接受大学教育，但这不应该成为牺牲成千上万其他学生公平竞争机会的理由。

实际上，我们可以找到其他的一些途径来弥补农村和城市学生之间的差距。首先，政府应该拨出更多的资金，用于那里的教育基础设施的建设和设备方面。这将从根本上解决问题。其次，我们可以派遣一些优秀的教师到农村地区工作一两年。这些老师会把最好的学习方法带给这些背景贫穷的学生。同时，政府也应该拿出一些资金培训那些农村地区的教师。只有老师的水平提高了，那里的学生取得好成绩才是现实。他们也不会感到很难有机会接受大学教育了。

反复考虑这个问题之后，我最后得出一个结论，那就是我们应当努力改善农村地区的学习环境。特别待遇对那些贫穷的学生将来的发展没有好处。就像建筑物，如果是建在沙滩上，很快就会坍塌。如果没有坚实的基础，就算可以接受更高的教育，学生们还是会落在后面。

闪光词汇

★ **access to** 有……机会，有权使用

Citizens may have free **access to** the library. 市民可以自由使用图书馆。

★ **privilege** ['privilidʒ] *n.* 特权，特别待遇

Education should not be considered to be a **privilege** in a modern society. 在一个现代社会中，受教育不应该被看成是一种特权。

★ **fill the gap** 弥合差距

I need to **fill the gap** in my knowledge. 我需要弥补知识上的不足。

★ **allocate** ['æləukeit] *vt.* 分派，分配

The Red Cross had **allocated** a large sum for the relief of the sufferers of the disaster. 红十字会拨出了很大一笔钱救济灾民。

实用句型

I do not deny...**but**... 我不否认……但是……

这是一种让步句型，是雅思议论文辩论方式的一种，既先用 I do not deny... 表示承认某种观点的合理性，然后再用 but... 加以反驳，目的是用来强调另一种观点的正确性。这种句型使文章结构清晰，论点全面，是一种非常有效的表达手段。如范文中的这段话：

I do not deny the fact **that** it is difficult for the students from poor background to access to university education, **but** it cannot be the reason to sacrifice fairness at the expense of millions of other students.

我不否认贫困学生确实很难有机会接受大学教育，但这不应该成为牺牲成千上万其他学生公平竞争机会的理由。

类似考题

2005 年 4 月 2 日

Pressure on the school and university students is increasing and students are pushed to hard work when they are young. Do you think it is a positive or negative development?

2008 年 9 月 27 日

Students from poor back ground such as rural areas often find it is difficult to have access to university education, so some people think universities should make it especially easy for them to study at. To what extent do you agree or disagree?

2010年12月18日考题回顾

传统教学法的未来

WRITING TASK 2

You should spend about 40 minutes on this task.

Write about the following topic：

Some people think that traditional teaching method with a teacher and students in a classroom will not exist by the year 2050. Do you agree or disagree?

Give reasons for your answer and include any relevant examples from your own knowledge or experience.

Write at least 250 words.

题目解释

一些人认为一位老师在教室教很多学生的传统教学法到2050年以后将不复存在。你同意还是不同意?

高分范文

The widespread of telecommunication technology has opened up a new range of possibilities for distance-learning. By gathering information from a wide variety of sources, such as the Internet, mobile phones, E-libraries, online training courses, students nowadays enjoy infinite and flexible access to knowledge. It is often argued that traditional teaching will die out someday in the future.

It has to be admitted that modern technology has a large number of benefits. It overcomes the geographical barriers and accelerates the flow of information, thus facilitating students' learning process and assisting them to take in information in a more efficient way. With access to the Internet, a huge amount of information and knowledge is just a click away. Moreover, online courses offer students greater flexibility and enable them to create a timetable in line with their specific needs. For students with physical handicaps and those who live far away from the school, online education is remarkably favorable.

However, communication technology is not very likely to replace a physical school if its drawbacks are not removed. Apart from knowledge and skills, young students in school also learn how to behave themselves, how to abide by rules and regulations of the society. In this sense, modern technology fails to function as effectively as a traditional teacher, who delivers ethical principles and moral values face to face. In addition, a computer or the Internet can only respond to questions which have been programmed into it, but fail to answer any unusual, non-standard and unprecedented question. By contrast, through timely interaction with a teacher, students can receive well-tailored answers.

My view is that conventional school teaching will keep its status as a dominant education provider. At the same time, students will also continue to make full use of various modern technologies as assistence or useful supplement to the teachers.

范文翻译

通信技术的普及为远程教育开辟了一系列新的可能。通过从各个渠道获取信息，如互联网、手机、电子图书馆、在线培训课程等，如今的学生可以通过多种方式灵活地获取无限的知识。经常有争论认为传统的教学方式在将来的某天会消失。

不得不承认现代科技有很大益处。它跨越了地理障碍，加速了信息流通，从而促进了学生的学习进程，并协助他们以更有效的方式获取信息。通过访问互联网，大量的信息和知识只需要一个点击即可获得。此外，在线课程为学生提供更大的灵活性，使他们能够根据自己的需求自行安排课程表。对于那些有生理缺陷和距离学校远的学生来说，网络教育是非常有利的。

然而，如果通信技术的不足不被消除，那么它是不大可能取代实体学校的。除了知识和技能，在校青年学生还要学习如何做人，如何遵守社会规章制度。从这个意义上讲，现代技术则不如传统教师有用，教师能面对面地向学生传达道德准则和价值观。另外，计算机或互联网只能回应已经编入电脑程序里的问题，而无法回答不寻常的、非标准的和以前未遇到的问题。相比之下，通过和教师的及时互动，学生则可以得到很好的答案。

我的观点是，传统的学校教学将继续保持其在教育中的主导地位。与此同时，学生也将继续充分利用各种现代技术作为教师教学的辅助或有用补充。

闪光词汇

★ **infinite** ['infinit] *adj.* 无限的

The universe seems **infinite.** 宇宙似乎是无限的。

★ **flexible** ['fleksəbl] *adj.* 灵活的

We need a foreign policy that is more **flexible.** 我们需要一种更灵活的外交政策。

★ **geographical** [ˌdʒiə'græfikəl] *adj.* 地理的

The current survey will have a wider **geographical** spread. 当前的调查将在更广泛的地域范围内进行。

★ **facilitate** [fə'siliteit] *vt.* 促进，使便利

Tractors **facilitate** farming. 拖拉机使耕作便利。

★ **in line with** 符合

The new proposal is **in line with** our general line. 新建议和我们总的原则是一致的。

★ **favorable** ['feivərəbl] *adj.* 有利的

The weather seemed **favorable** for the race. 这天气似乎很适合赛跑。

★ **ethical** ['eθikəl] *adj.* 伦理的

It is necessary to get the youth to have a high **ethical** concept. 必须使青年具有高度的道德观念。

★ **unprecedented** [ʌn'presidəntid] *adj.* 没有前例的

The air crash caused an **unprecedented** number of deaths. 这次空难的死亡人数是空前的。

★ **dominant** ['dɔminənt] *adj.* 支配的，统治的

The British were formerly **dominant** in India. 英国人从前统治印度。

★ **supplement** ['sʌplimənt] *n./v.* 补充

He had to get a job to **supplement** the family income. 他不得不找一份工作以贴补家庭收入。

类似考题

2008 年 11 月 15 日

More and more people work and study at home with the development of computer technology. Do you think it is positive or negative development?

2009 年 4 月 25 日

Some people think computers and the Internet are important in children's study, but others think students can learn more effectively in schools and with teachers. Discuss both views and give your opinion.

2008 年 1 月 26 日考题回顾

失业与教育程度

WRITING TASK 2

You should spend about 40 minutes on this task.

Write about the following topic：

> *Unemployment is becoming increasingly serious in many countries. Some people think students only need to receive primary education, while others think secondary education is necessary. What's your opinion?*

Give reasons for your answer and include any relevant examples from your own knowledge or experience.

Write at least 250 words.

题目解释

失业问题在许多国家变得日益严重。一些人认为，学生只需要接受初等教育，而另一些人认为，中等教育是必要的。你的观点是什么？

高分范文

Economic situation is not optimistic all over the world because of the widespread crisis. Unemployment rate keeps surging in many countries. Some people think students only need to receive primary education, while others think secondary education is necessary. I am convinced that education is not a catalyst to unemployment. On the contrary, education can be a restrainer to it.

First of all, some people may think more education is a financial burden to the family which is always hard because of unemployment, and letting youngsters work immediately would better the miserable situation. Only short-sighted people hold this kind of view. We should analyze what is the cause of losing jobs. People are out of work not because they are well-educated but because they are incapable. And the effective way to improve their capability is education. Financial burden is a temporary difficulty. Well-educated people can avoid their parents' fate of being laid-off.

Secondly, well-educated people are needed by our society. An ignorant person can only be fit for simple work, while a knowledgeable man may create ten times more wealth than the former. New technologies are used in many areas, and mastering them is a necessity before one works. And one with only primary education will certainly not be qualified.

Lastly, the current science and technology need to be innovated and renovated, which requires those with more education to finish. Productive forces are always improved by new technologies. And advanced productive forces will create more wealth, so that social welfare will be better. No one will worry about what to live on after losing jobs. And this prosperous future can only result from more education.

From the above comparison and contrast, anyone can safely conclude that secondary education is not a choice but a must. And unemployment should never become an excuse to reject secondary education.

范文翻译

世界经济形势因广泛蔓延的危机而变得不容乐观。很多国家的失业率持续攀升。有人认为学生只需接受初等教育即可，还有人认为中等教育是必要的。我深信，教育并不是失业问题的催化剂。相反，教育可能会还会对失业起到抑制作用。

首先，有人会认为接受更多的教育对于那些因为失业一直都很困难的家庭来说是一个经济负担，让年青人立即参加工作可以缓解困境。只有那些目光短浅的人才会持这种观点。我们应该分析一下失业的原因。人们失业不是因为他们受过良好的教育，而是由于能力不够。而提高能力最有效的方法就是接受教育。经济负担只是暂时的困难。接受过良好教育的人可以避免他们父母下岗的命运。

其次，接受过良好教育的人为社会所需。无知的人只适合做简单的工作，而具备知识技能的人可以创造出比前者多十倍的财富。很多领域都在使用新技术，一个人参加工作前掌握这些技术是必要的。仅接受初等教育的人显然不具备相应的资质。

最后，目前的科技需要改革和创新，这也需要具备高知识水平的人来完成。生产力的进步通常依赖于新技术。同时，先进的生产力又能促进财富的增长，从而使社会福利变得更好，人们也就不会再为失业后的生存问题发愁。而这些光明的前景只能靠更好的教育才能达到。

通过上面的比较和对比，任何人都能有把握地得出结论：中等教育不是一种选择而是一种必需。失业永远不应该成为拒绝中等教育的借口。

闪光词汇

★ **temporary** ['tempərəri] *adj.* 暂时的，临时的

They are all **temporary** workers. 他们都是临时人员。

★ **be fit for** 适合于

He turned out to **be fit for** the position. 结果证明他是胜任这一职务的。

★ **knowledgeable** ['nɔlidʒəbl] *adj.* 知识渊博的

He's very **knowledgeable** about football. 他的足球知识很丰富。

★ **necessity** [ni'sesiti] *n.* 必要性，需要

Out of **necessity** or out of interest, people go back to school for the common goal—to improve themselves. 不管是出于需要，还是出于兴趣爱好，人们重返学校是为了一个共同的目标，就是提高自己。

★ **innovate** ['inəuveit] *v.* 改革，创新

It is necessary to **innovate** and develop military theories. 创新和发展军事理论很有必要。

★ **productive forces** 生产力

Man is the most decisive factor in **productive forces**. 人是生产力中最具有决定性的力量。

★ **live on** 靠……生活

They **live on** vegetarian food. 他们靠吃素食活着。

★ **prosperous** ['prɔspərəs] *adj.* 繁荣的

His business is **prosperous**. 他的事业兴旺发达。

★ **result from** 由……产生

Nothing has **resulted from** his efforts. 他的努力终成泡影。

实用句型

From the above comparison and contrast, anyone can safely conclude that ... 通过上面的比较和对比，任何人都能有把握地得出结论：

在议论文写作中，经常要在结尾表达自己的观点。这句话虽然说“任何人”都能有把握地得出结论，实际是强调作者观点的合理性。

请看范文中的这句话：

From the above comparison and contrast, anyone can safely conclude that secondary education is not a choice but a must. And unemployment should never become an excuse

to reject secondary education.
通过上面的比较和对比，任何人都能有把握地得出结论：中等教育不是一种选择而是一种必需。失业永远不应该成为拒绝中等教育的借口。
类似的常用表达还有：**As far as I am concerned**... 和 **From my point of view**...

类似考题

2006 年 3 月 11 日考题

In many countries more and more young people are leaving school but unable to find jobs. What problems do you think youth unemployment will cause to the individual and the society? What measures should be taken to reduce the level of unemployment among youngsters?

2007 年 12 月 8 日考题

Many people believe that the main aim of university education is to help graduates to find better jobs，while some people believe that university education has wider benefit for individuals and society. Discuss both views and give your opinion.

2008 年 3 月 1 日考题回顾

各种课程的重要程度

WRITING TASK 2

You should spend about 40 minutes on this task.

Write about the following topic：

> ***Schools offer a wide range of courses such as physical education，music，economics，philosophy，math，English，geography，physics and history. Among all these subjects，which one do you think is the most important and which one is the least important?***

Give reasons for your answer and include any relevant examples from your own knowledge or experience.

Write at least 250 words.

题目解释

学校提供广泛的课程，例如体育、音乐、经济、哲学、数学、英语、地理、物理和历史。在所有的这些科目当中，哪一个你认为是最重要的，哪一个是最不重要的？

高分范文

With the rapid development of modern education, schools tend to provide a wide range of courses for students, such as physical education, music, economics, philosophy, math, English, geography, physics and history. However, I do not think all the courses are necessary to be studied. Talking of which subject is the most important and which one is the least important, I would like to say that English is number one, and philosophy is the last one.

For my part, English is the most important subject among these courses. English, as an international language, is used for different countries to communicate with each another. If someone is good at English, he will have more opportunities. And now, more and more foreigners settle in China. English helps us make friends with them easily. Furthermore, one of the requirements of studying abroad is having a high score of English.

On the other hand, philosophy is the least important subject. I never think learning philosophy can make students more logical to analyze matters as teachers have said. In fact, many theories oppose each other. Most of my classmates were confused with the different theories when we learned philosophy. It is unnecessary to learn something incompatible and useless. So I can say, it is not useful for everyone.

As to other courses, they have different advantages. For example, physical education helps students stay healthy. History helps students know more about the development of the country and the world. Geography helps students figure out the time in different parts of the world.

Based on the above discussion and analysis, we can see that English is most important, and everyone needs to master it. Meanwhile, philosophy, not as important as others, should be learned as an optional course.

范文翻译

随着现代教育的发展，学校往往给学生提供的课程范围很广泛，例如体育、音乐、经济学、哲学、数学、英语、地理、物理以及历史。然而，我认为并不是所有的这些课程都有必要学习。要说哪一个科目最重要，哪一个科目最不重要，我认为英语最重要，而哲学最不重要。

在我看来，英语在这些课程当中是最重要的科目。作为一种国际语言，英语被不同国家用来进行交流。如果有人擅长英语，他就会有更多的机会。现在，越来越多的外国人定居在中国，英语有助于我们和外国人交朋友。而且，出国留学的要求之一就是有一个好的英语成绩。

另一方面，哲学是最不重要的科目。我从来不认为学习哲学能够使学生在分析问题时像老师说的那么理性。事实上，很多理论互相冲突。我的大多数同学在学习哲学的时候都被不同的理论所困惑。没有必要学习相互矛盾而且没有用的东西。因此我要说，哲学并不是对每个人都有用。

至于其他的课程，它们各有不同的优点。例如，体育可以帮助学生保持健康，历史可以帮助学生了解国家和世界的发展，地理可以帮助学生推断出世界不同地方的时间。

基于上述讨论和分析，我们可以看到，英语最重要，每个人都应该掌握。与此同时，哲学则不如其他课程重要，应该作为选修课来学习。

闪光词汇

★ **talk of** 谈到

Do not **talk of** bygones. 不要再提往事。

★ **communicate** [kə'mju:nikeit] *v.* 沟通，传达

I'd like to find a job with more chances to **communicate** with people. 我想找个与人打交道机会多的工作。

★ **logical** ['lɔdʒikəl] *adj.* 合乎逻辑的，合理的

His argument seems **logical**. 他的论据似乎有道理。

★ **oppose** [ə'pəuz] *v.* 反对，使对立

honor credibility and **oppose** cheating 讲诚信，反欺诈

★ **confused** [kən'fju:zd] *adj.* 困惑的，烦恼的

I am really **confused**. 我很困惑。

★ **Incompatible** [ˌinkəm'pætəbl] *adj.* 性质相反的，矛盾的

Water is **incompatible** with fire. 水火不相容。

★ **figure out** 计算出，解决

Can you **figure** the total cost **out**? 你能把全部成本算出来吗?

实用句型

Talking of...I would like to say that... 谈到……我宁愿说……

议论文的首段中，要引述题目给出的观点，之后再表明自己的观点。这时常用的句型就是首先用 **Talking of** 引出题目中的素材，再用 I would like to say that... 提出作者的立场。请看范文中的这句话：

Talking of which subject is the most important and which one is the least important, **I would like to say that** English is number one, and philosophy is the last one. 要说哪一个科目最重要，哪一个科目最不重要，我认为英语最重要，而哲学最不重要。

类似考题

2008 年 5 月 22 日

Some people think that schools should concentrate on academic classes because they are helpful for future career. But they do not think music and sports classes are useful. To what extent do you agree or disagree?

2008 年 6 月 5 日

Some people think that university students should specialize in one subject, while others think universities should encourage students to learn a range of subjects. Discuss both views and give your opinion.

2008 年 7 月 5 日

Nowadays, more university students choose to study some practical subjects (such as marketing, computer programming, etc.) instead of theoretical subjects (such as economy, math, chemistry). Some people suggest that universities should focus on practical subjects, but not theoretical subjects. Do you agree or disagree?

2008年4月24日考题回顾

老师在信息时代的作用

WRITING TASK 2

You should spend about 40 minutes on this task.

Write about the following topic:

> ***Teachers used to convey information, but now with wide resources of information, there is no role for teachers to play in modern education. Do you agree or disagree?***

Give reasons for your answer and include any relevant examples from your own knowledge or experience.

Write at least 250 words.

题目解释

老师过去是传递信息，但是现在，随着信息资源越来越广泛，教师在现代教育中没有用武之地了。你同意还是不同意这种观点?

高分范文

Thanks to the boom of information technology, the rapidly increasing prevalence of computers in education has been rendering people tremendous benefits. Some people, therefore, claim that teachers' roles are not significant any more in the information age given the convenience and efficiency of the Internet in terms of information access. To my mind, this is a partial and misleading idea.

To begin with, teachers help define clear educational goals and discover more suitable methods for students in different learning stages. Without a strong sense of purpose, learners tend to easily get distracted and frustrated over the complex and mountainous arrays of data easily available through countless sources, which not only consume a lot of time and energy, but also undermine their confidence. By following through the informative and enjoyable activities specially designed by the teacher, students could take control of their learning and reap academic achievements as well as further enthusiasm.

In addition, the role of the teacher contributes to the analytical capability and communicative skills of the students, which are crucial elements for their future career development. Fostering problem solving abilities is definitely beyond the functions of the Internet or the computer.

Last but not least, as schools prepare students for citizenship in an age of information, teachers are even more irreplaceable in terms of the education of morality standard, professional ethics and personal integrity. The influence of a charismatic teacher could not be overemphasized in shaping the character of students, which is more valuable than imparting knowledge itself and will continuously work as a paramount motivity for the children in their life time.

Admittedly, with the flexibility and efficiency furnished by the computer and the Internet, the education system has seen a dramatic change over the past decade. However, teachers will still wield a significant influence in streamlining the learning process, developing practical abilities, and helping accomplish educational goals for students.

范文翻译

随着信息技术的发展，电脑在教育领域越来越广泛的应用给人们带来了巨大的好处。因此有些人指出，由于互联网在获取信息方面的便利与高效，使得老师在信息技术时代的作用不再那么重要了。在我看来，这种说法是有失全面并且容易误导的。

首先，教师可以为身处不同学习阶段的学生确立清晰的教育目标并找到更适合的学习方法。如果没有一个很强的目的性，学生往往会面对纷繁复杂、渠道多样、堆积如山的信息而迷失主题，感觉挫败。这种学习过程不仅耗时、费力，而且还会打击他们的学习信心。而通过全程参与老师特别规划过的信息量大并充满趣味的学习活动，学生在学习时采取主动，更容易取得学习成果和培养进一步学习的兴趣。

此外，教师的作用有利于培养学生分析问题的能力和交流技巧，这对于他们的未来职业发展是十分关键的。培养解决问题的能力，是电脑或互联网本身很难做到的。

最后但很重要的一点，随着学校为信息时代不断培养合格公民，教师在培养学生道德标准、职业道德、正直诚信等方面的作用更加无法取代。一个充满人格魅力的教师会帮助塑造学生的品格，这一影响怎么强调都不过分，它比知识的传授更为重要，并将在学生日后的生涯中作为一个重要的驱动力不断鞭策学生前进。

诚然，受益于电脑和互联网带来的灵活性和高效率，教育体系在过去的十年里发生了显著变化；但是，教师将依然会在提高学习效率、培养实际能力和帮助学生实现教育目标方面发挥重要作用。

闪光词汇

★ **prevalence** ['prevələns] *n.* 流行

The **prevalence** of cigarette smoking was much higher in young people. 吸烟在年轻人中更为盛行。

★ **thanks to** 由于，归功于

Thanks to his effort，it is more successful than we have expected. 由于他的努力，获得了比我们预期的更大的成功。

★ **prevalence** ['prevələns] *n.* 传播，流行，普及

I'm shocked at the **prevalence** of bribery among these officials. 我对这些官员的普遍受贿感到震惊。

★ **enthusiasm** [in'θju:ziæzəm] *n.* 热情，热心

His refusal iced our **enthusiasm**. 他的拒绝浇熄了我们的热情。

★ **overemphasize** ['əuvə'emfəsaiz] *vt.* 过分强调

We cannot **overemphasize** the importance of learning a foreign language. 我们无论怎么强调学习外语的重要性也不过分。

★ **flexibility** [ˌfleksə'biliti] *n.* 弹性，适应性

He enjoyed the **flexibility** of his working arrangement. 他对工作的适应性很强。

实用句型

Admittedly...**However**... 诚然……然而……

用在文章的结尾，Admittedly 表示让步，However 表示转折。

单边支持的作文通常会配合一个让步的结尾以避免论证听起来有失偏颇，而让步要注意一是避重就轻，二是双重转折。Admittedly 这个词引出的往往是辩论对手表面上合理的主张，实际上是为了强调自己的论据更具说服力。接下来配合 However，指出教师的作用依然很重要。恰当地运用这种结构，会让议论文结构清晰，富有逻辑性。

请看范文的结尾部分：

Admittedly，with the flexibility and efficiency furnished by the computer and the Internet，the education system has seen a dramatic change over the past decade. **However**，teachers will still wield a significant influence in streamlining the learning process，developing practical abilities，and helping accomplish educational goals for students.

诚然，受益于电脑和互联网带来的灵活性和高效率，教育体系在过去的十来年发生了显著变化。但是，教师将依然会在提高学习效率，培养实际能力和帮助学生实现教育目标方面发挥重要作用。

类似考题

2006 年 3 月 18 日

Some people think that teachers should be responsible for teaching students to judge what is right and wrong so that they can behave well. Others say that teachers should only teach students academic subjects. Discuss both views and give your opinion.

2007 年 5 月 19 日

Computers are increasingly used in education. In which areas do you think computers are more important and in which areas teachers are more important?

2009 年 1 月 15 日

Some people think students at school and university can learn more from teachers and lessons than from TV and the Internet. To what extent do you agree or disagree?

2008 年 8 月 30 日考题回顾

学生应该集体学习还是单独学习

WRITING TASK 2

You should spend about 40 minutes on this task.

Write about the following topic：

Some people think that students should be organized into groups to study，while others argue that students should be made to study alone. What are the benefits of each study method and which one do you think is more effective?

Give reasons for your answer and include any relevant examples from your own knowledge or experience.

Write at least 250 words.

题目解释

一些人认为，学生应该组成小组集体一起学习，而另一些人认为学生应该单独学习，两种学习方法各有哪些优点？你认为哪一种更有效？

高分范文

The heated debate over whether studying in group is superior to studying alone has long been in existence and educational experts are deeply divided over this issue. From an objective perspective, I am strongly convinced that both methods have their own advantages.

One of the major superiorities of group study is that it provides an environment in which students can exchange ideas with each other. It is well known that knowledge knows no bounds, so it is almost impossible for even an eminent professor at university to have a good command of everything, let alone an ordinary student. In consequence, students should be divided into different groups or classes so that they can communicate with, learn from and help each other.

Another obvious advantage of studying in group is that students have the opportunity to learn to socialize with others. Many sociologists point out that people in modern society are more isolated than those in ancient times mainly because they do not have enough opportunities to get along with others. Under such circumstances, it is unreasonable to deprive the students of the chance to socialize by arranging them to study alone.

However, we should not overlook the fact that studying alone also has its unique merit—effectiveness. In a big class, top students might feel bored because the teacher does not give them enough materials to learn whereas poor students might feel just the opposite because the teacher gives them too many materials to digest. In other words, the teacher usually slows down the pace of progress or reduces the content of his lesson in the light of students with lower ability.

Comparing the benefits of both sides, I deem group study more effective only if the class or group is not too big.

范文翻译

关于集体学习是否比独立学习好的话题的激烈讨论一直存在，教育家分为观点截然不同的两派。从客观的角度来讲，我坚信两种方法都有他们自己的优点。

集体学习的一个最主要的优点就是它给学生提供了一个彼此交流思想的环境。众所周知，知识无界，因此，对于一个大学的知名教授来说他不可能掌握一切，更不用说是一个普通的学生了。因此，学生应该被分成不同的组或者是班级，以便于他们互相交流、学习和彼此帮助。

集体学习的另外一个明显优势就是学生有机会学习与他人交往。许多社会学家指出，现代社会的人比古代的人更加孤单，因为他们没有足够的机会与他人相处。在这样的情况下，安排学生独立学习，从而剥夺他们与他人交往的机会是不合理的。

然而，我们也不能忽视一个事实，独立学习有它独一无二的优点，那就是效率。在一个大的班级，尖子学生可能觉得无聊，因为老师没有给他们足够的资料来学习；而成绩差的学生的感觉可能恰恰相反，因为他们感到老师给了他们太多的资料去消化。换句话说，老师通常放慢进度或者减少课程的内容，以照顾学习差的学生。

比较两者的优点，我认为集体学习更有效，只要是这个班级或者是集体不太大。

闪光词汇

★ **superior** [sjuː'piəriə] *adj.* 较好的，出众的

Superior wisdom derives from experience. 卓越的智慧来源于经验。

★ **perspective** [pə'spektiv] *n.* 观点，看法

We should see the events in historical **perspective**. 我们应该用历史的观点看待这些事件。

★ **convinced** [kən'vɪnst] *adj.* 确信的，深信的

But not everyone is **convinced** so. 但不是人人都这么想。

★ **eminent** ['eminənt] *adj.* 显赫的，杰出的

He is **eminent** among scientists. 他在科学家中是杰出的。

★ **deprive** [di'praiv] *vt.* 剥夺，使丧失

The court ruling **deprived** us of any share in the inheritance. 法庭裁决剥夺了我们全部的继承权。

★ **unique** [juː'niːk] *adj.* 唯一的，独特的

This is indeed a **unique** arrangement. 这确是独有的安排。

★ **digest** [di'dʒest; dai'dʒest] *v.* 消化，融会贯通

Cheese does not **digest** easily. 干酪不易消化。

实用句型

The heated debate over... 关于……的热烈争论

雅思写作中，很多考题会谈到当代社会的某个话题，不同人对这些话题会有不同的观点，甚至会有激烈的辩论。因此，第一段就可以用这个词组引出话题。如范文中的这句话：

The heated debate over whether studying in group is superior to studying alone has long been in existence and educational experts are deeply divided over this issue. 关于集体学习是否比独立学习好的话题的激烈讨论一直存在，教育家分为观点截然不同的两派。

debate 也可以替换成 controversy，意思是“争论”。

类似考题

2005 年 1 月 15 日

Some teachers say students should be organized into groups to study. Others argue students should be made to study alone. Tell the benefits of each study method. Which one do you think is more effective?

2008年9月6日考题回顾

老师和父母对孩子的影响

WRITING TASK 2

You should spend about 40 minutes on this task.

Write about the following topic:

> ***Once children start school, teachers have more influence on their intellectual and social development than parents. To what extent do you agree or disagree?***

Give reasons for your answer and include any relevant examples from your own knowledge or experience.

Write at least 250 words.

题目解释

一旦孩子开始上学，老师对他们的智力和社会发展的影响就比父母对他们的影响更多。你同意还是不同意这个观点？

高分范文

Parents would find themselves well-expressed in their young kids' early periods of life, during which time children are identical reflection of their parents in many aspects. However, this situation no longer lasts after their entrance to schools, even primary school. There they will get much greater influence from their teachers and peers, especially from their teachers and this kind of influence can be ever-lasting. We can find this to be true from the following aspects.

First of all, teachers can influence children in intellectual aspects in most of their school age. Kids have to spend most of their time in schools, together with many teachers in various disciplines. Their major period at home is their holidays, which is quite negligible compared with their normal school life. Therefore, parents are no peers when compared with teachers in school in this regard.

Also, due to their longtime company with children, teachers can significantly influence the social behavior of children. In many cases, parents can never have the chances to deal with the problems kids encounter at school. But teachers are professional in this regard and they are also psychologically trained to cope with many situations that parents can not even dream of. Parents can be the most intimate ones to listen to their children's confession, but they can never compare with teachers at school.

So I am one of the many people who feel that once children start school, teachers have more influence on their intellectual and social development although parents also play an important role in their development.

范文翻译

父母会发现他们在孩子很小的时候被很好地模仿，那段时间，他们在很多方面的反映是与父母相同的。然而，这种情形在他们入学甚至之后就不再存在了。一上小学，他们就会更多地受到他们的老师和同学们的影响，尤其是他们的老师，对他们的这种影响可能会一直持续。我们可以从以下几个方面来看。

首先，老师在孩子们的学生时代会在智力方面影响他们。孩子须花大量的时间在学校，和各科目的许多老师在一起。他们在家的时间主要就是假期，这和他们正常的学校生活比起来简直就是微不足道。因此，在这方面，父母和学校的老师没法比。

其次，由于长期和孩子相伴，老师能够对孩子的社会行为产生很大的影响。在很多情况下，父母永远没有机会处理孩子们在学校遇到的问题。但是老师在这方面是专家，他们也受过心理学方面的训练，知道如何处理很多父母连做梦都不会想到的情况。父母可能是孩子表白的最亲密的倾听者，但是他们永远都不能和学校的老师比。

因此，和许多人一样，我也认为孩子一旦上学，老师对他们的智力和社会发展的影响就更多，虽然父母在他们的发展过程中也扮演着很重要的角色。

闪光词汇

★ **identical** [ai'dentikəl] *adj.* 同一的，同样的
Their opinions are **identical**. 他们的意见完全一致。

★ **negligible** ['neglidʒəbl] *adj.* 可以忽略的
This will have a **negligible** effect on the temperature. 这对温度的影响将是微乎其微的。

★ **due to** 由于，应归于
Some people fail to pay their dues on time **due to** poverty. 一些人由于贫穷而不能及时交付会费。

★ **encounter** [in'kauntə] *v.* 遭遇，遇到
We did not **encounter** fierce resistance anywhere. 我们在任何地方都没有遭遇到顽强抵抗。

★ **psychologically** [ˌsaikə'lɔdʒikəli] *adv.* 心理上地，心理学地
He is **psychologically** stable. 他心理状态稳定。

实用句型

have more influence on... 对……有更大的影响
在雅思写作中，特别是在讨论有关影响话题的文章中，经常要谈到某人或某事对其他的人或事的影响，上面的表达方式就经常用到。类似的句型还有 **exert an influence on**... 对……施加影响。
请看范文中的这句话：
So I am one of many people who feel that once children start school，teachers **have more influence on** their intellectual and social development although parents also play an important role in their development.
因此，和许多人一样，我也认为孩子一旦上学，老师对他们的智力和社会发展的影响就更多，虽然父母在他们的发展过程中也扮演着很重要的角色。

类似考题

2009 年 10 月 8 日
Some people think that family life and parents have great influence on children's development，while others consider that external influence plays a more important role in children's life. Discuss both views and give your own opinion.

2008 年 12 月 6 日考题回顾

重复记忆在教育中的作用

WRITING TASK 2

You should spend about 40 minutes on this task.

Write about the following topic：

> ***Memorization of information by frequent repetition (rote learning) plays a role in education system. To what extent do you agree or disagree?***

Give reasons for your answer and include any relevant examples from your own knowledge or experience.

Write at least 250 words.

题目解释

通过不断重复记忆信息在教育中扮演重要的角色。你同意还是不同意?

高分范文

Learning is a complex process that involves different strategies and stages. As a key approach of learning, memorization of information by repetition contributes to the overall effectiveness of an education system, while the limitations should also be admitted.

Learning by repetition is an effective strategy in learning. For example, Chinese people believe that one will get the gist of a book after reading it for a hundred times. Researchers have found that rote learning is particularly useful for young learners. When teaching children how to use a computer, instructors will demonstrate how the computer works over and over again until they can perform tasks correctly. Moreover, for certain kinds of learning at an early stage, the understanding involved is often minimal. Naturally rote learning plays an important role.

It is true that rote learning can help students learn things by heart, but it can do little to improve their analytical ability and creativity. We need to bear it in mind that meaningful learning is more essential for our education system. When students grow older and study in higher grades, the scope and depth of their learning grow. There has been strong criticism that some schools overemphasize the importance of memorization of knowledge and produce students with great weaknesses in applying knowledge in practice. The solution to such a problem can be that schools and students put in more effort on meaningful learning.

All in all, I should say that as learning is a complex progress, students should employ different strategies at various stages. Rote learning is important in education system, but meaningful learning is more vital for students in developing advanced abilities and skills.

范文翻译

学习是一个复杂的过程，包括不同的策略和阶段。作为学习的一个重要手段，对信息的重复记忆在教育体系中是行之有效的。但我们也应该承认其局限性。

重复是有效的学习策略。例如，中国人认为一本书读过一百遍之后就能掌握其要旨。研究者发现机械学习对年轻人尤为有效。教孩子如何使用计算机的时候，教师们要一遍又一遍地演示电脑是如何工作的，直到学生能够正确地完成任务。而且，在某些学习的早期阶段，其中的理解成分常常很少。自然，机械学习扮演着重要的角色。

诚然，机械学习确实可以帮助学生牢牢记住事情，但对提高其分析能力和创造力却帮助甚微。我们应该牢记理解学习在教育体系中具有更重要的地位。当学生逐渐长大进入高年级的时候，学习的范围和深度都会有所增长。一直有一种严厉的批评，说一些学校只强调记忆知识的重要性，培养出来的学生应用知识的实践能力却很弱。解决此问题的办法就是学校和学生应当在理解学习方面投入更多的精力。

总之，我想说的是，学习是一个复杂的过程，学生在不同的阶段可以采取不同的策略。机械学习在教育体系中很重要，但是理解学习在学生获取高级技能方面更为重要。

闪光词汇

★ **contribute** [kən'tribjuːt] *v.* 捐助，贡献

Exercise **contributes** to better health. 锻炼能促成更强健的体魄。

★ **gist** [dʒist] *n.* 要点，要旨

He is quick in grasping the **gist** of a book. 他敏于了解书的要点。

★ **perform** [pə'fɔːm] *v.* 履行，执行

They continue to **perform** the experiment. 他们继续做试验。

★ **bear in mind** 记住

I'll **bear** your suggestion **in mind**. 我会记住你的建议的。

★ **essential** [i'senʃəl] *adj.* 绝对必要的　*n.* 要素，实质

Here patience is **essential**. 在这里，耐心是绝对必要的。

★ **put in** 花费，付出

They have **put in** more money for the rebuilding of the highway. 他们已为这条高速公路的重建花更多的钱了。

2008 年 12 月 13 日考题回顾

更多年轻人上大学的利弊

WRITING TASK 2

You should spend about 40 minutes on this task.

Write about the following topic：

> ***Some people believe that a country benefits greatly with a high percentage of young people who go to university，while others argue that it only leads to graduate unemployment. Discuss both views and give your opinion.***

Give reasons for your answer and include any relevant examples from your own knowledge or experience.

Write at least 250 words.

题目解释

一些人认为一个国家极大地得益于高比例的年轻人上大学，而另一些人认为这样只会导致毕业生失业。讨论这两种观点并给出你的观点。

高分范文

Education is far more complicated than we can imagine. In China, we used to encourage more students to go to college. But now the graduate unemployment has become a serious social problem, which cannot be solved in a short period of time. I disagree that a country benefits greatly with a high percentage of young people who go to university.

The society we live in is a gigantic system which needs all kinds of people to make it run properly. And university graduates are only a small part of them. We need peasants, drivers, soldiers, policemen, workers, etc. For example, a qualified driver only needs to get a driving license after training. This occupation usually does not need the knowledge of politics, algebra, geometry, astronomy or calculus. So, higher education is a waste to some extent.

It is true that nowadays, too many students going to university causes graduate unemployment in China. Last month, it was reported that a graduate with a doctor degree was forced to choose selling pork for a living; and over a thousand university graduates competed for several posts. So many Chinese families especially those poor ones think it is not worthy to send their children to the university. On the contrary, the graduates from vocational schools are in bad need by employers.

From the above analysis, we can conclude that a proper portion of university graduates suits the development of society, and too many of them would cause serious effects, such as graduate unemployment.

范文翻译

教育比我们想象的要复杂得多，在我国，过去常常鼓励更多的学生去上大学。但是现在，大学毕业生失业已经成为一个严重的社会问题，在短期内得不到解决。一个国家的发展极大地得益于大比例的年轻人上大学，我不同意这个说法。

我们生活的这个社会是一个庞大的系统，需要各种各样的人使其正常运转。大学毕业生只占其中一小部分。我们需要农民、司机、士兵、警察、工人，等等。例如，一个合格的司机只需要在培训后获得驾驶执照。这种职位通常并不需要政治、代数、几何、天文或微积分方面的知识。因此，高等教育在某种程度上就是一种浪费。

如今的实际情况是，在中国，太多的学生上大学导致大学毕业生失业。上个月，据报道，有个拥有博士学位的大学毕业生为了生存不得不选择卖猪肉；一千多个大学毕业生竞争几个职位。因此，很多中国家庭尤其是那些贫困家庭认为不值得将其子女送入大学。相反，职业学校的毕业生是老板们急需的。

根据以上分析，我们可以得出结论，适当比例的大学毕业生适合社会的发展，太多了就会造成严重的后果，例如大学毕业生失业。

闪光词汇

★ **complicated** [ˈkɔmplikeitid] *adj*. 复杂的，难解的

His theory was too **complicated** for us to understand. 他的学说对我们来说太复杂了，以至于不能了解。

★ **in a short period of time** 在一段短时间内

In a short period of time he grew into a great communist fighter. 在很短时期中，他成长为一名伟大的共产主义战士。

★ **qualified** [ˈkwɔlifaid] *adj*. 有资格的

Jane is well **qualified** for this teaching job. 简很适合担任这份教师工作。

★ **compete for** 为……竞争

Chances are that firms from across the country will come to **compete for** the contract. 很可能全国各地的公司都会来争订这个合同。

★ **vocational** [vəuˈkeiʃənəl] *adj*. 职业的

She was given some quick training at the **vocational** school. 她在职业学校受过速成训练。

类似考题

2007 年 1 月 13 日

Some people think universities should provide graduates with the knowledge and skills needed in the workplace in the future. Others think the true function of the university is to give access to knowledge for its own sake. What do you think are the main functions of a university?

2007 年 9 月 1 日

Some people think that studying in a college or university is the best way for students to prepare for their future career. But others think they should leave school as soon as possible to develop their career through work experience. Discuss both views and give your own opinion.

Unit 2

Working and Ideology

工作生活与意识形态

2011年3月12日考题回顾

竞争力的影响和利弊

WRITING TASK 2

You should spend about 40 minutes on this task.

Write about the following topic:

Competitiveness is becoming an important quality for people to have in our society. How does competitiveness affect individuals? Do you think it is a positive or a negative development?

Give reasons for your answer and include any relevant examples from your own knowledge or experience.

Write at least 250 words.

题目解释

竞争力在社会中正成为人们的一种重要品质。竞争力如何影响到个人？你认为这种发展是积极的还是消极的？

高分范文

The discussion as to whether the competitiveness is a blessing or a curse arouses most people's interests. A sizable percentage of people hold the opinion that one can only survive through fierce competition. Others, nevertheless, think quite differently on the question. For my part, I think competitiveness is becoming an important quality for people to have in our society. It affects individuals in two completely opposite ways.

On the one hand, competitiveness helps to enhance one's overall ability and social development. Take myself for example. It is a very obvious case. Competition means if I do not work hard and prevail against other people, I will be definitely substituted by the one who is more capable. So if I want to keep my position in a company or any other organization, I should always keep competitiveness in mind, which means I will have to make efforts and progress. We can also say, everyone is facing the same problem and wants to be more competitive. To sum all individuals' progress up, that would be a gigantic trend of progress for the human society.

However, on the other hand, struggling for competitiveness has its own weakness. Sometimes, competition is connected to fierceness, cold blooding and cruelty. Surely, these words are used to describe negative feelings and moods. If one lives in a competitive and hostile environment for a long time, he often becomes agitated, anxious and depressed in the end. And the relations around him can only be described as intense, unfriendly and frail. If this situation is extended infinitely, we cannot image how horrible the society would become. In a world without affection, love and tenderness, the only subject everyone persists is competition. I cannot see any positive signs.

To sum up, it is not completely correct whether we put competitiveness in a supreme position or we deserted it like evil. It is a scientific way for us to use the competitiveness properly so that we can make huge progress and at the same time maintain a harmonious society.

范文翻译

关于竞争力是一件好事还是坏事的讨论引起了大多数人的兴趣。有相当一部分人认为人们只能通过激烈的竞争才能生存。然而，其他人在这个问题上的看法相当不同。在我看来，竞争力在社会中正成为人们的一种重要品质。它以两种截然相反的方式影响着人们。

一方面，竞争力有助于提高人的整体能力，促进社会的发展。以我自己为例，这是个非常明显的例子。竞争意味着如果我不努力工作并且胜过别人，我将会被更胜任的人所取代。所以，如果我想在公司或其他任何组织保住我的职位，就必须时常牢记保持自己的竞争力。这意味着我必须努力，不断进步。我们也可以说，每个人都面临着同样的问题，都希望更具竞争力。所有个人进步的总和，必将带来人类社会巨大的进步。

但是，另一方面，努力取得竞争力也有其自身的弱点。有时候，竞争与激烈、冷血和残酷相关。当然，这些词是用来形容负面情绪和心情的。一个人如果长时间生活在充满竞争和敌对的环境中，他常常会变得激动、焦虑，并最终变得抑郁。他周围的关系只能用紧张、不友好和脆弱等词来形容。如果这种情况无限延伸下去，我们无法想象社会将会变得多么可怕。一个没有感情、爱和温柔的世界里，每个人唯一的目标就是竞争。我看不到任何积极的迹象。

综上所述，将竞争力放在至高无上的地位或者将其视为邪恶都是不完全正确的。对于我们来说，科学的做法是正确利用竞争力，以便取得重大的进步，同时还要保持社会的和谐。

闪光词汇

★ **survive** [sə'vaiv] *v.* 生存

These plants cannot **survive** in very cold conditions. 这些植物在严寒中不能存活。

★ **fierce** [fiəs] *adj.* 激烈的

What he said met with **fierce** opposition. 他的话语遭到激烈反对。

★ **gigantic** [dʒai'gæntik] *adj.* 巨大的

He has a **gigantic** appetite and eats gigantic meals. 他食量很大，能吃很多的食物。

★ **agitated** ['ædʒiteitid] *adj.* 激动的

Don't get all **agitated**! 不要那么激动！

★ **supreme** [sjuː'priːm] *adj.* 至高的

The Pope is the **supreme** leader of the Roman Catholic Church. 教皇是罗马天主教的最高领袖。

★ **harmonious** [hɑː'məunjəs] *adj.* 和谐的

They can build a more **harmonious** society once inequality and exploitation are removed. 消除了不均与剥削，他们就能建立一个更为和谐的社会。

实用句型

1. **The discussion as to whether…is a blessing or a curse arouses most people's interests.** 关于……是一件好事还是坏事的讨论引起了大多数人的兴趣。这种句型一般用于第一段，介绍背景，同时引出话题。

请看范文中的这句话：

The discussion as to whether the competitiveness **is a blessing or a curse arouses most people's interests.** 关于竞争力是一件好事还是坏事的讨论引起了大多数人的兴趣。

2. **A sizable percentage of people hold the opinion that…Others, nevertheless, think quite differently on the question.** 有相当一部分人认为……。然而，其他人在这个问题上的看法相当不同。这种句型一般用于第一段，介绍双方观点。

请看范文中的这句话：

A sizable percentage of people hold the opinion that one can only survive through fierce competition. **Others, nevertheless, think quite differently on the question.** 有相当一部分人认为人们只能通过激烈的竞争才能生存。然而，其他人在这个问题上的看法相当不同。

2011 年 3 月 19 日考题回顾

在家工作和学习的利弊

WRITING TASK 2

You should spend about 40 minutes on this task.

Write about the following topic：

> ***Around the world more adults can work at home and more children can study at home. Computer technology development makes it accessible. Do you think it is a positive or a negative development?***

Give reasons for your answer and include any relevant examples from your own knowledge or experience.

Write at least 250 words.

题目解释

在全世界范围内，更多的成年人能够在家工作，更多的孩子能够在家学习。计算机技术的发展使之很容易实现。你认为这是一种积极的发展还是消极的发展?

高分范文

Benefiting from the rapid development of computer and the Internet technology, more adults can work at home and more children can study at home. This phenomenon has caused a heated public debate among us. Some people are of the opinion that doing job at home is a retrogression, while there are also quite a few people who are strongly opposed to their opinion. Before giving my opinion, I think it is important to look at the argument on both sides.

On the one hand, we should acknowledge its advantages. Working or studying at home can make people travel less in a large scale, which will reduce the possibility of traffic accidents and relieve the traffic jam and fatherly contribute much to the environment protection. From another point of view, we should not neglect its positive consequence in enhancing the child-parent relations. Since the whole family can stay at home working and studying, they spend comparatively more time together. The family will undoubtedly build closer relations.

On the other hand, we should not overlook the disadvantages. The worst one I would say is that it will isolate people farther and farther. For example, more people rely on the modern technology and are reluctant to get in touch with others. Moreover, the efficiency of long-distance education is in doubt. Children, not like the adults, need to be supervised and guided. When they are left at home to study through the Internet, most of them tend to slack off. In addition, intensive use of computer is not good for one's health. The screen will harm the sights, making people become short-sighted. And sitting before computer for long time will damage the spinal column of children who are in the period of growth.

Now, after close examination, it is not difficult to draw the conclusion that the phenomenon has both merits and demerits. And my opinion is that adults' working at home should be encouraged, and children's studying at home should not be recommended.

范文翻译

受益于快速发展的计算机和互联网技术，更多的成年人可以在家工作，更多的孩子可以在家学习。这种现象在我们中已经引起了热烈的公开讨论。一些人认为在家做事情是一种退步，但也有一些人强烈反对他们的观点。在给出我的观点之前，我认为看一看问题的两面是很重要的。

一方面，我们应该承认它的优点。在家工作或学习可以在很大程度上减少人们的出行，这将降低交通事故的可能性，减少交通阻塞，进而大大促进环境保护。从另一方面来看，我们也不应该忽视它在改善子女和父母关系方面的积极效果。因为全家人在家工作或学习，他们相对来说要花更多的时间在一起。家庭无疑会建立更紧密的联系。

另一方面，我们也不能忽视它的缺点。我要说的最糟糕的一点是它会使人们越来越隔阂。例如，更多的人依靠现代技术而不愿意与他人接触。此外，远程教育的效率也值得怀疑。不像成年人，儿童需要被监督和指导。当他们被留在家里通过互联网学习，他们当中的很多人会懈怠。而且，大量使用计算机对健康不利。屏幕会损害视力，使人们变得近视。而且，长时间坐在电脑前会损害正在成长的儿童的脊柱。

现在，在仔细考虑后，不难得出这个结论：这种现象既有益处也有不足。我的看法是成年人在家工作应该被鼓励，而孩子在家学习不应该被提倡。

闪光词汇

★ **retrogression** [ˌretrəuˈgreʃən] *n.* 退步

Persist in progress and oppose **retrogression**. 坚持进步，反对倒退。

★ **comparatively** [kəmˈpærətivli] *adv.* 相当地

He was **comparatively** calm and concentrated on judging how to defeat his opponent. 他相对冷静沉着，聚精会神地判断如何打败对手。

★ **isolate** [ˈaisəleit] *vt.* 使隔离

Do not **isolate** yourself from others. 不要把自己孤立起来。

★ **supervise** [ˈsjuːpəvaiz] *v.* 监督，管理

The architect **supervised** the building of the house. 建筑工程师监督房子的施工。

★ **slack off** 松懈，偷懒

It's natural to **slack off** towards the end of a hard day's work. 辛苦工作了一天，快结束时有所松懈是很自然的。

实用句型

1. **Before giving my opinion, I think it is important to look at the argument on both sides**. 在给出我的观点之前，我认为看一看问题的两面是很重要的。这种句型一般用于第一段，引出下文。
2. **On the one hand, we should acknowledge its advantages.** 一方面，我们应该承认它的优点。这种句型一般用做第二段的中心句，表示开始分析有利的方面。
3. **On the other hand, we should not overlook the disadvantages.** 另一方面，我们也不能忽视它的缺点。这种句型一般用做第三段的中心句，表示开始分析不利的方面。
4. **Now, after close examination, it is not difficult to draw the conclusion that the phenomenon has both merits and demerits.** 现在，在仔细考虑后，不难得出这个结论：这种现象既有益处也有不足。这种句型一般用于结尾段开头，表示总结全文。

类似考题

2008 年 10 月 23 日

Many people use distance-learning programs to study at home, but some people think that it cannot bring the benefit as much as attending college or university. To what extent do you agree or disagree?

2008 年 11 月 15 日

More and more people work or study at home with the development of computer technology. Do you think it is a positive or a negative development?

2009 年 12 月 12 日

Recently some people can work at home using modern technology. Some people say this only benefits the workers, but not the employers. To what extent do you agree or disagree?

2009 年 2 月 28 日考题回顾

改善公众健康的措施

WRITING TASK 2

You should spend about 40 minutes on this task.

Write about the following topic:

> ***Some people believe that to improve public health governments should increase the number of sports facilities; others believe that it has little effects and need other measures to improve public health. Discuss both views and give your opinion.***

Give reasons for your answer and include any relevant examples from your own knowledge or experience.

Write at least 250 words.

题目解释

一些人认为要改善公众健康政府应该增加体育设施的数量，另一些人认为这样做没有什么效果，需要其他的措施来改善公众健康。讨论这两种观点并且给出你的观点。

高分范文

The construction of new sports facilities is definitely needed in an environment where people's health is in a declining state. However, there are those who believe that the way of improving people's health should lie in other measures that governments have to come up with to enable people to live more healthily.

In many countries, the lack of sports facilities has directly led to a sharp decline in the general public's involvement in sports activities, which is the major reason for overweight nowadays. If a wider range of sports and fitness facilities (swimming pools, basketball courts and gymnasiums etc.) were available, people would be more willing to spend time in taking exercise, instead of watching television, playing video games or using computers at home.

However, the building of such facilities may become a waste of time and taxpayers' money if they are built far away from the place where people live or if they are too expensive to use. In these cases, the government should spend more on advertising healthier lifestyle instead of just wasting money on facilities which are not going to be actively used by the people. For example, it is important for people to know that little things like jogging or taking the stairs provide as many benefits as using exercising equipment in a sports club.

From what has been discussed above, I suppose that the government should spend more money on the campaigns of getting the public to be more involved in a healthier lifestyle instead of wasting taxpayers' money on sports facilities which are barely used by the general public. This is by far the best way of improving the health of a nation as a whole.

范文翻译

在人们的健康正处于下降状态下的环境中，建造新的体育设施是非常必要的。然而，也有一些人相信，改善人们的健康应依赖于其他措施，政府必须提出这些措施，使人们更加健康地生活。

在许多国家，缺乏体育设施直接导致广大市民参与体育活动的机会急剧减少，这是如今人们超重的主要原因。如果有更多的体育和健身设施（游泳池、篮球场和健身房等）可利用，那么人们会更愿意花时间锻炼，而不是看电视、玩游戏或在家里使用电脑。

但是，如果这些设施被建在远离人们住处的地方或者使用起来太昂贵，这种建设可能是浪费时间和纳税人的金钱。在这些情况下，政府应该更多地宣传健康的生活方式，而不只是在设施上浪费金钱，而这些设施是不会被人们积极利用的。例如，像慢跑或爬楼梯这样的小事和使用体育俱乐部里提供的健身设施一样有好处，让人们知道这一点很重要。

通过上面的讨论，我认为，政府应该花更多的钱动员人们更多地参与健康的生活方式，而不是在体育设施上浪费纳税人的钱，这些设施很少被广大民众使用。这是提高整个民族健康水平的最佳途径。

闪光词汇

★ **improve** [im'pru:v] *v.* 改善，改进
We must always endeavour to **improve** our work. 我们总要努力改进自己的工作。

★ **measure** ['meʒə] *n.* 方法，措施
Feed by **measure** and defy physicians. 饮食有节制，医生无用处。

★ **available** [ə'veiləbl] *adj.* 可得到的，可利用的
The funds are not otherwise **available**. 这些资金没有别的方法可以获得。

★ **benefit** ['benifit] *n.* 利益，好处
This dictionary will be of great **benefit** to me. 这部字典将对我有很大裨益。

★ **barely** ['bɛəli] *adv.* 仅仅，刚刚，几乎不能
He could **barely** exist on such a low wage. 他很难靠这么低的工资生存。

实用句型

From what has been discussed above，I suppose that ... 通过上面的讨论，我认为……
用这种句型结构作为结尾段的第一句，表示对全文的内容做出总结，并给出建议。
请看范文中的这句话：
From what has been discussed above，I suppose that the government should spend more money on the campaigns of getting the public to be more involved in a healthier lifestyle instead of wasting taxpayers' money on sports facilities which are barely used by the general public. 通过上面的讨论，我认为，政府应该花更多的钱动员人们更多地参与健康生活方式，而不是在体育设施上浪费纳税人的钱，这些设施很少被广大民众使用。

2008 年 1 月 19 日考题回顾

老年人的传统观念对年轻人的作用

WRITING TASK 2

You should spend about 40 minutes on this task.

Write about the following topic：

The old generation often holds some traditional ideas on the correct way of life，thinking and behavior. However，some people think these ideas are not helpful for the young generation to prepare for modern life. What's your opinion?

Give reasons for your answer and include any relevant examples from your own knowledge or experience.

Write at least 250 words.

题目解释

关于正确的生活方式、思想和行为，老一代通常有一些传统的观点。然而，一些人认为这些传统的观点对年轻的一代人为现代生活做准备没有什么帮助。你的观点是什么？

高分范文

Views are subjective, and have much to do with one's life experience and the social environment. The old generation has formed some traditional ideas about what the correct way of life is, what one's thinking and behavior should be. However, many people hold the view that these ideas are not helpful for the young generation to prepare for modern life. I find the statement is narrow to some extent.

Some basic viewpoints of life such as honesty, industriousness and thrift are consistent no matter how time changes, which have been inherited by the old generation and should be passed on from generation to generation. They are the core part of the long-standing civilization. Without these virtues the whole society would fall into chaos.

However, not all of the ideas of the old generation are correct. Some of them are out of date, and some of them can be completely wrong. For example, not many old people are familiar with the Internet, which they think is unreal and refuse to accept. Nonetheless, the Internet makes our life more convenient than ever and no one could imagine what the modern life would be without the Internet. What's more, many old people in China think divorce is not acceptable. Even though marriage is inharmonious, they try hard to prevent it from breaking up. Now young people liberate themselves from all these bondages. If they think marriage is a barrier to happiness, they will get rid of the relationship. They are brave enough to pursue their own happiness.

To sum up, views and ideas should be changed with the development of modern society. To inherit all the ideas from the old generation will do nothing but harm to the young generation. It is right for the young to take the essence and discard the dregs.

范文翻译

观点是主观的，与个人人生经历和社会环境息息相关。老一代人关于正确的生活方式、一个人的思想和行为应该是什么样的，形成了一些传统的观念。然而，许多人认为这些观念对年青一代为现代生活做准备没有帮助。我认为这个观点有一点儿狭隘。

无论时代如何变迁，一些基本的生活观念像诚实、勤俭和节约都不会改变，它们已经被老一代继承，并且应当一代一代地传下去。它们属于长期存在的文明的核心部分。没有了这些美德，整个社会将会陷入混乱。

然而，并不是老一代人的所有观念都是正确的。有些已经过时，有些可能完全错误。比如说，很少有老年人熟悉互联网，他们认为互联网是不真实的并且拒绝接受。但是，互联网给人们的生活带来了前所未有的便捷，无法想象，如果没有互联网，现代生活会是什么样子的。另外，中国的许多老年人认为离婚是不可接受的。即使婚姻不和睦，他们也会尽力维持而不离婚。现在的年轻人已从这些束缚中解脱出来。如果婚姻成了幸福的一个障碍，他们会解除这种关系。他们敢于追寻自己的幸福。

总之，观点和想法应该随着现代社会的发展而改变。继承老一代人的所有观点只会对年轻的一代有害。对于年轻人来说，取其精华、去其糟粕才是正确的。

闪光词汇

★ **subjective** [sʌb'dʒektiv] *adj.* 主观的，个人的

This is a very **subjective** judgment of her abilities. 这是对她能力的一种非常主观的判断。

★ **prepare for** 为……做准备

Will you help me **prepare for** the party? 你能否帮我为这次聚会做好准备工作?

★ **acceptable** [ək'septəbl] *adj.* 可接受的，合意的

What is the minimum salary you would find **acceptable**? 你能接受的最低工资是多少?

实用句型

...**will do nothing but harm to** ...**It is right for sb. to**（do sth.）……只会对……有害。对于某人来说做……是正确的。

这种句型结构用于表明作者的观点，先用...will do nothing but harm to ... 表示反对的内容，再用 It is right for sb. to（do sth.）表示赞同什么样的做法或者提出建议。

请看范文中的这句话：

To inherit all the ideas from the old generation **will do nothing but harm to** the young generation. **It is right for the young to** take the essence and discard the dregs. 继承老一代人的所有观点只会对年轻的一代有害。对于年轻人来说，取其精华、去其糟粕才是正确的。

2008年2月14日考题回顾

居住在大城市还是小城市

WRITING TASK 2

You should spend about 40 minutes on this task.

Write about the following topic:

> ***An increasing number of people choose to live in big cities. What problems will this bring about? Should the government encourage people to live in small towns?***

Give reasons for your answer and include any relevant examples from your own knowledge or experience.

Write at least 250 words.

题目解释

越来越多的人选择居住在大城市，这会引起什么样的问题？政府应该鼓励人们居住在小城市吗？

高分范文

Big cities have more convenient infrastructure facilities and opportunities, so an increasing number of people choose to live there. However, problems of living in big cities are appearing. And the government is working out measures to cope with them. Encouraging people to live in small towns is a practical one.

For individuals, living in big cities may encounter many problems. Firstly, the rent and the price of houses are higher there. So it costs more to live. Secondly, there are too many people to compete for the limited jobs. Competition is furious and some of them become jobless. Thirdly, traffic is congested in big cities. It takes more time for people to go to and off work every day.

Meanwhile, as far as society is concerned, this trend leads to disparity of resource allocation and other difficult problems. In the first place, more people choose to live in big cities, and fewer people remain living in the countryside or small towns. Agriculture is weakened for lack of laborers. In the second place, attracted by big cities, talented people choose to study and work there. This makes big cities more attractive and small towns poorer. Lastly, many people in big cities have their own cars; and more exhaust gas is emitted. So the air in many big cities is usually badly polluted.

Therefore if we take the situation into careful consideration, it is not difficult to draw the conclusion that encouraging people to live in small towns would be a pragmatic solution to problems mentioned above. Governments should give preferable policies to small towns so that people can benefit from living there.

范文翻译

大城市有更多便捷的基础设施和机会，因此越来越多的人选择居住在那里。然而，住在大城市的诸多问题也显现出来。政府正出台措施来应对。鼓励人们在小城市生活就是很实际的一项。

对于个人而言，生活在大城市可能会遇到很多问题。首先，那里的房租和房价都较高，因此生活在那里花费的成本更高。其次，有太多的人竞争数量有限的工作。竞争很激烈，他们当中的一些人就会成为失业者。再次，大城市的交通很拥挤，人们每天都要花更多的时间上下班。

同时，就社会而言，这种趋势导致资源分配的不均衡和其他难题。首先，更多的人选择在大城市生活，较少的人留在乡村或小城市。由于缺乏劳动力，农业被削弱。其次，有才能的人受大城市吸引，他们选择在那里学习和工作，这使大城市更具魅力，而小城镇会变得更加贫困。最后，许多大城市里的人都有他们自己的小汽车，更多的废气被排放出来，所以，大城市的空气通常污染严重。

所以，如果我们认真地考虑一下形势，不难得出结论，鼓励人们居住在小城市是解决上面提到的这些问题的一个很实际的办法。政府应该给小城市一些优惠政策，让居住在这里的人们获益。

闪光词汇

★ **convenient** [kən'viːniənt] *adj.* 便利的，方便的

When is the most **convenient** time for you? 你什么时候最方便?

★ **cope with** 应付

We adopted several measures to **cope with** it. 我们采用了几种方法来应付它。

★ **flood into** 涌进

The early 90's witnessed an unprecedented tide of rural workers **flooding into** big cities in China.

(20 世纪) 90 年代初期，一股历史上从未有过的农民工的潮流涌进了中国的大城市。

★ **congested** [kən'dʒestid] *adj.* 拥挤的

The main streets in the centre of the city are always very **congested**. 城市中心的街道总是很拥挤。

★ **preferable** ['prefərəbl] *adj.* 更可取的，更好的，更优越的

He finds country life **preferable** to living in the city. 他感到在乡村生活比在城市生活要好些。

实用句型

as far as ...**be concerned** 就……而言，谈到……

一般用于段落的开头，引出论点；或者用于结尾，总结观点。

请看范文中的这句话：

Meanwhile, **as far as** society **is concerned**, the trend leads to disparity of resource allocation and other difficult problems. 同时，就社会而言，这种趋势导致资源分配的不均衡和其他的难题。

类似考题

2006 年 5 月 13 日

Housing shortage in big cities can cause severe social consequences. Some people think only government action can solve this problem. To what extent do you agree or disagree?

2008 年 2 月 16 日考题回顾

明天重要还是今天重要

WRITING TASK 2

You should spend about 40 minutes on this task.

Write about the following topic：

> ***An American film actor once said，“Tomorrow is important and precious.” Some people think individuals and society should pay more attention to the future than to the present. Do you agree or disagree?***

Give reasons for your answer and include any relevant examples from your own knowledge or experience.

Write at least 250 words.

题目解释

一位美国电影演员曾经说过：“明天是重要而且珍贵的。”一些人认为个人和社会应该更关注将来而不是现在。你同意还是不同意？

高分范文

An American film actor once said，“Tomorrow is important and precious.” But another saying goes like this：“Yesterday is history；tomorrow is mystery；only today is a present.” In my opinion，individuals and society should pay more attention to the present than to the future.

Tomorrow is always a day after today. What the actor said really means that tomorrow is hope and the hope is important and precious，which we should never give up. If someone loses hope，he will lose all the motivations and even the courage to live. When people are in despair，they could not see through misery and find the hope. So the words are intended to encourage people to be strong and try hard.

However，only hope can not achieve anything. We also should grab the present to work hard and to get near to the hope. What's more，a high-quality life needs to enjoy the present. If we always think tomorrow would be better and we should enjoy tomorrow，when the next day comes，another tomorrow is ahead. Thus，there is no day for us to enjoy life forever. To all the people on this earth，life is a single trip ticket. No one could restart his life，so every moment is important and precious to us. We spend every minute seriously and carefully. Together we will have a splendid life. If we spend every present moment idly waiting for the so called important and precious tomorrow to come，life will surely be meaningless. Many philosophers and great thinkers have noticed this question and most of their answers are the present is more important and precious than the future and the future is based on what we are doing today.

From the above analysis，we could draw the conclusion that what we are doing at present decides what tomorrow would be like，and that the present is important and precious.

范文翻译

有位美国电影演员曾说过："明天是重要且宝贵的。"但还有一句谚语提到："昨天是历史，明天是未知，只有今天才是现在。"依我看来，个人和社会都应当更多地关注现在而不是未来。

明天永远是今天后面的一天。那位演员说的明天实际上指的是希望，希望是重要且宝贵的，我们永远都不应该放弃。如果某人失去了希望，他将失去所有的动力，甚至会丧失活着的勇气。当人们绝望的时候，是不可能穿越迷雾并找到希望的。因此，这句话是鼓励人们要坚强和努力。

然而，只有希望并不能获得任何东西。我们必须抓住此刻，努力工作，以期靠近希望。另外，高质量的生活需要享受现在。如果我们总是想着明天更美好，想着我们应该享受明天，当第二天来临的时候，又一个明天会展现在眼前。因此，永远没有任何一天可以享受生命。对于地球上的每个人，生命都是一张单程票。没有人可以重新开始，因此生命的每一刻对我们来说都是重要且珍贵的。我们严肃认真地对待每一分钟，这样就可以享有精彩的一生。如果把现在的每一刻都耗费在等待所谓的重要和珍贵的明天上，生命势必会没有意义。很多哲学家和伟大的思想家都已意识到这个问题，他们给出的答案大都是此刻比未来更加重要和宝贵，而未来是建立在今天所做的一切的基础之上的。

通过上面的分析，我们可以得出结论，我们今天所做的将决定明天将是什么样子，现在是重要和珍贵的。

闪光词汇

★ **precious** ['preʃəs] *adj.* 宝贵的，贵重的

When a thing is scarce，it is **precious**. 物以稀为贵。

★ **pay more attention to** 多注意

We hope that you'll **pay more attention to** the quality of your goods in the future. 希望贵方将来多注意产品的质量问题。

★ **splendid** ['splendid] *adj.* 壮丽的，辉煌的

We've had a **splendid** evening and thanks for having us. 我们过了一个美好的傍晚，谢谢您的款待。

★ **analysis** [ə'nælisis] *n.* 分析

He has given an acute **analysis** of the situation. 他对形势做了深刻的分析。

实用句型

From the above analysis，we could draw the conclusion that ... 通过上面的分析，我们可以得出……结论。

这种句型结构用在最后一段，对全文的分析加以总结，给出结论。

请看范文中的这句话：

From the above analysis，we could draw the conclusion that what we are doing at present will decide what tomorrow would be like，and that the present is important and precious. 通过上面的分析，我们可以得出结论，今天所做的将决定明天将是什么样子，现在是重要和珍贵的。

2008 年 4 月 12 日考题回顾

忙于工作的原因和影响

WRITING TASK 2

You should spend about 40 minutes on this task.

Write about the following topic:

> *More people are busy with work and have no enough time to spend with their families and friends. Why does this happen? What are the effects on family life and society as a whole?*

Give reasons for your answer and include any relevant examples from your own knowledge or experience.

Write at least 250 words.

题目解释

越来越多的人忙于工作，没有足够的时间与他们的家人和朋友一起度过。为什么会发生这种情况？这对家庭生活和整个社会有哪些影响？

高分范文

It is generally acknowledged that more working people are busy with work and have no enough time to spend with their families and friends. Obviously, there are many factors which influence one's attitude to job and lifestyle directly or indirectly.

More people have become workaholics. We may look into two possible reasons. In the first place, job satisfaction is increasingly becoming an essential element, if not the most important one of individual well-being. Another reason is that they would be fired if they spent too much time with friends and families and turned a deaf ear to the boss. That is to say, sometimes, people are forced to act like this. This situation has very profound effects on family life and society as a whole.

On the one hand, undoubtedly, working can be a win-win approach, that is, it will benefit both family life and the whole society. In fact, you devote 10 hours each day to working furiously to make money, reach goals, and give your families the best. At the same time, people who devote themselves to working can bring more benefits to society. They can enhance productivity of society and create more fortune. As a result, the entire society will be more wealthy and harmonious.

On the other hand, the situation also has negative impacts. People are busy with work and often feel extremely tired when they are off duty and have to ignore their families and friends. So friends and family members may become more separated and colder to one another. None of us want to see this happen with pleasure.

In my opinion, the following tips can help the workaholic refocus and get the best out of life and keep healthy and alive in the long run, too. First, be resolved to keep Saturdays and Sundays strictly to your family and friends. Second, always bear it in mind that you work so that you can provide your family with a rich and colorful life.

范文翻译

众所周知，更多参加工作的人忙于他们的工作，没有足够的时间陪伴他们的家人和朋友。显然，有许多因素直接或间接地影响一个人对待工作和生活方式的态度。

越来越多的人变成了工作狂。我们可以看到两方面的原因。首先，工作带来的满足感日益成为一个人幸福的非常重要的组成部分，即使不是最重要的组成部分。另一个原因就是，如果花太多的时间与朋友和家人在一起而不听老板的，他们将会被解雇。也就是说，有时，人们这样做是被迫的。这种状况对家庭生活和整个社会都有很深远的影响。

一方面，毋庸置疑，工作是一个双赢的途径，那就是，它既有利于家庭生活，也有利于整个社会。事实上，你每天花 10 小时发疯地工作：赚钱，实现目标，为家人创造最好的生活条件。同时，人们努力工作也给社会带来益处。他们能提高社会生产力，创造更多的财富。结果就是，整个社会更加富有而和谐。

另一方面，这种情况也有消极的影响。人们忙于工作，下班后经常感到极度疲惫，因此不得不忽略他们的家人和朋友。因此，朋友和家人之间变得越来越隔阂和疏远。这是我们都不愿意看到的。

在我看来，下面的办法可以帮助工作狂汲取生活的精华，并且活得更健康长寿。第一，确保周末要留给家人和朋友。第二，要记住，你工作是为了使你的家庭过上富有而多彩的生活。

闪光词汇

★ **be busy with** 忙于

We **are** now very **busy with** preparation. 我们正忙着准备呢。

★ **workaholic** [ˌwəːkəˈhɔlik] *n.* 工作第一的人，工作狂

More people have become **workaholics**. 许多人已经变成了工作狂。

★ **look into** 观察

We may **look into** two possible reasons. 我们可以看到两个可能的原因。

★ **devote to** 把……献给

We should **devote** ourselves assiduously and faithfully **to** the duties of our profession. 我们应当勤奋地而忠诚地献身于我们的专业职责。

★ **turn a deaf ear to** 不理睬

He dug in and **turned a deaf ear to** our reasoning. 他固执己见，对我们讲的道理根本不听。

★ **bear in mind** 记住

Bear it in mind that you'll have to practice economy. 记住要厉行节约。

类似考题

2006 年 10 月 28 日考题

As most people spend a major part of their adult life at work, job satisfaction is an important element of individual well-being. What are the factors that contribute to job satisfaction? How realistic is the expectation of job satisfaction for all workers?

2008 年 5 月 31 日考题回顾

身体和精神状态在体育运动中的作用

WRITING TASK 2

You should spend about 40 minutes on this task.

Write about the following topic：

Some people argue that the fittest and strongest individuals and teams can achieve the greatest success in sports. But other people think the success is much related to the mental attitude. Discuss both views and give your opinion.

Give reasons for your answer and include any relevant examples from your own knowledge or experience.

Write at least 250 words.

题目解释

一些人认为，身体最好、最强壮的个人和团队在体育运动中能取得最大的成功。但是另一些人认为，体育运动中的成功与精神状态的关系更密切。讨论这两种观点并给出你的看法。

高分范文

In contemporary society，an increasing number of people enjoy sports. They play hard，they play often，and they play to win. Some argue that the strong always beat the weak and the fit win the ill. While others insist that the mental attitude can also affect the result of a sports game. But I deem that a sound mind is in a sound body. And the decisive factors of success in sports are related to both spirit and body.

In some sports pageants，such as the Olympic Games，World Championship Match，and World Cup Match，competition is extremely furious. In some of the matches，like judo，marathon，weight-lifting，shooting and boxing，only the fittest and strongest athletes can attain their aim：winning. In some other group matches，such as football，basketball and volleyball，only every member in the group is fittest and strongest，may the team achieve the greatest success in the competition.

Meanwhile，in some games，such as shooting and dash，the candidates must be in the best mental state. In these matches，success is much more closely related to the mental attitude，which matches one of ancient Chinese says—when there is an unavoidable confrontation，the brave win.

To sum up，whether body or mental attitude is decisive in sports is dependent on the kind of games. As a matter of fact，Competition in most of the matches is highly severe，and both physical condition and mental attitude can influence the result，but neither of them is definitely decisive. In most of the games，only the best individuals and teams who are fittest and strongest both in body and in spirit can achieve the greatest success.

范文翻译

在当今社会，越来越多的人喜欢体育运动。他们努力比赛，不懈拼搏，以取胜为目标。一些人认为，强壮的总是打败弱小的，身体健康的战胜身体不好的。而另一些人坚持认为，精神状态也能影响一次体育比赛的结果。但是我认为，有健康的身体，才有健康的精神。体育运动中成功的决定性因素与精神和身体都有关系。

在一些体育盛会中，例如奥运会、世锦赛和世界杯等，竞争是非常激烈的。在其中的一些比赛中，包括柔道、马拉松、举重、射击和拳击等，只有身体最好、最强壮的运动员才能达到他们的目标：胜利。在另外一些团体比赛中，像足球、篮球和排球等，只有团队中的每一个成员都是身体最好、最强壮的，整个团队才有可能在竞争中取得最大的成功。

与此同时，在一些比赛中，例如射击和短跑等，参赛选手必须处于最佳的精神状态。在这些比赛中，成功与精神状态的关系更密切，这正应了中国的一句古话——狭路相逢，勇者胜。

总之，是身体还是精神状态在体育运动中起决定性作用依比赛的种类而定。其实，在大部分的比赛中，竞争都是非常激烈的，身体状况和精神状态都能影响结果，但其中任何一个都不完全是决定性因素。在绝大多数比赛中，只有最好的个人和团队，也就是身体和精神都处于最好状态的个人和团队才能取得最大的成功。

闪光词汇

★ **mental** ['mentl] *adj*. 精神的，智力的

He got the answer by **mental** arithmetic. 他用心算得出了答案。

★ **sound** [saund] *adj*. 健全的，可靠的

I've repaired the roof and it's quite **sound** now. 我修了屋顶，现在它挺坚固的。

★ **decisive** [di'saisiv] *adj*. 决定性的

★ Two factors had a **decisive** influence. 有两个因素有决定性的影响力。

★ **relate** [ri'leit] *v*. 联系

Happiness does not always **relate** to wealth. 幸福不总与财富相关。

★ **pageant** ['pædʒənt] *n*. 盛会，庆典

The Olympic Games is a sports **pageant** for the people of the world. 奥运会是世界人民的体育盛会。

★ **competition** [ˌkɔmpi'tiʃən] *n*. 竞争

He takes part in a swimming **competition**. 他参加游泳比赛。

★ **dependent** [di'pendənt] *adj*. 依靠的，由……决定的

All effects are **dependent** on their causes. 一切的结果都基于它们的原因。

2008 年 11 月 8 日考题回顾

穿时尚衣服的原因和影响

WRITING TASK 2

You should spend about 40 minutes on this task.

Write about the following topic：

> *More and more people now choose to wear fashionable clothes. Why? What positive and negative effects does this trend have on society?*

Give reasons for your answer and include any relevant examples from your own knowledge or experience.

Write at least 250 words.

题目解释

现在，越来越多的人选择穿时尚的衣服，这是为什么？这种趋势对社会的积极影响和消极影响都有哪些？

高分范文

Fashion refers to the style of dressing that is popular in a culture at any given time. In present day, more and more people choose to wear fashionable clothes. There are no less than two reasons as follows:

In the first place, what a person chooses to wear can reflect his personality or likes. When people who have cultural status start to wear new or different clothes, a fashion trend may start. People who like or respect them may start to wear clothes of a similar style. In the second place, advertising can also influence people's choice to a large degree. Whenever we switch the channels, we are bombarded with lots of TV commercials. Young people are easily affected, and it is possible for them to try the new fashion, feel the new taste and have new experience. They easily respond to advertising because it is part of their nature, which is normal.

Fashion's impacts on society as a whole include both positive and negative aspects. The positive sides are two-fold. Firstly, fashion can support garment industry which can accelerate the economic development. Secondly, the development of garment industry can offer more job opportunities to young people, which may reduce the rate of unemployment. But on the other hand, fashionable clothes are made in small quantities to guarantee exclusivity, so they are rather expensive. The attitude of people toward fashion has resulted in a new prophecy—consumerism, which is a negative impact against a background of the world financial crisis.

From the analysis above, we can conclude that fashion has more positive effects than negative effects on society. And people should be encouraged to wear fashionable clothes as long as they like and have enough money.

范文翻译

时尚是指在任何特定时间和文化范围内流行的服饰。当前，越来越多的人选择穿流行的服装，有以下两个原因：

首先，一个人选择穿什么能反映他的个性和喜好。当一个有文化地位的人开始穿新的或者是不同的服装的时候，流行趋势可能就开始了。喜欢或尊敬他们的人们就会开始穿相似风格的服装。其次，广告也在很大程度上影响人们的选择。无论什么时候我们转换频道，我们都会面对大量的电视商业广告。年轻人很容易受到影响，并且他们有可能尝试新时尚，感受新体验，收获新经历。他们很容易对广告作出回应，因为那对于他们来说很自然，很正常。

时尚对社会整体的影响包括积极的和消极的两个方面。积极的影响有两点：首先，时尚能支持服装工业，促进经济发展。其次，服装工业的发展能为年轻人提供更多的就业机会，从而降低失业率。但是另一方面，时尚的服装为了保证独特性，数量都很少，因此它们都很贵。人们对时尚的态度已经导致新的预言，即消费至上主义，这在世界金融危机爆发的情况下的影响是消极的。

基于以上分析，我们可以得出结论：时尚对社会的积极影响超过了消极影响。人们应该被鼓励穿时尚服装，只要他们喜欢并且有足够的钱。

闪光词汇

★ **personality** [ˌpəːsəˈnæliti] *n.* 个性，人格

Though their **personalities** differed, they got along as friends. 虽然他们性格迥异，但却相处友好。

★ **switch** [switʃ] *v.* 转换，转变

He **switched** the conversation to a lighter subject. 他把谈话转移到一个更轻松的话题。

★ **accelerate** [ækˈseləreit] *v.* 加速，促进

We must seize all opportunities to **accelerate** development. 必须抓住一切机遇加快发展。

★ **guarantee** [ˌgærənˈtiː] *n.* 保证，保证书 *v.* 保证，担保

The insurance company **guarantees** to replace any parts of the car which are stolen. 保险公司保证赔偿汽车上任何被偷的零部件。

★ **prophecy** [ˈprɔfisi] *n.* 预言

His **prophecy** has now come true. 他的预言果然应验了。

★ **consumerism** [kənˈsjuːmərizəm] *n.* 用户至上主义，消费主义

American shopping malls and supermarkets are palaces of **consumerism**. 美国的购物中心和超市是消费主义的地盘。

Unit 3

Environment and Animal Protection

环境与动物保护

2010 年 9 月 11 日考题回顾

动物实验

WRITING TASK 2

You should spend about 40 minutes on this task.

Write about the following topic:

> ***Some people think that the use of animals for experiment is not right. Others think it is beneficial for medical testing. Discuss both views and give your own opinion.***

Give reasons for your answer and include any relevant examples from your own knowledge or experience.

Write at least 250 words.

题目解释

有些人认为利用动物进行实验是不对的。另外一些人认为这有益于医疗实验。讨论这两种观点，并给出你自己的看法。

高分范文

Could the use of animals in scientific experiments be justified? Recently, this phenomenon has been brought to public attention with people standing on both sides.

Those who hold that it is barbaric to exploit animals for our own purposes list the reasons as follows. To begin with, it is psychologically unacceptable. Suppose we are a pet owner. When someone asks to take away our lovely dog for a scientific experiment, we will certainly cry out and claim that he or she is a devil. This is just the reaction we are expecting, for it is love and concern for others that make human beings human, and this kind of love and care is not only existing among ourselves, but also between us and the nature. Also, it is a sheer violation of animal's right of subsistence. All lives enjoy the equality to live in this world and every creature on the earth is a gift. It must be a nightmare to live in a world where people kill animals for any purpose they like.

However, to get a fuller view of such a controversial issue, we should put ourselves in another position. Scientific experiments using animals have contributed a lot in medical development. In other words, we can derive the first-hand information about diseases from animal testing. Thanks to that, cures for many kinds of disease, which have killed thousands of people in the past few decades, have been found now and many lives are saved. If we were one of those with that kind of disease, we would definitely support using animals in scientific experiments that could save our lives, which reflects the rule of the nature—the fittest survives. Moreover, it is helpful to lessen the risks on conducting experiments on human beings directly. In fact, animals are the substitution of human beings during the risky testing so that we can avoid being hurt by some unknown medicine or therapy.

From what has been discussed above, we can see that it is extremely hard to reach an absolute conclusion. After pondering this question on many occasions, I think the correct attitude is that we should make good use of the animals while at the same time loving and protecting them, since it is not only for our own sake but also for the sake of the harmony that exists in the natural world.

范文翻译

在科学实验中使用动物是否合理？近来，这个现象引起了公众的关注，人们持两种对立的观点。

一些人认为出于个人目的而利用动物是野蛮的，理由如下。首先，这在心理上是不能被接受的。假设我们是宠物的主人。如果有人想拿走我们可爱的小狗做科学实验，我们一定会大叫，称这人是魔鬼。这仅仅是我们预期的反应，因为正是这种对别人的爱心和关怀，才使人类之所以成为人，这种爱和关心不仅仅存在于人类之间，也存在于人类和自然之间。此外，这也是对动物生存权利的彻底侵犯。一切生命在这个世界上享有平等生存的权利，地球上的每个生物都是天赐。生活在人们可以随意杀死动物的世界必定是件可怕的事情。

但是，为了更全面地分析这样一个有争议的问题，我们应当把自己放在另一个位置上。科学实验使用动物对医学发展做出了很多贡献。换言之，我们从动物实验中得到了很多有关疾病的第一手资料。正因为如此，过去几十年来夺去无数人生命的多种疾病，现在已经发现了治愈方法，这挽救了很多生命。如果我们患上了这些疾病，就一定会支持在科学实验中使用动物，这可以挽救我们的生命，这反映了大自然的规则——适者生存。此外，它有利于降低用人体直接进行实验的风险。其实，在危险的试验中，动物是人的替代品，使我们能够避免被一些未知的药物或治疗所伤害。

通过上面的讨论，我们可以看到，很难得出一个绝对的结论。多次考虑这个问题后，我想正确的态度是，我们应该在利用好动物的同时爱护它们，因为这不仅仅出于我们自身的利益，同时也是为了与自然和谐共处。

闪光词汇

★ **barbaric** [bɑː'bærik] *adj*. 野蛮的

This **barbaric** practice should be banned immediately. 这种野蛮行径应立刻予以禁止。

★ **violation** [ˌvaiə'leiʃən] *n*. 违反；侵害

This is one of the commonest traffic **violations**. 这是最常见的违反交通规则之例。

★ **subsistence** [sʌb'sistəns] *n*. 生存

Their main mode of **subsistence** is hunting. 他们主要以打猎为生。

★ **controversial** [ˌkɔntrə'vəːʃəl] *adj*. 争论的，争议的

The topic of argument is **controversial**. 这个议题是很有争议的。

★ **derive from** 得自

Many English words are **derived from** Latin and Greek. 很多英语单词都源出于拉丁文和希腊文。

★ **lessen** ['lesn] *v*. 减轻

Regular exercise can help to **lessen** the pain. 经常运动有助于减轻痛感。

★ **substitution** [ˌsʌbsti'tjuːʃən] *n*. 代替

We use saccharin in **substitution** for sugar. 我们用糖精代替糖。

★ **ponder** ['pɔndə] *v*. 考虑

We **pondered** whether to tell him. 我们考虑是否要告诉他。

★ **for the sake of** 为了

We made concessions **for the sake of** peace. 为了和平我们做出了让步。

实用句型

1. **Recently, this phenomenon has been brought to public attention with people standing on both sides.** 近来，这个现象引起了公众的关注，人们持两种对立的观点。这种句型一般用于第一段，引出话题和观点。
2. **Those who hold that...list the reasons as follows.** 一些人认为……，理由如下。这种句型一般用做第二段的中心句，表示开始分析一方的观点和理由。
请看范文中的这句话：
Those who hold that it is barbaric to exploit animals for our own purposes **list the reasons as follows**. 一些人认为出于个人目的而利用动物是野蛮的，理由如下。
3. **However, to get a fuller view of such a controversial issue, we should put ourselves in another position**. 但是，为了更全面地分析这样一个有争议的问题，我们应当把自己放在另一个位置上。这种句型一般用做第三段的中心句，表示开始分析与前一段不同的观点和理由。
4. **From what has been discussed above, we can see that it is extremely hard to reach an absolute conclusion. After pondering this question on many occasions, I think the correct attitude is that we should**··通过上面的讨论，我们可以看到，很难得出一个绝对的结论。多次考虑这个问题后，我想正确的态度是我们应该……。这种句型一般用于结尾段，表示总结全文，并提出自己的观点。
请看范文中的这句话：

From what has been discussed above, we can see that it is extremely hard to reach an absolute conclusion. After pondering this question on many occasions, I think the correct attitude is that we should make good use of them while at the same time love and protect them. 通过上面的讨论，我们可以看到，很难得出一个绝对的结论。多次考虑这个问题后，我想正确的态度是，我们应该在利用好动物的同时爱护它们。

类似考题

2005年9月17日

Some people think that using animals for experimentation purpose is cruel, but other people think that it is necessary for the development of science. Discuss both views and give your opinion.

2006年5月27日

Some people think that using animals for experimentation purpose is cruel, but other people think that it is necessary for the development of science. Discuss both views and give your opinion.

2009 年 2 月 21 日考题回顾

个人在环境保护中的作用

WRITING TASK 2

You should spend about 40 minutes on this task.

Write about the following topic：

> ***Some people think that environmental problems are too big for individuals to deal with. Others，however，think that each individual should take some actions. Discuss both views and give your own opinion.***

Give reasons for your answer and include any relevant examples from your own knowledge or experience.

Write at least 250 words.

题目解释

一些人认为，环境问题对于个人来说太大而无法应付。然而，另一些人认为，每一个人都应该采取行动。讨论这两种观点并给出你的观点。

高分范文

It is true that our individual actions often seem insignificant compared with the scale and complexity of global environmental problems such as pollution, deforestation and depletion of natural resources. But that does not relieve our duty as individuals to do as much as we can to deal with these problems.

Individual actions, small as they may be, can prove more effective than we realize. We can avoid driving the car, and take public transit, walk, or bicycle instead. This will reduce the use of fuel and cut pollution. Saving energy at home, like turning on the air conditioner only when we have to, or turning water heater down a few degrees, is also ultimately good for the environment. Individual actions can also turn into united power when, for example, the whole neighborhood is mobilized to participate in a local campaign to oppose environmentally damaging policies.

There are, however, obstacles that stand in the way of individual actions towards environmental protection. The first obstacle is the lack of professional knowledge needed to cope with serious environmental problems like soil erosion and salinity, which require a significant amount of investigation and research. Another obstacle which makes individual actions almost impossible is an environmental emergency or accident, e. g. an oil spill near the border line, which would necessitate government intervention or even international coordination.

In conclusion, when it comes to environmental problems, individual actions are indispensable in the problem solving process. But the most pressing and complicated problems go far beyond an individual's capability and so require the concerted effort of the government as well as the global community.

范文翻译

诚然，我们个人的行动与全球环境问题，例如污染、砍伐森林和自然资源损耗等的程度和复杂性相比，似乎是微不足道的。但是，这并不减少我们作为个人尽最大能力去处理这些问题的职责。

个人的行动虽然小，但能证明比我们意识到的更有效。我们可以避免开车，改为乘坐公共交通、步行或者骑自行车，这样会减少燃料的使用和环境污染。在家里节约能源，只有必要时才打开空调，或将热水器调低几度，这对环境也是绝对有好处的。个人行动也可以转变成团队的力量，例如，当整个社区被动员参加当地活动，反对破坏环境的政策时。

然而，个人在保护环境的行为过程中也存在障碍。第一个障碍是缺乏必要的专业知识，以处理严重的环境问题，像土壤侵蚀和盐碱化，这些需要大量的调查和研究。另一个障碍是当一次紧急的环境情况或者事故发生时，例如：边界线附近漏油，个人行动几乎是不可能的，这使政府的干预甚至国际协调成为必要。

总之，当涉及环境问题时，个人行动在问题的解决过程中是必不可少的。但是，一些最紧迫和复杂的问题远远超出了个人的能力，因此需要政府以及国际社会的一致努力。

闪光词汇

★ **individual** [ˌindiˈvidjuəl] *n.* 个人，个体 *adj.* 个别的，单独的，个人的

The rights of the **individual** are considered to be the most important in a free society. 在自由的社会里个人权利被认为是最重要的。

★ **complexity** [kəmˈpleksiti] *n.* 复杂的事物，复杂性

The controversy pointed to the **complexity** of the problem. 这场争论有力地说明这个问题的复杂性。

★ **ultimately** [ˈʌltimətlɪ] *adv.* 最后，终于

Responsibility for the disaster must **ultimately** lies with the government. 这场灾难的责任最终必定还是在于政府。

★ **mobilize** [ˈməubilaiz] *v.* 动员

We must go all out to **mobilize** the masses. 我们要大力发动群众。

★ **obstacle** [ˈɔbstəkl] *n.* 障碍，妨害物

We seem to have removed every **obstacle** to agreement. 我们似乎已扫除了达成一致的所有障碍。

类似考题

2007 年 2 月 3 日

Individuals can do nothing to improve the environment. Only governments and large companies can make a difference. To what extent do you agree or disagree with this opinion?

2008 年 9 月 13 日

Many people think it is very important to protect the environment but they make no effort to do it themselves. Why does it happen? How to solve this problem?

2009 年 10 月 31 日

The environment problems facing today's world are so great that there is little ordinary people can do to improve the situation. Governments and large companies should be responsible for reducing the amount of damage being done to the environment. To what extent do you agree or disagree?

2008 年 2 月 2 日考题回顾

对动物的利用

WRITING TASK 2

You should spend about 40 minutes on this task.

Write about the following topic:

> ***Some people think people can exploit animals for any purpose they need, while others do not think so. What is your opinion?***

Give reasons for your answer and include any relevant examples from your own knowledge or experience.

Write at least 250 words.

题目解释

一些人认为，人们可以为了任何他们需要的目的对动物进行利用，而另外一些人却不这么认为。你的观点是什么？

高分范文

Mankind is the superior ruler of the earth. Therefore, some think that people can exploit animals for any purpose. This aggressive idea sounds dangerous to all animals and even to mankind. People should not treat animals as their own property, and do whatever they like to animals. The reasons are as follows.

First of all, this behavior may break the balance of nature and incur punishment to mankind. For example, long ago, a national campaign was launched in China to extinguish sparrows because they were considered as harmful birds which eat grain grown by farmers. A large number of sparrows were killed, but no one expected that in the next years the disaster of pests spread across the country and brought even larger loss. And people got to know the positive effects of sparrows, that is, they also eat pests.

Second, vastly exploiting animals may cause the extinguishment of rare species. The number of Tibetan antelopes keeps decreasing from over one million fifty years ago to no more than 50,000 nowadays, because cruel and greedy people chase and kill them to get their furs to make expensive shawls. The situation in the ocean is not optimistic, either. Whales are killed by many countries for meat and producing medicines and other stuff, and Japan is on top of the slaughters' list.

For the reasons discussed above, I strongly commit to the notion that human beings can make good use of animals but not exploit them for any purpose they need. No one could imagine what the world would be like, were mankind the only living creature in the world. So, we should stop exploiting animals without measure.

范文翻译

人类是地球的高级统治者。因此，一些人认为人们可以为了任何目的利用动物。这种激进的观点听起来对所有动物甚至人类都是很危险的。人们不应当把动物当作自己的财产来对待，对动物为所欲为。原因列举如下：

首先，这种行为可能会打破自然平衡，招致对人类的惩罚。例如，从前，一场全国灭雀运动在中国掀起，因为麻雀被认为是有害的鸟，它们吃农民种植的庄稼。大量麻雀被捕杀，但谁也没料到，在随后几年，害虫灾害蔓延全国，造成了更大的损失。人们才开始意识到麻雀的积极作用，那就是它们也吃害虫。

其次，对动物的大量开发利用会造成稀有物种的灭绝。藏羚羊的数量已从 50 年前的超过 100 万只减少到现在的不足 5 万只，就是因为残酷和贪婪的人们追杀藏羚羊，获取藏羚羊毛来制作昂贵的披肩。海洋的情形也不容乐观。有很多国家为了食用、生产药物和其他材料，捕杀了很多鲸鱼。其中日本是捕杀最多的国家。

基于以上理由，我强烈主张人类可以合理利用动物，但不应为了他们需要的任何目的利用动物。谁也无法想象只有人类存活的世界会是什么样子。所以，应该停止对动物的不正当利用。

闪光词汇

★ **superior** [sjuːˈpiəriə] *adj.* 较高的，上级的

Hold off the attacks of a numerically **superior** enemy. 顶住在数量上占优势的敌人的进攻。

★ **exploit** [iksˈplɔit] *v.* 利用

We shall **exploit** our rich resources to expand the economy. 我们应该利用我们丰富的资源发展经济。

★ **extinguish** [iksˈtiŋgwiʃ] *v.* 消灭

You can not **extinguish** the love of liberty. 你不能消灭对自由的热爱。

★ **make good use of** 充分利用

We must **make good use of** our time. 我们要很好利用时间。

实用句型

For the reasons discussed above，I strongly commit to the notion that … 因此，我强烈主张……

这一句型用于结尾，表明作者的立场。strongly 强烈地，表示强调。

请看范文中的这句话：

For the reasons discussed above，I strongly commit to the notion that human beings can make good use of animals but not exploit them for any purpose they need. 基于以上理由，我强烈主张人类可以合理利用动物，但不应为了他们需要的任何目的利用动物。

类似考题

2005 年 9 月 17 日

Some people think that using animals for experimentation purpose is cruel，but other people think that it is necessary for the development of science. Discuss both views and give your opinion.

2006 年 5 月 27 日

Some people think that using animals for experimentation purpose is cruel，but other people think that it is necessary for the development of science. Discuss both views and give your opinion.

2008 年 4 月 5 日考题回顾

国际旅行是否应该禁止用飞机

WRITING TASK 2

You should spend about 40 minutes on this task.

Write about the following topic：

> ***Aircraft uses more fuel than cars and produces more pollution. Some people suggest the non-essential use of aircraft like international travel should be discouraged. Do you agree or disagree?***

Give reasons for your answer and include any relevant examples from your own knowledge or experience.

Write at least 250 words.

题目解释

飞机比小汽车燃烧更多的油料并且产生更多的污染。一些人建议像国际旅行等不必要使用飞机的情况应该被限制。你同意还是不同意这种观点？

高分范文

Facts and evidence prove that the fuel consumed by an aircraft in one long-distance flight such as international travel can be used by a car for several years, and the amount of pollution produced by the aircraft is even more. Therefore, some people suggest that non-essential flights like international travel should be discouraged. Personally, I totally disagree with this argument.

On the one hand, it is right to take action to save the increasingly diminishing fossil fuel and reduce emission of greenhouse gases. However, to simply discourage only one means, such as international travel, makes no sense. It is advisable for governments to find new ways that are technically and economically more feasible and practical.

On the other hand, anyone who is sensible will agree that traveling by air is essential in terms of international communications. Superb systems of air communications make it possible for modern travelers to visit far-away places at a moderate cost within hours. If air travel were discouraged, how would people travel across the oceans and high mountains? Actually, traveling by air has so far been the best way for people to travel around the world, considering the distance covered, the number of passengers transported and travel time.

After careful consideration of the facts and reasons above, we can safely come to the conclusion that international travel by air has so far been the most economical and efficient way which should not be discouraged only because it uses more fuel.

范文翻译

事实和证据表明，一架飞机在一次长途国际旅行飞行中所消耗的燃料可以供一辆小汽车使用好几年时间，而且飞机产生的污染甚至更多。因此，一些人建议，一些不是非常重要的飞行，像国际旅行，应该被限制。在我看来，我完全不赞同这种说法。

一方面，采取行动来节省日益减少的石油燃料并且减少温室气体的排放是正确的。然而，仅仅限制一种方式，例如国际旅游，是没有用的。对于政府来说，找到在技术上和经济上更可行和更实际的新途径是可取的。

另一方面，任何一个明智的人都会承认在国际交流方面乘飞机是必要的。完善的航空系统使现代的旅行者支付适量成本在几个小时之内就能到很远的地方游览成为可能。如果航空被限制，人们如何飞越海洋和高山？实际上，考虑到所旅行的路程，运送的旅客数量和旅行的时间，乘飞机旅行是迄今为止环游世界最好的方式。

通过认真考虑上述事实和原因，我们可以得出这样一个结论：乘飞机国际旅行是迄今为止最经济、最有效的方式，不能仅仅因为耗费更多油料而被限制。

闪光词汇

★ **sense** [sens] *n.* 意义，理性 *v.* 感到，理解

There's no **sense** in waiting three hours. 等三小时是毫无道理的。

★ **feasible** ['fi:zəbl] *adj.* 可行的，切实可行的

This plan is **feasible** for carrying out. 这计划是可以实行的。

★ **staggering** ['stægəriŋ] *adj.* 令人惊愕的

I find their decision simply **staggering**. 我觉得他们的决定简直太惊人了。

★ **sensible** ['sensəbl] *adj.* 有感觉的，明智的

He is **sensible** of the danger of his position. 他发觉他处境危险。

★ **in terms of** 在……方面

Think of it **in terms of** an investment. 从投资的角度来考虑那件事。

★ **superb** [sju:'pə:b] *adj.* 极好的

They've designed us a **superb** plan. 他们给我们设计了一个极好的计划。

★ **moderate** ['mɔdərit] *adj.* 中等的，适度的 *v.* 缓和

The storm has moderated. 风暴平静下来了。

★ **consideration** [kənsidə'reiʃən] *n.* 体谅，考虑

Safety is the most important **consideration** in choosing a car. 在选择汽车时安全是最重要的考虑因素。

实用句型

Facts and evidence prove that... 事实和证据表明……

这种句型结构用来提出某种观点或者现象。

请看范文中的这句话：

Facts and evidence prove that the fuel consumed by an aircraft in one long-distance flight such as international travel can be used by a car for several years, and the amount of pollution produced by the aircraft is even more. 事实和证据表明，一架飞机在一次长途飞行例如国际旅行中所消耗的燃料可以供一辆小汽车使用好几年时间，而且产生的污染甚至更多。

类似考题

2006 年 2 月 18 日

Some people believe that air travel should be restricted because it causes serious pollution and uses up the world's fuel resources. To what extent do you agree or disagree?

2006年3月25日

One long-distance flight consumes fuel which a car uses for several years, but they cause the same amount of pollution. So some people think that we should discourage non-essential flights, such as tourist travel, rather than to limit the use of cars. To what extent do you agree or disagree?

2008年6月14日

Many people think cheap air travel should be encouraged because it gives ordinary people freedom to travel further. However, others think this leads to environmental problems, so air travel should be more expensive in order to discourage people from having it. Discuss both sides and give your own opinion.

2008 年 7 月 26 日考题回顾

国际合作对环境和贸易的作用

WRITING TASK 2

You should spend about 40 minutes on this task.

Write about the following topic：

> ***Some people think that international cooperation has brought benefits to the protection of the environment. Others believe that the greater benefits have been achieved in world business. Discuss both views and give your opinion.***

Give reasons for your answer and include any relevant examples from your own knowledge or experience.

Write at least 250 words.

题目解释

一些人认为国际合作对保护环境有利。另一些人认为更大的利益在于世界贸易。讨论这两种观点并给出你的观点。

高分范文

There is no doubt that international cooperation, from private enterprises to governments, has become increasingly prevalent in recent years. It is conducive to almost every country in many aspects such as the protection of the environment and world business.

On one hand, some people claim that international cooperation is good for environmental protection. They are well aware that every country has its unique way of protecting environment. For example, the Dutch do well in disposing of wastes. If their advanced technology can be introduced into the developing countries that can hardly invent it, not only some countries or groups but also perhaps all of the people living on earth will benefit a lot. To be sure, the countries that have invented these technologies may have to suffer economic losses at a certain level unless their intellectual property rights are protected by the governments.

On the other hand, others hold the view that the main advantage of international cooperation is evident in terms of business. It is true that import and export trade plays a major role in a country's economic development. For instance, a modern car often consists of different components from various countries. However, to some extent, this cooperation between local businesses and foreign companies has brought about more intense competition around the world.

Therefore, in my opinion, the merits of international cooperation lie in both environmental protection and business transactions, even though it may face some challenges. The improvement of environment and world economy has been an international focus in recent years. Only by working together internationally, can people solve the increasingly serious problems worldwide like global warming and give a boost to the expansion of world trade.

范文翻译

近年来从私企到政府，国际合作变得日益广泛，这点是毫无疑问的。几乎所有国家在各方面都从中获益，例如环境保护和世界贸易。

一方面，一些人认为国际合作有利于环境保护。他们意识到每个国家在环境保护方面都有自己的考虑。例如，荷兰在垃圾处理方面做得很好。如果他们的先进技术能够被引入到那些几乎没有研发能力的发展中国家，不仅仅是一些国家或团体，可能是所有居住在地球上的人类都会受益。当然，发明这些技术的国家可能会在经济方面蒙受一定的损失，除非他们的知识产权受到政府的保护。

另一方面，还有一些人认为，国际合作的主要优势显然是在商业领域。诚然，进出口贸易在一个国家的经济发展中扮演着重要的角色。例如，一辆现代小汽车往往由几个国家生产的配件组装而成。然而，在某种程度上，本地企业与国外公司间的这种合作在全球范围内已引发了更为激烈的竞争。

因此，我的观点是，国际合作的价值存在于环境保护和商业交易两方面，尽管这种合作可能会面临一些挑战。环境的改善和世界经济的发展一直是近年来国际关注的焦点。只有通过国际合作，人们才能解决一些日益严重的世界性问题，如全球变暖，并且促进世界贸易的增长。

闪光词汇

★ **conducive** [kən'dju:siv] *adj.* 有益于

Fresh air is **conducive** to health. 新鲜空气有助于健康。

★ **consist** [kən'sist] *v.* 由……组成，在于，一致

Health doesn't **consist** with smoking. 健康与吸烟不相容。

★ **merit** ['merit] *n.* 优点，价值

You may not like him，but he has his **merits**. 你也许不喜欢他，不过他有自己的优点。

★ **even though** 即使

I will try it，**even though** I may fail. 即使我可能失败，我也要试一下。

实用句型

...**even though** ... 即使……

作者在总结自己的观点时，用 even though 表示让步，可以避免观点过于绝对化。

请看范文中的这句话：

Therefore，in my opinion，the merits of international cooperation lie in both environmental protection and business transactions，**even though** it may face some challenges. 因此，我的观点是，国际合作的价值存在于环境保护和商业交易两方面，尽管这种合作可能会面临一些挑战。

Unit 4

Science and Technology

科技

2011 年 1 月 8 日考题回顾

机器人的利弊

WRITING TASK 2

You should spend about 40 minutes on this task.

Write about the following topic:

Some people think that robots are very important to humans' future development, while others think that they are dangerous and have negative effects on society. Discuss both views and give your own opinion.

Give reasons for your answer and include any relevant examples from your own knowledge or experience.

Write at least 250 words.

题目解释

一些人认为机器人对于人类的未来发展很重要，另一些人却认为机器人很危险，对于社会有负面影响。讨论双方的观点并给出你的意见。

高分范文

As one of the most important inventions, robots have a wide application in all aspects of our lives. As to the artificial intelligence, people hold divergent views whether it is a blessing or a curse for human beings. Speaking for myself, the advent of robots has both advantages and disadvantages.

There is no denying that robots can enhance the work efficiency and relieve people from the heavy work. It is reported that robots can perform some risky and repetitive tasks for human being. For example, in some countries, robots can work in the factories, hospitals and shops to replace the human labor. Therefore, people can have more leisure time. What is more, it is a fresh idea that robots can take good care of the senior citizens in the aging society, which is a growing tendency in many countries.

However, it must be admitted that robots are never without the downsides. For one thing, people tend to be over dependent on the work of the robots, which leads to people's deteriorating creativity, imagination and flexibility both in work and life. For another, with more robots coming into the work force, more people may become unemployed and it is difficult for people to make a living in this sense. In the more competitive world, robots make the job hunting tougher than before.

Taking into account of all these factors, we may reach the conclusion that robots indeed make it possible for people to achieve the high efficiency and have helpers in work and life. But they create the new problems for human beings as well. On balance, robots present the chances and new challenges in reality. What we should consider is that we can accept the advantages of robots while staying away from the drawbacks.

范文翻译

作为最重要的发明之一，机器人在我们生活的各个方面有着广泛的应用。关于人工智能对于人类是福是祸，人们持有不同的意见。在我看来，机器人的出现既有优点又有缺点。

无可否认，机器人可以提高工作效率，把人从繁重的工作中解脱出来。据报道，机器人可以替人执行一些冒险和重复性的工作。例如在一些国家，机器人可以取代人力在工厂、医院和商店工作。因此，人们可以有更多的闲暇时间。此外，有一个新的想法，就是机器人可以在老龄化社会中照顾好老年人，而老龄化在许多国家呈现一种上升的趋势。

然而，必须承认，机器人不是没有缺点。一方面，人们往往过度依赖机器人的工作，从而导致人们在工作和生活中的创造力、想象力和灵活性都日益退化。另一方面，随着更多的机器人进入劳动大军的队伍，更多的人可能面临失业，从这意义上说，人们谋生就很困难。在更具竞争性的世界里，机器人使求职比以前更加困难。

考虑所有这些因素，我们可以得出这样的结论，即机器人确实有可能使人们实现高效率，成为工作和生活的助手。但是，它们也给人类带来了新的问题。总而言之，机器人在现实中提供了机遇和新的挑战。我们应该考虑的是，我们可以接受机器人的优点，同时远离机器人的弊端。

闪光词汇

★ **artificial intelligence** 人工智能

This computer represents the pinnacle of **artificial intelligence**. 这台计算机代表了人工智能的最高水平。

★ **divergent** [dai'vəːdʒənt] *adj.* 分歧的

Their differences can be seen from their **divergent** conceptions on the plan. 两者之间的差异性，由彼此对于计划之构想的不同可见一斑。

★ **deteriorate** [di'tiəriəreit] *v.* 退化

His sight has begun to **deteriorate**. 他的视力已经开始下降。

实用句型

1. **As to**…, **people hold divergent views whether it is a blessing or a curse for human beings. Speaking for myself, the advent of**…**has both advantages and disadvantages**. 关于……对于人类是福是祸，人们持有不同的意见。在我看来，……的出现既有优点又有缺点。这种句型一般用于第一段，引出话题，同时表明自己的观点。

请看范文中的这段话：

As to the artificial intelligence, **people hold divergent views whether it is a blessing or a curse for human beings. Speaking for myself, the advent of** robots **has both advantages and disadvantages**. 关于人工智能对于人类是福是祸，人们持有不同的意见。在我看来，机器人的出现既有优点又有缺点。

2. **There is no denying that**…**can enhance**…**and relieve** … 无可否认，……可以提高……，并且减轻……。这种句型一般用做第二段的中心句，表示开始分析有利的方面。

请看范文中的这句话：

There is no denying that robots **can enhance** the work efficiency **and relieve** people from the heavy work. 无可否认，机器人可以提高工作效率，把人从繁重的工作中解脱出来。

3. **However, it must be admitted that**…**are never without the downsides**. 然而，必须承认，……不是没有缺点。这种句型一般用做第三段的中心句，表示开始分析不利的方面。

请看范文中的这句话：

However, it must be admitted that robots **are never without the downsides.** 然而，必须承认，机器人不是没有缺点。

4. **Taking into account of all these factors, we may reach the conclusion that** … 考虑所有这些因素，我们可以得出这样的结论……。这种句型一般用于结尾段，表示总结全文。

请看范文中的这句话：

Taking into account of all these factors, we may reach the conclusion that robots indeed make it possible for people to achieve the high efficiency and have helpers in work and life. 考虑所有这些因素，我们可以得出这样的结论，机器人确实有可能使人们实现高效率，成为工作和生活的助手。

类似考题

2010年3月20日

More and more work has been done by the machines. What are the impacts on individuals and society? What's your opinion?

2010 年 4 月 24 日考题回顾

每人都拥有小汽车、电视和冰箱的利弊

WRITING TASK 2

You should spend about 40 minutes on this task.

Write about the following topic:

> ***It has been suggested that everyone in the world wants to own a car, a TV and a fridge. Do you think the disadvantages of such a development to the society outweigh the advantages?***

Give reasons for your answer and include any relevant examples from your own knowledge or experience.

Write at least 250 words.

题目解释

据说世界上的每个人都想拥有一辆小汽车、一台电视和一个冰箱。你认为这种发展对社会是弊大于利吗?

高分范文

I firmly believe that if everybody owned a car, a TV, and a refrigerator, the benefits to society would far outweigh the detrimental effects. That being said, I'm also assuming that "everybody" means every family, not every individual person, and that these consumer goods would not spring into existence over night. If, on the other hand, everybody received these products immediately, I think they would be useless without proper infrastructure such as paved roads and electrical transmission lines and fueling stations. Even a modest attempt to provide these services to many parts of the world, this would most likely throw the economy there into turmoil from competition and reallocation of resources and labor, and then quickly exhaust those limited resources.

But, if the process were more gradual as currently is, I believe the goal of putting a TV, a refrigerator, and a car in every family's possession is a good idea. As technology improves, we will find more efficient and sustainable methods of producing power, and most of the negative effects will be negligible, such as pollution and global warming. What we need to ensure this positive outcome is a reliable source of electricity, such as fusion power, which doesn't come with all the garbage of using fossil fuels or other conventional power sources.

If everybody had these basic consumer products that so many of us take for granted, most people would consider their living standards to be much improved, and would be much happier. On a basic level, improved transportation, better food preservation, and access to news and entertainment are what every family wants to have. In turn, I think it would encourage widespread social stability, and integrate large portions of the world population into the global mainstream.

范文翻译

我坚信如果人人都拥有一辆小汽车、一台电视和一个冰箱，这对社会的益处将会大大超过有害的影响。话虽如此，我同样假设“人人”是指每个家庭，并不是指每个单独的个人，而且这些消费品不会在一夜之间涌现存在。从另一方面来讲，假如每个人都很快地得到了这些产品，我认为没有适当的基础设施也是无用的，例如铺设好的道路、电力传输线路和加油站等。即使采用合适的方式将这些设施提供给世界上的许多地区，也很可能会导致经济处于资源和劳动力的激烈竞争与再分配的混乱之中，然后迅速耗尽那些有限的资源。

但是，如果这个过程是循序渐进的，比如目前这种情况，那么我相信每个家庭拥有一台电视机、一个电冰箱、一辆小汽车的目标是个不错的想法。随着技术水平的提高，我们将会发现更多生产能量的有效、可持续的方法，大部分的负面影响将变得微不足道，如污染和全球变暖。为了确保取得积极成果，我们必须采用可靠的电力来源，比如说核能发电，这样就可避免使用化石燃料或其他传统能源所带来的麻烦。

如果每个人都拥有了我们许多人认为理所当然的这些基本消费产品，大多数人会认为他们的生活水平大大提高了，也会感到更幸福。基本上，改善交通、更好的食品保鲜及新闻和娱乐的获得是每个家庭都想拥有的。反过来讲，我认为这会促进更大范围的社会稳定，并将更多的世界人口融入全球化的主流中来。

闪光词汇

★ **detrimental** [ˌdetri'mentl] *adj*. 有害的

Poor eating habits are **detrimental** to health. 不良的饮食习惯对健康有害。

★ **infrastructure** ['infrə'strʌktʃə] *n*. 基础设施

Vast sums are needed to maintain the **infrastructure**. 保养基础设施需要巨额款项。

★ **turmoil** ['tə:mɔil] *n*. 混乱

The robbery put the village in a **turmoil**. 抢劫使全村陷入混乱。

★ **negligible** ['neglidʒəbl] *adj*. 可以忽略的

The damage to my car is **negligible**. 我的汽车的损坏程度可忽略不计。

★ **integrate** ['intigreit] *vt*. 使一体化

Immigrants are **integrated** into the community. 移民与该地区的居民融为一体。

类似考题

2007 年 9 月 8 日

The unlimited use of cars may lead to many problems. What are these problems? In order to reduce these problems, people should be discouraged from using cars. To what extent do you agree or disagree?

2010 年 11 月 20 日考题回顾

人们是否都获益于现代通讯技术

WRITING TASK 2

You should spend about 40 minutes on this task.

Write about the following topic:

> ***Some people think people have benefited from modern communications technology, but others do not think some people have benefited from it at all. To what extent do you agree or disagree with the opinion?***

Give reasons for your answer and include any relevant examples from your own knowledge or experience.

Write at least 250 words.

题目解释

一些人认为人们从现代通讯技术中获益，但是其他人认为一些人根本没有从中获益。你在多大程度上同意或不同意这种观点？

高分范文

Nowadays, even if we have recognized the face-to-face communication, within high-speed exchange and timely feedback, is far more needed in our society, the modern communications technology development brings other advantages to us. Those benefits cover a large scope. But some people argue that we cannot take advantage of it at all. Obviously I do support the former opinion.

The instant message software or mobile technology has been used by us to change the way to contact with our friends, which is one symbol of modern communications technology. In the past, we contacted with friends by sending letters. If your friend lived far from you, you might receive his letter half a month later and it was possible that your friend got your reply after a month since he sent it. Nowadays, however, you can convey far more information during the chatting process by instant message software, such as MSN, QQ, Fetion (made by China Mobile for sending free messages). And the colorful image and important profile can be easily exchanged and shared online.

Furthermore, the Internet technology improvement allows people to collaborate online, which can collect various resources in different places. Especially for some international corporations, the top office might not understand local situation, and problem solving groups or subsidiary companies in different countries should get requirement to finish each part of the task through the videoconference by parent company. Therefore, without modern communications technology, the cooperation must incur added communication cost and the task may not be finished well.

To conclude, modern communications technology has great influence on our daily life and social work. Even if the residents in some poor and remote areas almost have nothing to do with modern communications technology, they also get useful information by it indirectly. Therefore, it is impossible for them to have no benefit from it at all.

范文翻译

现在，即使我们认识到可以快速交流并及时收到反馈的当面沟通在我们的社会中必不可少，但现代通信技术的发展也给我们带来了一些其他的优势。这些益处覆盖范围很广。不过有些人认为我们根本不能从中获益。很明显，我支持第一种观点。

我们利用即时消息软件或者移动技术来改变我们与朋友交流的方式，这是现代通讯技术的一个标志。在过去，我们通过书信的方式与朋友联系。如果你的朋友离你很远，你可能半个月之后才能收到信件，而你的朋友可能在他发出信件之后的一个月才能收到你的回信。然而，如今，你可以在聊天时通过即时信息软件发送更多的信息，例如 MSN、QQ、飞信(中国移动为发送免费信息而设的平台)。丰富多彩的照片及重要的图片都可以很容易地在线进行交换和分享。

此外，互联网技术的改善使得人们可以在网上进行合作，这样可以整合不同地区的多方面的资源。尤其是对于一些跨国公司来说，总部可能不了解当地形势，问题解决小组或位于不同国家的子公司需要通过视频会议获悉母公司要求它们完成的任务中的每一个部分。因此，如果没有现代通信技术，合作必然会产生额外的通信成本，而且任务可能不会被完成得很好。

总之，现代通信技术对我们的日常生活和社会工作都产生了很大影响。即使一些偏僻贫穷地区的人们几乎与现代通信技术无关，但他们也会间接地通过它获取有用的信息。因此，对于他们来说，一点也不从现代通信技术中获益是不可能的。

闪光词汇

★ **feedback** [ˈfiːdbæk] *n.* 反馈

The more **feedback** we get from viewers，the better. 从观众那儿得到的反馈越多越好。

★ **contact** [ˈkɔntækt] *vt.* 联系

We agreed to **contact** again as soon as possible. 我们同意尽快再次联系。

★ **symbol** [ˈsimbəl] *n.* 象征

The white colour is a **symbol** of purity. 白色是纯洁的象征。

★ **convey** [kənˈvei] *vt.* 传递

I can't **convey** my feelings in words. 我无法用言语来表达我的情感。

★ **collaborate** [kəˈlæbəreit] *vt.* 合作

Two writers **collaborated** on the script for the film. 两个作家合写了这部电影的脚本。

★ **subsidiary** [səbˈsidjəri] *adj.* 附属的

This question is **subsidiary** to the previous one. 这个问题是辅助上一个问题的。

★ **remote** [riˈməut] *adj.* 遥远的

The thing happened in the **remote** past. 这件事发生在遥远的过去。

类似考题

2009 年 1 月 17 日

Today，people can work and live anywhere they want because of the improvement of communication technology and transport. Do the advantages of this development outweigh the disadvantages?

2008 年 6 月 28 日考题回顾

老年人使用手机和网络

WRITING TASK 2

You should spend about 40 minutes on this task.

Write about the following topic：

> ***With the rapid development of technology，more and more young people begin to use mobile phones and the Internet，but old people have little chance to be exposed to them. In what ways could mobile phone and the Internet be useful to old people? How should old people be encouraged to use this new technology?***

Give reasons for your answer and include any relevant examples from your own knowledge or experience.

Write at least 250 words.

题目解释

随着科技的飞速发展，越来越多的年轻人开始使用移动电话和网络，但是老人们很少有机会接触它们。移动电话和网络在哪些方面对老年人是有帮助的？老年人应该如何被鼓励去使用这项新技术？

高分范文

It is obvious that advanced technologies such as mobile phone and the Internet not only bring a lot of fun to youngsters, but also have an important impact on the life of senior citizens who would like to keep pace with the times.

Today, mobile phones are increasingly popular with old people. Unlike young people who fancy playing games or taking photos with phones, the old seem to be interested in their most basic function—communication. It is easily found that keeping in touch by mobiles with their children who live separately or study overseas has become a necessary thing in their everyday life. What's more, if old people feel physically uncomfortable or get in danger outdoors and alone, they can immediately make an emergency call or inform their relatives or friends by using mobile phones.

The Internet is as important as mobile phones in old people's life now. Apparently, some elderly people tend to surf on the Internet, learning something that they are fascinated with. Some like to meet new friends online or chat with their friends on the Internet. Others become accustomed to shopping online or running their own small businesses by E-mail.

However, I must confess that some old people are afraid to try new technologies probably because they have not yet understood or experienced them. So they should be encouraged to take part in some activities that are held in their community with the aim of teaching them to use the new technologies. Meanwhile, they are really supposed to be a bit more confident and fearless to try.

范文翻译

显然，技术的进步，例如手机和网络，不仅给年轻人带来很多的乐趣，而且对那些喜欢跟上时代步伐的老年人也有很重要的影响。

如今，手机在老年人当中日益普及。与那些喜欢用手机玩游戏和拍照片的年轻人不同，老年人似乎感兴趣的是它们最基本的功能——沟通。很容易发现，通过手机和他们那些分开居住或留学海外的孩子保持联系已经成为他们每日生活中很重要的事情。还有，如果老年人感到身体不舒服或者是单独在户外遇到了危险，他们可以立即用移动电话进行紧急呼救或者通知他们的亲戚或是朋友。

和手机一样，网络在老年人的日常生活中同样重要。很显然，一些老年人喜欢网上冲浪，学习一些他们感兴趣的东西。一些人喜欢在网络上结交新朋友或者通过网络和他们的朋友聊天。还有一些人喜欢网上购物或者通过电子邮件经营他们自己的小生意。

然而，必须承认，一些老年人害怕尝试新技术，这可能是因为他们还没有理解或者使用过它们。因此，他们应该被鼓励参加一些在他们社区举行的活动，这些活动旨在教他们如何使用这些新技术。同时，他们真的应该更自信并且更勇敢地尝试。

闪光词汇

★ **keep pace with** 并驾齐驱

Cultural developments are **keeping pace with** economic ones. 文化的发展紧跟经济的发展。

★ **apparently** [ə'pærəntli] *adv.* 显然地

Apparently the weather is changing. 显然天气在变。

★ **surf** [sə:f] *n.* 激浪　*v.* 做冲浪运动；在……冲浪

You can **surf** the Internet with this computer here. 你可以用这台计算机上网。

★ **fascinate** ['fæsineit] *v.* 使着迷，使神魂颠倒；迷人，有吸引力

I am quite **fascinated** by his adventure in Africa. 他在非洲的冒险活动使人着了迷。

★ **and so forth** 等等

They discuss investment，the state of the economy **and so forth**. 他们讨论了投资和经济状况等问题。

★ **accustomed** [ə'kʌstəmd] *adj.* 惯常的，习惯的

He is **accustomed** to hard work. 他习惯于做艰苦的工作。

★ **confess** [kən'fes] *v.* 承认，坦白

I must **confess** my error. 我必须承认我的错误。

★ **take part in** 参与，参加

They **take** an active **part in** scientific experiments. 他们积极参加科学实验。

★ **be supposed to** 应该

You **are supposed to** be responsible for them. 你是应当对他们负责的。

★ **confident** ['kɔnfidənt] *adj.* 自信的，确信的

He feels **confident** of success. 他对成功很有信心。

类似考题

2006 年 1 月 14 日

There are social，medical and technical problems associated with the use of mobile phones. What forms do they take? Do you agree that the problems outweigh the benefits of mobile phones?

2008 年 7 月 12 日考题回顾

农业领域的新发展

WRITING TASK 2

You should spend about 40 minutes on this task.

Write about the following topic：

Some people support the development in agriculture such as factory farming and scientific creation of new type of fruits and vegetables. Some people oppose it and support other development. Discuss both views and give your opinion.

Give reasons for your answer and include any relevant examples from your own knowledge or experience.

Write at least 250 words.

题目解释

一些人支持在农业领域有所发展，例如工厂农业和新型水果和蔬菜的科技创新。一些人对此持反对态度并且支持其他发展。讨论这两种观点并给出你的观点。

高分范文

Taking a historical view about agriculture, we can quite easily understand how much we rely on this trade, including the mode of life and the way we think. As a result of population increase, many methods that have been unthinkable before can now be adopted, such as factory farming and inventing new types of fruits and vegetables. Many stand for these, while many others oppose them.

The proponents argue that traditional agriculture has always been slow and lacked efficiency in mass production of food, which is already a serious problem in many countries. At the same time, factory farming can be very profitable since we can just get rid of the impact from climatic factors and pest invasion. New varieties of plants can also be a part of industrial production of food, since geneticists can be employed for more high-yielding species and new breeds of vegetables.

The opponents list the harms of factory production of agriculture, ranging from genetic disaster to the overuse of fertilizers. For them, the concern of natural and organic food is above all other factors, and they can even ignore the high price of fruits and vegetables, only if they are organic and grown in the field, which may mean safety.

I personally agree with the former. As we can easily see, human population has been explosively growing in the last half century, much faster than any period of history. Traditional modes of agriculture may be just too slow and monotonous to fulfill the need of global citizens. Therefore, the trend from the field to the workshop just cannot be resisted.

范文翻译

从历史的角度看农业，我们很容易理解我们是多么依赖它，包括我们生活和思考的方式。由于人口的增长，许多以前不可思议的方式现在都可以采取了，例如工厂农业以及研发新型的水果和蔬菜。许多人对此很支持，而另一些人则持反对的态度。

支持者认为，传统的农业在食物的批量生产方面效率低下，这在许多国家一直都是一个严重的问题。同时，既然我们可以利用工厂农业消除季节因素的影响和害虫的侵害，那么它是很有利可图的。既然遗传学者能够被请来研发更高产的物种和新的蔬菜种子，新的植物种类也可能是食物工业化生产的一部分。

反对者列举了农产品在工厂生产的害处，包括基因的危害和肥料的过度使用。对于他们来说，对天然和有机食物的关注比其他因素都重要，他们甚至可能忽视水果和蔬菜的高价格。只要它们是有机的并且生长在田野里，它们就是安全的。

我个人赞同前一种观点。显而易见，在上半个世纪，人口一直在爆炸性地增长，比历史上的任何时期都要快。传统的农业方式可能太慢而且太单调，不能满足全球人们的需求。因此，从田间到工厂的趋势不可抵挡。

闪光词汇

★ **rely on** 依赖，依靠

Blind people **rely** a lot **on** touch. 盲人在很大程度上依靠触觉。

★ **unthinkable** [ˈʌnˈθiŋkəbl] *adj.* 不能想象的，不可思议的

Failure at this late stage is **unthinkable**. 在这么一个后期阶段失败简直难以相信。

★ **profitable** [ˈprɔfitəbl] *adj.* 有利可图的

I think the cooperation will be **profitable**. 我觉得此次合作会有很大的收益。

★ **get rid of** 摆脱，除去

You are supposed to **get rid of** carelessness，for it often leads to irretrievable errors. 你们一定要克服粗枝大叶，因为粗枝大叶常常引起无可挽回的错误。

★ **explosively** [iksˈpləusivli] *adv.* 爆发地，引起爆炸地

The population in Central America is growing **explosively**. 中美洲的人口飞速增长。

2008 年 11 月 29 日考题回顾

现代和传统游戏对儿童的影响

WRITING TASK 2

You should spend about 40 minutes on this task.

Write about the following topic:

> ***Some people think modern children's games can help them to develop a wide range of skills, but other people argue that traditional games can be much better for developing such skills. State your opinion.***

Give reasons for your answer and include any relevant examples from your own knowledge or experience.

Write at least 250 words.

题目解释

一些人认为，现代儿童游戏能帮助他们发展更广泛的技能，但是另一些人认为传统游戏能够更好地发展这些技能。阐述你的观点。

高分范文

Nowadays, it is widely acknowledged that games can develop children's intelligence, widen their horizons and stimulate their inquisitiveness. However, the discussion about the discrepancy between traditional games and modern games are greeted by the public with great enthusiasm. As far as I am concerned, I consent to the following statement: in some cases, modern games can do better.

With the computer and the Internet widespread, there are categories of online games whose visual effects and engrossing plots lead the children into a wonderland. Racing games can practice the kids' sensibility. Puzzle games can develop their intelligence and dressing up games can cultivate the children's art appreciation. These modern games are more suitable to our children's appetite. There is no denying the fact that modern children's computer skills and creativity are better than their parents' in many respects. In my own opinion, modern games contribute considerably to this.

It must be emphasized that traditional games are not neither rhyme nor reason. On the contrary, traditional games can also sparkle in our eyes. For example, playing team games, like Word Puzzle, Game of Life and so on can enhance our family relationship and help the children build up collective conception and team spirit. But through a meticulous comparison between traditional games and modern games, I must say that in terms of functions for children, modern games can do a better job.

In a nutshell, modern games have more merits in comparison with traditional games, but to eliminate the disadvantages of modern games, parents, schools and games companies should avoid the kids' games addiction. And modern games will definitely do good to our children and society.

范文翻译

如今，大家一致认为游戏能开发孩子的智力，拓宽他们的视野，并且激发他们的好奇心。然而，关于传统游戏和现代游戏矛盾的讨论引起了人们的热情响应。在我看来，在一些情况下，我同意下面的观点，那就是现代游戏更好。

随着计算机和互联网的普及，有很多种在线游戏，这些游戏的视觉效果和引人入胜的情节把孩子们带入了一个奇妙的世界。竞赛游戏能锻炼孩子的敏感性；迷幻游戏能开发他们的智力；伪装游戏能培养孩子的艺术鉴赏力。这些现代游戏更合孩子们的胃口。不可否认，现代孩子们的计算机技术和创造力在很多方面比他们的父母要强，在我看来，现代游戏起了很大的作用。

必须强调的是，传统游戏并非一无是处。相反，传统游戏也很耀眼。例如，玩团队游戏，像猜字谜，以及生命游戏等能增强家庭成员之间的关系，帮助孩子树立集体观念和培养团队精神。但是通过仔细比较传统游戏和现代游戏，我必须指出，在对儿童的许多功能方面，现代游戏做得更好。

综上所述，现代游戏比传统游戏有更多的优点，但是，为了消除现代游戏的缺点，父母、学校和游戏公司应当避免儿童沉迷于游戏。现代游戏定将会对我们的孩子和社会都有好处。

闪光词汇

★ **discrepancy** [dis'krepənsi] *n.* 差别，差异，矛盾
There was a **discrepancy** in the two reports of the accident. 在该事件的两个报告中有不一致之处。

★ **engrossing** [in'grəusiŋ] *adj.* 引人入胜的，极有趣的
He is Listening to an **engrossing** symphony. 他正在听一首引人入胜的交响乐。

★ **wonderland** ['wʌndəlænd] *n.* 仙境，奇境
I feel as if in a **wonderland**. 我觉得像是置身仙境中了。

★ **sensibility** [ˌsensi'biliti] *n.* 敏感性
She has an unusual **sensibility** for colors. 她对色彩非常敏感。

★ **cultivate** ['kʌltiveit] *v.* 培养；耕作
The school **cultivate** excellent students. 那所学校培养优秀的学生。

★ **suitable to** 适合
The shoes are **suitable to** travel. 这鞋适用于旅行。

★ **considerably** [kən'sidərəbəli] *adv.* 相当地
Women's health conditions have improved **considerably**. 妇女的健康状况极大地改善了。

★ **neither rhyme nor reason** 毫无道理，一无是处
His demand seems to have **neither rhyme nor reason**. 他的要求似乎完全不合理。

★ **on the contrary** 相反
On the contrary，it serves the interests of the peace-loving people. 相反，这是符合爱好和平的人民的利益的。

★ **build up** 树立，增进，增大
His analysis **builds up** their confidence. 他的分析增强了他们的信心。

实用句型

Nowadays，It is widely acknowledged that ...**However，the discussion about**...**As far as I am concerned**... 如今，众所周知的是……然而，关于……的讨论……在我看来。
这种句型结构首先介绍话题，接下来引出题目中的观点，实际上就是对题目的改写。最后再表明作者的观点。这是议论文第一段的完整框架，考生注意临摹。
请看范文中的这句话：
Nowadays，it is widely acknowledged that games can develop children's intelligence，widen their horizons and stimulate their inquisitiveness. **However，the discussion about**

discrepancy between traditional games and modern games are greeted by the public with great enthusiasm. **As far as I am concerned**, I consent to the following statement: in some cases, modern games can do better. 如今，大家一致认为游戏能开发孩子的智力，拓宽他们的视野，并且激发他们的好奇心。然而，关于传统游戏和现代游戏矛盾的讨论引起了人们的热情响应。在我看来，在一些情况下，我同意下面的观点，那就是现代游戏更好。

Unit 5

Crime

犯 罪

2011 年 1 月 22 日考题回顾

反社会行为的原因和解决办法

WRITING TASK 2

You should spend about 40 minutes on this task.

Write about the following topic:

> ***Some individuals tend to act in an antisocial way (violence, crimes), society in general is to blame. What causes the antisocial behaviour? Who should be responsible to deal with it?***

Give reasons for your answer and include any relevant examples from your own knowledge or experience.

Write at least 250 words.

题目解释

一些人倾向于用反社会的方式行事（暴力、犯罪），整个社会难辞其咎。是什么原因导致反社会的行为？谁应该来负责处理呢？

高分范文

Throughout much of the world, rapid proliferation of antisocial behaviors seems to be an increasingly widespread problem. The public cry for more prisons and tougher sentences, which outweighs prevention and treatment of criminal acts. However, it is more urgent to identify the underlying root causes of these antisocial actions, rather than to deal with the symptoms through punishment measures.

The most common factor responsible for crimes is poverty. People who cannot afford to make their own ends meet are very likely to commit crimes as a last resort. It goes without saying that poor and unemployed individuals have much higher likelihood of committing crimes. Exposure to violence is another factor that contributes to crimes, especially youth crimes. Without proper parental guide, some young adults get deeply addicted to the Internet and spend too much time on it. Some of them are contaminated by violence and pornography online, which is closely linked to their aggressive behaviors.

Crime prevention requires the joint efforts of the entire society. The government should popularize education and create more jobs. The availability of education and job opportunities would allow citizens to secure employment and earn regular income, thereby reducing the crime rate to a minimum. To tackle youth crime, parents should play more supportive and loving roles, attaching more importance to their children's emotional needs and limiting their access to unfavorable contents on the Internet by creating more interesting after-school entertainment.

To sum up, this unpleasant phenomenon can be attributed to several factors, including poverty and lack of parental supervision. The government should take more effective measures to raise living standards of those economically impoverished individuals and parents should give correct and immediate instruction to young adults.

范文翻译

在世界的许多地方，迅速增加的反社会行为似乎是一个越来越普遍的问题。公众呼吁建立更多的监狱和实施更严厉的刑罚，这超过了对犯罪行为的预防和改造的呼吁。但是，更迫切的事情是要找出这些反社会行为的根本原因，而不是通过处罚措施来处理这个问题。

犯罪最常见的因素是贫穷。那些无法维持生计的人，很容易将犯罪作为最后的手段。不用说，贫穷和失业人员犯罪的可能性更高。接触暴力是犯罪的另一个因素，特别是青年犯罪。由于没有父母正确的引导，一些年轻人沉迷于互联网，因此花费很多时间在上面。他们当中的一些受到在线暴力和色情的污染，这些与他们的过激行为有着密切的关联。

预防犯罪需要来自于整个社会的共同努力。政府应当普及教育，创造更多的就业机会。获得教育和就业机会可以保证公民就业并赚取固定收入，从而将犯罪率降至最低。为了解决青少年的犯罪行为，父母扮演的角色应当更具支持性和更有爱心，更加重视子女的感情需要，通过创造更有趣的课后娱乐活动，限制他们访问互联网上不好的内容。

总的来说，这种不好的现象可以归咎于几个因素，包括贫穷以及缺乏父母的监管。政府应该采取更有效的措施，提高那些经济贫困的人们的生活水平，同时家长应当给予孩子正确和及时的指导。

闪光词汇

★ **proliferation** [prəuˌlifəˈreiʃən] *n.* 扩散

Nuclear **proliferation** threatens world peace. 核扩散威胁世界和平。

★ **antisocial** [ˈæntiˈsəuʃəl] *adj.* 反社会的

It is **antisocial** to play music loudly enough to annoy everyone else in the street. 在大街上闹嚷嚷地奏乐，使大家受干扰，这是损害社会秩序的。

★ **cry for** 要求

Charles **cried for** his mother to stay with him. 查尔斯哭着要妈妈和自己待在一起。

★ **symptom** [ˈsimptəm] *n.* 症状

The doctor told her to watch out for **symptoms** of measles. 医生叫她注意麻疹出现的症状。

★ **afford** [əˈfɔːd] *vt.* 供应得起

She cannot **afford** the expense. 她花不起这笔钱。

★ **commit** [kəˈmit] *vt.* 犯（错误）

He has **committed** a serious fault. 他犯了严重错误。

★ **resort** [riˈzɔːt] *n.* 手段，凭借

Friends are the best **resort** in trouble. 在困难中，朋友是最好的可以求助的人。

★ **addicted** [əˈdiktid] *adj.* 沉溺于某种嗜好中的

She's become **addicted** to love stories. 她迷上了言情小说。

★ **pornography** [pɔːˈnɔgrəfi] *n.* 色情文学，色情作品

Police have seized several consignments of **pornography**. 警方没收了好几批运来的色情物品。

★ **popularize** [ˈpɔpjuləraiz] *v.* 普及

The company is trying to **popularize** its new products. 公司努力推广新产品。

★ **supportive** [səˈpɔːtiv] *adj.* 支持性的

Most of the staff who responded to the questionnaire were **supportive**. 回答了问卷的职员大多数表示支持。

★ **attach importance to** 重视

The old man **attaches importance to** his health very much. 这位老人很重视他的健康。

实用句型

1. **Throughout much of the world，…seems to be an increasingly widespread problem.** 在世界的许多地方，……似乎是一个越来越普遍的问题。这种句型一般用于第一段，介绍背景，同时引出话题。

请看范文中的这句话：

Throughout much of the world，rapid proliferation of antisocial behaviors **seems to be an increasingly widespread problem.** 在世界的许多地方，迅速增加的反社会行为似乎是一个越来越普遍的问题。

2. **The most common factor responsible for…is…** ……最常见的原因是……。这种句型一般用做第二段的中心句，表示开始分析问题产生的原因。

请看范文中的这句话：

The most common factor responsible for crimes **is** poverty. 犯罪最常见的因素是贫穷。

3. …**requires the joint efforts of the entire society.** ……需要来自于整个社会的共同努力。这种句型一般用做第三段的中心句，表示提出解决问题的对策。

请看范文中的这句话：

Crime prevention **requires the joint efforts of the entire society.** 预防犯罪需要整个社会的共同努力。

类似考题

2005 年 1 月 22 日

Statistics suggest that nowadays an increasing number of crimes are committed by the young people. What are its causes and how can we solve this problem?

2009 年 12 月 19 日

Crime is a problem all over the world and there is nothing that can be done to prevent it. To what extent do you agree or disagree?

2010 年 1 月 30 日

Today there is a great increase in antisocial behavior and lack of respect to others. What are the causes of this? What measures can be taken to reduce this problem?

2010 年 8 月 5 日

In many parts of the world，the incidence of violence/crimes is increasing. Give possible reasons，recommendations of punishment and measures to the situation.

2008 年 1 月 12 日考题回顾

对犯罪分子的惩罚

WRITING TASK 2

You should spend about 40 minutes on this task.

Write about the following topic:

Some people think that criminals should be given longer terms in prison, so as to reduce the crime rate. To what extent do you agree or disagree?

Give reasons for your answer and include any relevant examples from your own knowledge or experience.

Write at least 250 words.

题目解释

一些人认为犯罪分子应该更长时间被关在监狱里，以便降低犯罪率。你同意还是不同意这种观点？

高分范文

In recent years, a growing number of people have begun to insist that criminals should be given longer terms in prison, so as to reduce the crime rate. They argue that law offenders should be punished severely. In my opinion, they should be locked up in prisons longer, too.

Just as an old saying goes, mercy to the criminals may be cruelty to the public. For criminals like thieves, robbers, rapists or even murderers, it is improper or even dangerous to let them out of jails, because they could still pose threat to our society. Longer terms in prison can ensure a safe and comfortable living environment to those law-abiding citizens.

More important, the longer imprisonment of criminals can deter the potential criminals. The would-be criminals must think twice before they commit crimes because they are in dread of the severe punishment. Researches reveal that there is a direct link between the longer imprisonment of criminals and the decline of crime rate. If we were too lenient with criminals, the world would be in great danger and full of blood and violence.

In addition, when criminals are given longer terms in prison, their behavior would be under control. They have to spend more time in prison before they are set free. This can prevent them from committing crimes again and will save the police much trouble to catch them.

From what I have discussed above, I firmly hold to the belief that criminals should be given longer terms in prison and at the same time receive compulsory reclaim.

范文翻译

近年来，越来越多的人认为犯罪分子应该更长时间被关在监狱里，以便降低犯罪率。他们认为，违法者应该受到严厉的处罚。我也认为，罪犯应该更长时间被关在监狱里。

正如一句俗语说的，对罪犯的仁慈就是对百姓的残忍。因为像小偷、抢劫犯、强奸犯甚至杀人犯，释放他们是不合理甚至是非常危险的，因为他们仍然是社会的威胁。而把罪犯长期关在监狱里可以为守法者营造一个安全舒适的生活环境。

更重要的是，对罪犯的长期关押还是对潜在犯罪的一种威慑。由于害怕严厉的惩罚，那些想要犯罪的人在犯罪之前必定三思。研究表明，在对罪犯的长期关押和犯罪率的降低之间有着直接的联系。如果我们对罪犯过于宽容，世界将会处于危险之中，充满了血腥与暴力。

另外，当罪犯被长时间关在监狱中的时候，他们的行为会得到控制。在他们被释放前不得不花更长的时间在监狱里。这样就可以阻止犯罪分子再次犯罪，减少给警察的抓捕带来的麻烦。

如上所述，我坚信：罪犯应该更长时间被关在监狱中，同时接受强制改造。

闪光词汇

★ **severely** [si'viəli] *adv.* 严格地，激烈地

His courage was **severely** tried. 他的勇气受到严峻的考验。

★ **pose threat to** 对……构成威胁

Pollution **poses** a great **threat to** our existence. 污染对我们的生存造成巨大威胁。

★ **imprisonment** [im'prizənmənt] *n.* 关押

The criminals got ten year's **imprisonment**. 这个罪犯被判 10 年徒刑。

★ **deter** [di'təː] *v.* 阻止

Failure did not **deter** him from trying again. 失败并没有阻止他再度尝试。

★ **think twice** 三思

You should **think twice** before you take this step. 你在采取这一步骤之前，应当三思。

★ **commit a crime** 犯罪

If you **commit a crime** you can never escape being punished. 你要是犯罪，就逃脱不了要受惩罚。

★ **in dread of** 畏惧

They are **in** daily **dread of** earthquakes. 他们天天在担心地震。

★ **under control** 被控制住

Everything is **under control**. 一切都处于控制之下。

★ **save trouble** 减少麻烦

They have **save** me a lot of **trouble**. 他们使我省了许多麻烦。

★ **compulsory** [kəm'pʌlsəri] *adj.* 强制性的，必须做的，必修的

In most schools，sports are **compulsory**. 在多数学校中体育活动是必须参加的。

实用句型

Just as an old saying goes 常言道，俗话说
这种句型结构的作用主要有两点：其一是引出要论证的观点，其二是借古说今，从而使论证的观点更有说服力。
请看范文中的这句话：
Just as an old saying goes，mercy to the criminals may be cruelty to the public. 正如一句俗语说的，对罪犯的仁慈就是对百姓的残忍。

类似考题

2005 年 6 月 18 日
Sending criminals to prison is not the best method of dealing with them. Education and job training are better ways to help them. Do you agree or disagree?

2007 年 10 月 25 日
Some people think the only purpose of imprisonment is to punish crime. Others think it has other functions. Discuss both views and give your opinion.

2008 年 9 月 18 日
Some people think that criminals should not be imprisoned. Instead，education and job training should replace the former to deal with criminals. To what extent do you agree or disagree?

2009 年 9 月 17 日
Some people think that all the lawbreakers should be sent into the jail，while others believe that they should also be made to do some work or learn some skills in the community. Discuss both views and give your own opinion.

Unit 6

Culture and Travel

文化与旅游

2011 年 1 月 27 日考题回顾

出国旅游还是通过网络和电视来了解其他国家

WRITING TASK 2

You should spend about 40 minutes on this task.

Write about the following topic：

> ***Some people think that it is necessary to travel abroad to learn about other countries, but other people think that it is not necessary to do so because all the information can be seen on TV and the Internet.***
>
> ***Discuss both opinions and give your own opinion.***

Give reasons for your answer and include any relevant examples from your own knowledge or experience.

Write at least 250 words.

题目解释

一些人认为要想了解其他国家就有必要出国旅游，但是另外一些人认为这么做没有必要，因为所有的信息都可以通过电视和互联网获取。讨论双方观点并给出你自己的观点。

高分范文

There aroused a heated debate as to whether we should learn about other countries by travelling abroad. People have different ideas about it. Some people think the most instant way of obtaining the knowledge about other countries is travelling to those countries, but other people argue that the TV and the Internet can provide us all the information, which make travelling abroad unnecessary. Admittedly, both sides are reasonable.

Those who favor travelling abroad to learn about other countries give their reasons as follows. Firstly, travelling abroad means one is really in that environment, and he experiences and feels the culture, transportation, hospitality and lodging there. So the most important benefit is that people can deeply "feel" the country and have a vivid impression there. In addition, by this way, one can know the country as a whole. There are mountains, rivers, cities, towns, villages and people who inhabit there. And people can see the historic relics and beautiful landscapes in person. So people will have a comprehensive understanding of the country they have visited.

However, there are also some others who contend that this method of knowing other countries is not suitable for most people, for the consideration of high expenses. For example, in current China, a large portion of the population does not have that much wealth and cannot afford travelling around the world. Moreover, there are many other economical ways to appreciate other places, among which the TV and the Internet are the fast, convenient and up-to-date ones. There are avalanches of articles, pictures and video clips on the TV and the Internet. And the contents almost include all the information one can imagine. No matter if one wants to learn the history or geography or the customs about other countries, he will be satisfied by them.

Both sides make sense. Therefore it is really hard for me to draw a definite conclusion. To my mind, I would say that the second way is the base and the first way is the top. The most feasible strategy is to go from the base to the top step by step.

范文翻译

我们是否应该通过出国旅游的方式了解其他国家引发了一场激烈的辩论。人们对此持有不同的看法。有些人认为，获取其他国家知识的最快方式是前往这些国家，但其他人认为电视和互联网可以为我们提供所有的信息，出国旅行是不必要的。诚然，双方都是合理的。

赞成那些出国去了解其他国家的人理由如下。首先，出国旅游意味着可以置身于其环境之中，亲身经历和感受那里的文化、交通、热情以及住宿等。因此，最明显的好处是，人们可以深切地感受那个国家，对那里有一个生动的印象。此外，通过这种方式，一个人可以全面地了解这个国家。那里有山川、河流、城市、城镇、村庄和居住在那里的居民。人们可以亲自领略历史遗迹和美丽的风景。因此，人们会对所访问的国家有一个全面的了解。

不过，也有一些人争辩说，考虑到高费用问题，通过这种方式了解其他国家并不适合大多数人。例如，在目前的中国，有很大一部分人口不具有那么多的财富，没有能力到世界各地旅行。而且，还有许多其他更经济实惠的方法可以用来了解其他的地方，其中电视和互联网是最快速、便捷和先进的方式。在电视和互联网上有大量的文章、图片以及视频。其中的内容几乎囊括了所有可想象到的信息。不管一个人想要了解其他国家的历史、地理还是习俗，都可以通过它们得到满足。

双方都很有道理。因此我很难得出一个明确的结论。我的意见是，第二种方式是基础，第一种方式是高端。最可行的策略是从基础逐步过渡到高端。

闪光词汇

★ **hospitality** [ˌhɔspiˈtæliti] *n.* 热情，好客

I received the **hospitality** of the family. 我受到这家人亲切的款待。

★ **relic** [ˈrelik] *n.* 遗迹

This custom is a **relic** of ancient times. 这习俗乃是古代遗风。

★ **comprehensive** [ˌkɔmpriˈhensiv] *adj.* 全面的

An objective test can be quite **comprehensive**. 客观测试相当全面。

★ **appreciate** [əˈpriːʃieit] *vt.* 鉴赏

We **appreciate** steady workers. 我们赞赏踏实的工人。

★ **avalanche** [ˈævəˌlɑːntʃ] *n.* 大量

She received an **avalanche** of mails. 她收到大量的邮件。

实用句型

1. **There aroused a heated debate as to whether... People have different ideas about it.** ……引发了一场激烈的辩论。人们对此持有不同的看法。这种句型一般用于第一段，介绍背景，引出话题。

请看范文中的这句话：

There aroused a heated debate as to whether we should learn about other countries by travelling abroad. **People have different ideas about it.** 我们是否应该通过出国旅游的方式了解其他国家引发了一场激烈的辩论。人们对此持有不同的看法。

2. **Admittedly, both sides are reasonable.** 诚然，双方都是合理的。这种句型一般用于第一段最后一句，引起下文。

3. **Those who favor...give their reasons as follows.** 赞成……的人给出如下理由。这种句型一般用做第二段的中心句，表示开始分析一方的观点和理由。

请看范文中的这句话：

Those who favor travelling abroad to learn about other countries **give their reasons as follows.** 赞成那些出国去了解其他国家的人理由如下。

4. **However, there are also some others who contend that...** 不过，也有一些人争辩说，……。这种句型一般用做第三段的中心句，表示开始分析另一方的观点和理由。

请看范文中的这句话：

However, there are also some others who contend that this method of knowing other countries is not suitable for most people, for the consideration of high expenses. 不过，也有一些人争辩说，考虑到高费用问题，通过这种方式了解其他国家并不适合大多数人。

5. **Both sides make sense. Therefore it is really hard for me to draw a definite con-**

clusion. To my mind, I would say that... 双方都很有道理。因此我很难得出一个明确的结论。我的意见是，……。这种句型一般用于结尾段，表示总结全文，并提出自己的观点。

请看范文中的这句话：

Both sides make sense. Therefore it is really hard for me to draw a definite conclusion. To my mind, I would say that the second way is the base and the first way is the top. 双方都很有道理。因此我很难得出一个明确的结论。我的意见是，第二种方式是基础，第一种方式是高端。

2011年2月12日考题回顾

旅游的利弊

WRITING TASK 2

You should spend about 40 minutes on this task.

Write about the following topic:

Tourism can be an excellent way for a country to develop, but it also causes harm. How can we ensure the continued development of the tourism?

Give reasons for your answer and include any relevant examples from your own knowledge or experience.

Write at least 250 words.

题目解释

旅游是一个国家极好的发展途径，但它也会带来不利。我们怎样才能确保旅游业的持续发展呢？

高分范文

With the steady growth in the country's economy as well as people's living standards, tourism is increasingly important. Some argue that the advantages of the increased tourism do outweigh the disadvantages, but others negate this view. As far as I am concerned, both of the two sides are reasonable to some extent.

The benefits of travel for a country are multifarious and prevalent. First of all, tourism industry can expand consuming requirement and support the development of commerce, including hotels, restaurants and marketplaces, which has turned to be the driving force in GDP growth. Next, it also has the magic to turn a backward town into a wonderland of prosperity, which can promote city development. In addition, some international travel can contribute to cultural exchange among different people, which helps to reduce prejudice and hostility.

But we should not neglect the harm that travel might cause. Firstly, many famous scenic spots of historical and cultural relics are near their maximum capacity. And increased tourism may break the local natural balances and pose potential risks to the reservation of cultural relics. Secondly, some of the international tourists may travel with illegal purposes, such as drug dealing or smuggling. Lastly, increased tourism brings serious threat of epidemics. Some of the diseases can spread from one place to another with tourists.

For the continued development of tourism in one country, some major aspects should be considered. First, the annual tourist population should be limited within a reasonable number. Any company or department who ignores the regulation should be punished by the law. Also, drug dealing, smuggling or any behavior which might cause serious eco-disasters should be prohibited by the law. In addition, travel agencies and governments have the obligation of educating both tourists and local residents to consciously cherish the tourism resources.

In general, we can list many other merits and demerits of travelling. But one thing we know for sure is that we can try our best to remove those drawbacks and amplify the advantages with long years of persistence.

范文翻译

随着国家经济和人民生活水平的稳定增长，旅游业也越来越重要。一些人认为，旅游业增长所带来的好处比坏处多，但其他人否定这种观点。就我而言，这两种观点在某种程度上都是合理的。

旅游对于一个国家来讲好处有很多。首先，旅游业可以扩大消费需求，促进商业发展，包括旅馆、饭店和商场，这些又是国内生产总值增长的驱动力。其次，旅游还有一种将落后城镇转变为繁华胜地的魔力，从而促进城市的发展。另外，一些国际旅游有助于不同人群之间的文化交流，有助于减少偏见和敌意。

但是我们也不能忽视旅游可能带来的损害。首先，许多著名的历史文化遗迹景点已经接近它们的最大承受能力。旅游业的增长可能会破坏当地的自然平衡，对文化遗产的保存构成潜在的风险。其次，一些国际旅客旅游时可能还有非法的目的，如毒品交易或走私。最后，日益增长的旅游业带来了流行病的严重威胁。一些疾病会随着游客从一个地方传至另一个地方。

对于一个国家旅游业的持续发展来说，下面的一些主要方面应当考虑。首先，每年的旅游人数应当限制在一个合理的数目之内。任何无视规定的公司或部门都应当受到法律的惩罚。此外，法律应当禁止毒品交易、走私或者其他任何可能导致严重生态灾难的行为。另外，旅行社和各国政府都有义务教育游客和当地居民自觉珍惜旅游资源。

总之，我们能够列出旅游方面的很多优点和缺点。但是我们确信一件事情，那就是我们能够通过尽最大努力来消除缺点，并且也能通过长期的坚持来增加优点。

闪光词汇

★ **negate** [ni'geit] *vt.* 否定

The decline of community life is **negating** the work of welfare services. 社区生活质量的下降否定了福利机构的工作。

★ **multifarious** [ˌmʌlti'fɛəriəs] *adj.* 各种各样的

It has a **multifarious** and bright prospect. 其发展前景是多样化而光明的。

★ **prevalent** ['prevələnt] *adj.* 普遍的

The habit of travelling by aeroplane is becoming more **prevalent**. 乘飞机旅行的习惯变得越来越盛行了。

★ **wonderland** ['wʌndəlænd] *n.* 奇境

I feel as if in a **wonderland**. 我觉得像是置身仙境中了。

★ **prosperity** [prɔs'periti] *n.* 繁荣

The new agreement raised hopes for conditions of **prosperity** and harmony. 新的协议唤起了人们对繁荣与和谐前景的期望。

★ **prejudice** ['predʒudis] *n.* 偏见

They accused him of having a **prejudice** against his women employees. 他们指责他歧视女雇员。

★ **hostility** [hɔs'tiliti] *n.* 敌意

There is open **hostility** between the two employees. 两位员工表现出公开的敌意。

★ **smuggling** ['smʌgliŋ] v. 走私

The evidence pointed to the existence of an international **smuggling** network. 证据表明很可能有一个国际走私网络存在。

★ **cherish** ['tʃeriʃ] *v.* 珍惜；珍爱

The old lady tenderly **cherished** her dog. 老妇人十分珍爱她的狗。

★ **amplify** ['æmplifai] v. 放大，增强

The new manager wants to **amplify** the company. 新经理想要扩大公司。

★ **persistence** [pə'sistəns] *n.* 坚持

He achieved success through dogged **persistence**. 他靠着坚持不懈取得了成功。

实用句型

1. **With the steady growth in the country's economy as well as people's living standards, ...is increasingly important.** 随着国家经济和人民生活水平的稳定增长，……也越来越重要。这种句型一般用于第一段介绍背景，引出话题。

请看范文中的这句话：

With the steady growth in the country's economy as well as people's living standards, tourism **is increasingly important.** 随着国家经济和人民生活水平的稳定增长，旅游业也越来越重要。

2. **Some argue that the advantages of...do outweigh the disadvantages, but others negate this view.** 一些人认为，……所带来的好处比坏处多，但其他人否定这种观点。这种句型一般用于第一段，介绍双方观点。

请看范文中的这句话：

Some argue that the advantages of the increased tourism **do outweigh the disadvantages, but others negate this view.** 一些人认为，旅游业增长所带来的好处比坏处多，但其他人否定这种观点。

3. **The benefits of...are multifarious and prevalent.** ……好处有很多。这种句型一般用作第二段的中心句，表示开始分析有利的方面。

请看范文中的这句话：

The benefits of travel for a country **are multifarious and prevalent.** 旅游对于一个国家来讲好处有很多。

4. **But we should not neglect the harm that...might cause.** 但是我们也不能忽视……可能带来的损害。这种句型一般用作第三段的中心句，表示开始分析不利的方面。

请看范文中的这句话：

But we should not neglect the harm that travel **might cause.** 但是我们也不能忽视旅游可能带来的损害。

5. **For..., some major aspects should be considered.** 对于……，下面的一些主要方面应当考虑。这种句型表示接下来要提出一些解决问题的对策。

请看范文中的这句话：

For the continued development of tourism in one country, **some major aspects should be considered.** 对于一个国家旅游业的持续发展来说，下面的一些主要方面应当考虑。

类似考题

2007 年 6 月 2 日

Many developing countries are currently expanding their tourist industries. Why is this the case? Is it a positive or a negative development?

2008 年 11 月 20 日

As we know，international travel has become cheaper. More and more countries open their doors and more tourists go abroad for traveling. Do the advantages of the increased tourism outweigh the disadvantages?

2010 年 6 月 26 日考题回顾

国际旅游带来偏见还是促进理解

WRITING TASK 2

You should spend about 40 minutes on this task.

Write about the following topic:

> ***International travel makes people prejudiced rather than broad-minded. What are its causes and what measures can be taken to solve this problem?***

Give reasons for your answer and include any relevant examples from your own knowledge or experience.

Write at least 250 words.

题目解释

国际旅游使人们变得偏见而不是心胸开阔。原因是什么？可以采取哪些解决措施？

高分范文

International tourism is booming. With all this coming and going, you would expect greater understanding to develop between the people of different countries in the world. Not a bit of it. International tourism may have some drawbacks. For example, it makes people prejudiced. It seems to me that the causes may be as follows.

Firstly, many tourist organizations are directly responsible for this state of prejudice. They deliberately set out to protect their clients from too much contact with the local population. So the modern tourists lead a sheltered life. They are allowed to see only what the organizers want them to see and no more. This makes it impossible for the tourists to communicate with local people. Language is always a barrier, so tourists are also happy to be protected in this way. Secondly, unbalanced regional development may increase the conflict between people who come from different nations. At the same time, history and religion are also very important factors. Again, different education background contributes to prejudice as well.

In present day, we should take proper measures to solve these problems. The most important one is that tourists should be given more chances to communicate with local people. Otherwise, they cannot have a full view of the local culture.

From the discussion above, we can see that as long as we take some measures, international tourism still can help people know more about the outside world and promote friendship and mutual understanding. In fact, travel is a very good means of broadening people's horizon.

范文翻译

国际旅游业正在蓬勃发展。看到人们之间的交往如此频繁，你会以为世界各国人民之间的相互了解比以前更深了。其实根本不是这么回事。国际旅游业也有一些缺点。例如，它会使人们怀有偏见。在我看来，引起偏见的原因主要有以下几点。

首先，许多旅游组织应该为这种状况负直接责任。他们处心积虑地把客户与当地居民隔离开来，不让他们有过多的接触。现代的游客过着一种受保护的生活。游客只能看到组织者允许他们看的地方，而不再有其他的。这使得游客根本不可能和当地人交流。由于还存在着语言障碍，他们也乐得被这样保护起来。其次，区域发展的不平衡也可能导致来自不同国家人们之间的冲突。同时，历史和宗教信仰也是非常重要的因素。再次，不同的教育背景也是引起偏见的重要原因。

如今，我们应该采取恰当的措施解决这些问题。最重要的就是应该让游客有更多的机会和当地人交流。否则，他们不可能全面了解当地文化。

从上述讨论我们可以看到，只要我们采取相应的措施，旅游仍然能够使人们更了解外面的世界，促进友谊和相互理解。实际上，旅游是拓宽人们视野的一个很好的办法。

闪光词汇

★ **prejudiced** ['predʒudist] *adj.* 怀有偏见的
Try not to be **prejudiced** in your judgements. 你做判断时要尽量做到不存偏见。

★ **deliberately** [di'lɪbərətli] *adv.* 故意地
He has **deliberately** deceived us. 他是有意欺骗我们。

★ **sheltered** ['ʃeltəd] *adj.* 受保护的；受庇护的
These plants must be **sheltered** from direct sunlight. 这种植物必须遮起来，免受阳光直射。

★ **mutual** ['mjuːtjuəl，'mjuːtʃuəl] *adj.* 相互的，共有的
They have **mutual** admiration and understanding. 他们彼此倾慕和理解。

类似考题

2006 年 5 月 20 日
International tourism has become a huge industry in the world. Do the problems of international travel outweigh its advantages?

2008 年 8 月 21 日
International travel makes people prejudiced rather than broad-minded. What are its causes and what measures can be taken to solve this problem?

2010 年 8 月 21 日考题回顾

特殊日期的意义

WRITING TASK 2

You should spend about 40 minutes on this task.

Write about the following topic：

> ***Nowadays many charities and other organizations publicize their activities by giving a name to a particular day every year, like National Non-smoking Day, National Children's Day, etc. Why do these organizations do this? How effective can these special days be?***

Give reasons for your answer and include any relevant examples from your own knowledge or experience.

Write at least 250 words.

题目解释

如今，很多慈善团体和其他组织每年通过给一些特殊日期命名来宣传他们的行为，像国际无烟日、国际儿童节等。这些组织为什么这样做？这些特殊的日子有什么样的效果？

高分范文

Nowadays, some charities and other organizations publicize their activities by giving a name to a particular day every year, like National Non-smoking Day, National Children's Day, etc. In this essay, I would analyze some possible reasons for the activities mentioned above and influence brought by these special days.

There are a number of reasons for these activities. First of all, by doing these, some institutions may gain more publicity and increase their influence. Take National Non-smoking Day as an example, which is a very obvious case. When companies which manufacture smoking cessation products publicize their activities in National Non-smoking Day, they then have a great confidence to promote their products. At the same time, their market share will be expanded due to the enlargement of their influence.

With regard to the effectiveness of these special days, those who favor them give their reasons as follow. To start with, in these days, such as National Non-smoking Day, the companies concerned can promote the public's awareness of the dangers of smoking. Meanwhile, people will also attach much importance to these institutions. Lastly, some other special days, such as National Children's Day and National Labors' Day, give some social groups a special reason for celebration.

However, the negative effects brought by the special days still exist. Firstly, the public may be confused by so many special days and will be at a loss to know what to do. Secondly, on most days of the year, ordinary citizens might ignore the significant issues promoted by these special days.

Although not all the "Special Days" can be effective enough to the public, some "Days" such as those mentioned above can bring people more benefits and will be supported by lots of people.

范文译文

如今，一些慈善团体和其他组织每年通过给一些特殊日期命名来宣传他们的活动，像国际无烟日、国际儿童节等。在这篇文章当中，我将分析上面提到的这些行为可能的原因以及这些特殊日期带来的影响。

举办这些活动有很多原因。首先，通过这些活动，一些机构可以提高它们的知名度，扩大影响力。以国际无烟日为例，这是一个非常明显的例子。当生产戒烟产品的公司在国际无烟日宣传它们的活动的时候，它们就会很有信心宣传它们的产品。同时，它们的市场份额会因为它们影响力的增大而增加。

当提到这些日子的影响的时候，那些支持它们的人给出了下面的理由。首先，在这些日子，例如国际无烟日，相关的公司能够提高公众对吸烟危险性的认识。同时，人们也会重视这些机构。最后，另有一些特殊的日子，例如国际儿童节和国际劳动节，给一些社会组织举行庆祝活动以一个特殊的理由。

然而，这些日子带来的负面影响依然存在。首先，公众可能对如此多的特殊日子感到困惑，而且不知所措。其次，在一年中的大多数日期，普通民众可能会忽视这些日子提出的问题的重要性。

尽管并不是所有的“特殊日期”对公众足够的有效，但是上面提到的那些日期能够给人们带来更多的好处，也会受到大多数人的支持。

闪光词汇

★ **publicize** ['pʌblisaiz] *vt.* 宣扬

The campaign is intended to **publicize** the service of the tourist board. 这次宣传运动目的在于为旅游部门的服务做广告。

★ **market share** 市场份额，市场占有率

The company is fighting to retrieve its **market share**. 这个公司正在为恢复其市场份额（占有率）而奋斗。

★ **celebration** [ˌseli'breiʃən] *n.* 庆祝，庆典

We had a **celebration** in the hall yesterday. 昨天我们在大厅里进行了庆祝。

★ **confused** [kən'fjuːzd] *adj.* 困惑的，烦恼的

They asked so many questions that I got **confused**. 他们问了那么多问题，都把我弄糊涂了。

实用句型

In this essay，I would analyze some possible reasons for...**and influence brought by**... 在这篇文章当中，我将分析……可能的原因以及……带来的影响。

雅思考试中，如果题目涉及对某种现象的原因和影响进行论述，就可以在第一段的最后一句使用这个句型。

请看范文中的这句话：

In this essay，I would analyze some possible reasons for the activities mentioned above **and influence brought by** these special days. 在这篇文章当中，我将分析上面提到的这些行为可能的原因以及这些特殊日期带来的影响。

类似考题

2008 年 12 月 20 日

Nowadays many charities and other organizations publicize their activities by giving a name to a particular day every year，like National Non-smoking Day，National Children's Day，etc. Why do these organizations do this? How effective can these special days be?

Unit 7

Media

媒体

2009 年 3 月 5 日考题回顾

报纸对人们的影响

WRITING TASK 2

You should spend about 40 minutes on this task.

Write about the following topic：

> ***Newspapers have become an enormous influence on people's ideas and opinions. Why is this the case? Is it a desirable or undesirable situation?***

Give reasons for your answer and include any relevant examples from your own knowledge or experience.

Write at least 250 words.

题目解释

报纸对人们的思想观念有巨大的影响。情况为什么是这样？这是一种理想的状况还是不理想的状况？

高分范文

In modern society, newspapers play an essential role in shaping people's thoughts on a wide range of issues and are always regarded as an indispensable source of information. In my opinion, this complex phenomenon can be boiled down to several key factors, and both its positive and negative aspects need to be analyzed thoroughly.

To begin with, human curiosity is an underlying factor in the growing popularity of newspapers. As the only species on the planet equipped with extraordinary intelligence, humans are inveterately curious about the latest events around the globe. Therefore, all kinds of newspapers prosper in such an age that is gushing with information, appealing to people's increasingly strong desire to know more about this constantly changing world.

To a large extent, this situation is a desirable one with its many positive aspects. First of all, most newspapers and magazines report actual events in a detailed way, providing not only factual information but also deep insights into complex social and political issues. In addition, major newspapers have smoothly operated branches, seasoned correspondents and a highly efficient system to collect local news with the swiftest actions. Most importantly, their coverage and insightful comments can encourage young readers to form their own opinions on current affairs.

On the other hand, people should be fully aware of the downside of the journalistic dominance. By furnishing citizens with prejudiced and self-opinionated reports on sensitive issues, newspapers can manipulate their perspectives and attitudes and exercise a sort of monopoly on their way of thinking.

In conclusion, while absorbing bits of information in the newspapers, readers are advised to adopt an objective approach and cast a discriminating eye on their way of presentation, comments and implicit assumptions.

范文翻译

在现代社会，报纸在人们形成对很多问题的看法方面一直扮演着关键的角色，并被始终当作是一个不可缺少的信息来源。在我看来，这种复杂的现象可以归结为几个关键因素，需要从积极和消极方面深入分析。

首先，人们的好奇心是报纸日益普及的一个根本因素。作为星球上唯一拥有特别智力的物种，人们对最近发生在全球各地的事件非常好奇。因此，在这种信息爆炸的时代，各类报纸涌现，并引起人们日益强烈的愿望去更多地了解这个不断变化的世界。

在很大程度上，这种情况是好的，有许多积极的方面。首先，大多数报纸和杂志详细地报道了真实的事件，不仅提供实际的信息，而且还深入地分析复杂的社会和政治问题。此外，各主流报纸有运转顺利的分支机构，经验丰富的记者，和迅速采取行动采集当地新闻的高效率的运作系统。最重要的是，其覆盖面和富有洞察力的评论能够鼓励年轻的读者就时事问题形成他们自己的观点。

另一方面，人们应该充分认识到新闻控制性这种不利的方面。在敏感问题上，通过给人们提供充满偏见和固执己见的报告，报纸能够操纵他们的观点和态度，并在他们的思维方式方面施加一种垄断。

总之，在阅读报纸信息时，建议读者采取一种客观的态度，并且用批判的眼光去看待他们报道的方式、评论和暗示的假设。

闪光词汇

★ **regard as** 把……当作

We **regard** labour **as** a matter of honour. 我们认为劳动是光荣的事。

★ **curiosity** [ˌkjuəriˈɔsiti] *n.* 好奇心

I caught the employer's attention and aroused his **curiosity**. 我吸引了雇主的注意力，并激起他的好奇心。

★ **intelligence** [inˈtelidʒəns] *n.* 智力，聪明，智能

Could I ask about your attitude to **intelligence** tests? 请问您对智力测验有什么看法？

★ **prosper** [ˈprɔspə] *v.* 昌盛，繁荣

We are bound to **prosper** beyond other countries. 我们肯定要比其他国家更兴旺繁荣。

★ **appeal to** 引起……的兴趣

Bright colours **appeal to** small children. 鲜艳的颜色吸引小孩儿。

★ **manipulate** [məˈnipjuleit] *vt.* （熟练地）操作，操纵

A clever politician knows how to **manipulate** his supporters. 一个聪明的政治家知道如何利用他的拥护者。

类似考题

2009 年 8 月 22 日

News media is more influential nowadays. Some people think it is a negative development. To what extent do you agree or disagree?

2008 年 1 月 10 日考题回顾

儿童看电视、录像和玩游戏的利弊

WRITING TASK 2

You should spend about 40 minutes on this task.

Write about the following topic：

Some people think children's spending time on TV，video and PC games is good，while others think it is bad. Discuss both views and give your own opinion.

Give reasons for your answer and include any relevant examples from your own knowledge or experience.

Write at least 250 words.

题目解释

一些人认为儿童花时间看电视、录像和玩电脑游戏有好处，而另一些人则认为不好。讨论这两种观点并给出你的看法。

高分范文

TV sets，video players and computers bring common people a lot of pleasure. However，children may be influenced by these high-tech products. Some people think children's spending time on TV，video and PC games is good，while others think it is bad. Speaking for myself，I would qualify both of the views to some extent.

Children's spending time on TV，video and PC games has some merits. Firstly，they widen children's horizons because they present a vivid world in front of the children. As to transmitting information，TV，video and PC games show it in pictures more powerful than words. Secondly，they are very entertaining. In particular，some cartoons are often broadcast lively so that the children feel as if they were participating. More important，sometimes，they can also play an educational role. For example，some English programs provide an excellent opportunity to learn English for children who are learning this language. Programs about historical events teach the children history.

However，TV，video and PC games can also be harmful. On the one hand，children are growing up addicted to the telly. Sometimes，food is left uneaten，homework undone and sleep is lost. On the other hand，sometimes，TV，video and PC games encourage passive enjoyment. For example，some children spend hours before the little screen，ignoring their study，outdoor activities and even their friends. Some parents say that their kids are indifferent to nearly everything and precocious somehow.

In my own opinion，it is not realistic to segregate TV sets，video players or computers from children，and proper use of these can have positive effects on them. So what we should do is to guide children to use these properly.

范文翻译

电视机、录像机和电脑给大众带来了很多乐趣。然而，孩子也受到了这些高科技产品的影响。有人认为孩子花时间看电视、录像，玩电脑游戏是有益的，而有人认为这是不好的。说到我自己，我要在一定程度上论证这两个观点。

孩子花时间看电视、录像，玩电脑游戏有一些好处。首先，它们开阔了儿童的眼界，因为电视、录像和电脑游戏给儿童呈现了一个生动的世界。就信息传递而言，电视、录像和电脑游戏以图片的形式展示，这比文字更有说服力。第二，它们非常有趣。尤其是播放一些生动的卡通的时候，孩子们感觉身临其境。更重要的是，有时它们也扮演着教育的角色。例如，一些英文节目为那些学习这种语言的孩子提供很好的机会，有关历史事件的节目让孩子了解历史。

然而，电视、录像和电脑游戏也是有害的。一方面，孩子们在对电视的迷恋中长大，有时饭不吃，家庭作业也不做，觉也不睡。另一方面，有时电视、录像和电脑游戏鼓励被动娱乐，例如一些孩子在小荧屏前度过了几个小时，忘了他们的学习、户外运动甚至是他们的朋友。有些父母说他们的孩子几乎对每一件事都漠不关心，并且有些早熟。

依我看来，不让孩子接触电视机、录像机和电脑的做法是不切实际的，而正确合理地使用这些会给孩子带来积极的影响。因此，我们所应当做的是引导孩子适当地使用它们。

闪光词汇

★ **entertaining** [entə'teiniŋ] *adj*. 愉快的，有趣的

The children staged an **entertaining** puppet show. 孩子们表演了一场十分有趣的木偶戏。

★ **participate** [pɑː'tisipeit] *vi*. 参与，参加

He goes to **participate** in the conference. 他去参加大会了。

★ **excellent** ['eksələnt] *adj*. 卓越的，极好的

Her English is **excellent**. 她的英文好极了。

★ **addicted** [ə'diktɪd] *adj*. 入了迷的，上了瘾的

She is **addicted** to drawing. 她酷爱绘画。

★ **indifferent** [in'difərənt] *adj*. 不关心的，冷漠的

I am **indifferent** to their arguments. 我对他们的争论毫不关心。

★ **precocious** [pri'kəuʃəs] *adj*. 早熟的

That child is far too **precocious**. 那孩子过于早熟。

类似考题

2008 年 5 月 10 日

Some children can learn efficiently by watching TV. Therefore, they should be encouraged to watch TV both at home and at school. To what extent do you agree or disagree?

2010 年 3 月 27 日

Studies suggest that children spend more time in watching TV than they did in the past and spend less in doing active or creative things. Why do you think? What methods can be used to tackle with it?

2010 年 9 月 25 日

Children nowadays spend too much time in watching television and playing video games. Describe the effects on children, families and society. Report the measures to solve the problem.

2010 年 11 月 4 日

Some parents need to spend time in reading or telling stories to Children, while others think children can read through a variety of sources, such as books, TV and Internet by themselves. Discuss both views and give your own opinion.

2008 年 8 月 16 日考题回顾

媒体应否报道犯罪细节

WRITING TASK 2

You should spend about 40 minutes on this task.

Write about the following topic:

> ***Some people think that the media should not report the details of crimes to the public. To what extent do you agree or disagree?***

Give reasons for your answer and include any relevant examples from your own knowledge or experience.

Write at least 250 words.

题目解释

一些人认为，媒体不应该向公众报道犯罪细节。你在多大程度上同意或者是不同意？

高分范文

Nowadays, it is universally accepted that the issue of crimes is becoming increasingly serious. But at the same time, controversy has arisen over whether the media should report the details of crimes. Some people assert that the media coverage of crime details should be banned, while others claim that such reports have their own advantages. As far as I am concerned, I would side with the former group.

On the one hand, we should acknowledge that reports of criminal details may carry great risks. In the first place, they render many citizens afraid of crimes and worried about their own safety. Obviously, a lot of city residents will fear that the same crimes will happen to them, which can even lead to serious psychological problems. Furthermore, media reports of criminal details are unfair for the victims of crimes. The victims who have suffered greatly from these crimes would feel they were forced to experience a nightmare again. Above all, potential criminals can learn from such reported details to avoid mistakes, which may add to the difficulty the police have in capturing criminals.

On the other hand, media reports of criminal details may carry certain benefits. The fundamental reason for this is that such reports keep the public alert to crimes. Should all these reports disappear from the media, it would be very hard for the public to know about the crimes occurring in society. Even so, it can be noted that the news of crimes spread by the media is often exaggerated. Therefore, the public may have a hard time deciding how dependable an alarming crime report would be.

To conclude, although detailed reports of crimes may have their own advantages, I firmly believe that they bring us great risks. Therefore, we should encourage the media to inform the public about criminal acts, but not in great detail.

范文翻译

如今，大家一致认为犯罪问题越来越严重。但是与此同时，关于媒体是否应该报道犯罪细节也引起了争论。一些人声称应该禁止报道犯罪细节，而另一些人认为，这样的报道也有他们自己的优点。就我个人而言，我支持前者。

一方面，我们应该承认对犯罪细节的报道可能带有一定的危险性。首先，它使很多市民害怕犯罪并且担心他们自己的安全问题。显然，很多人会害怕同样的犯罪会发生在他们自己身上，甚至会导致更严重的心理问题。此外，媒体报道犯罪细节对犯罪的受害人不公平。在犯罪中受到巨大伤害的受害人会感到他们被迫又经历了一次噩梦。更重要的是，潜在的犯罪分子从这种对细节的报道中学习，从而避免错误，这可能增加警察抓捕犯罪分子的难度。

另一方面，媒体报道犯罪细节可能有一定的好处。主要的原因是这样的报道使公众对犯罪保持警惕。如果这些报道都从媒体中消失，公众就很难了解到当今社会犯罪的发生情况。虽然如此，仍然可以注意到，被媒体传播的有关犯罪的新闻经常被夸张了。因此，公众可能很难确定一个令人震惊的犯罪报道在多大程度上是可靠的。

总之，尽管对犯罪细节的报道可能有它们自己的优点，但我坚信这样会带给我们巨大的危险。因此，我们应该鼓励媒体向公众报道犯罪行为而不是犯罪细节。

闪光词汇

★ **coverage** ['kʌvəridʒ] *n.* 报道，覆盖
Sports **coverage** on TV is quite extensive. 电视上的体育新闻报道很广泛。

★ **side with** 与（某人）站在同一边，和（某人）抱同样的见解
She always **sides with** me. 她总是站在我一边。

★ **render** ['rendə] *v.* 给予，致使，实施，提出
He had to **render** an apology for his rudeness. 他不得不因他的粗鲁作出道歉。

★ **suffer from** 忍受，遭受
She was **suffering from** a headache. 她正经受头痛之苦。

★ **nightmare** ['naitmɛə] *n.* 梦魇，噩梦，可怕的事物
Earthquake is a **nightmare**. 地震是一场噩梦。

★ **exaggerate** [ig'zædʒəreit] *v.* 夸大，言过其实，夸张
You **exaggerated** the difficulty. 你夸大了那些困难。

类似考题

2005 年 7 月 23 日

The detailed description about crime will affect the people and cause many social problems. Some people say that the media should be strictly controlled. Do you agree or disagree?

Unit 8

Economy

经　济

2011年2月26日考题回顾

是否应减少进口食品

WRITING TASK 2

You should spend about 40 minutes on this task.

Write about the following topic：

> ***Many people believe that countries should produce food for all population to eat and import food as little as possible. To what extent do you agree or disagree?***

Give reasons for your answer and include any relevant examples from your own knowledge or experience.

Write at least 250 words.

题目解释

许多人认为，国家应当生产所有国人的食品，进口尽可能少的食品。你在多大程度上同意或不同意这个观点?

高分范文

As a direct result of economic globalization, there has been a steady rise in the import of food throughout the world in recent years. This increasingly globalized food supply brings a wider selection of agricultural products to a country, making its population more nutritionally enriched.

Imports of food are vitally important in terms of ensuring consumer choice and nutritional standards. In some countries where certain fruits and vegetables hardly grow or are out of season, importing these goods guarantees a balanced diet throughout the year. In contrast, without food import, the range and quality of food choices available to consumers would be significantly reduced. In addition, when it comes to items with low domestic production, imports serve as a supplement to a country's food system. For example, an inland country may have to purchase seafood from overseas in order to ensure its availability in the market.

However, on the other hand, some people claim that food imports should be reduced to the minimum for the sake of a country's national fitness. They argue that imported goods are typically frozen and packaged, and less fresh due to added transportation and storage time. More importantly, trade with other countries in food has the potential to bring human and animal diseases.

From my point of view, after considering these two sides carefully, I would say that the merits outweigh the harm. Technical advance in the food processing industry has made it much easier to preserve fresh food over a long air flight. Public concern about food safety can be removed as long as detailed control measures for food imports are implemented in a country. So I think the positive attitudes should be taken towards importing food, which demonstrates a government's stance on the international trade. In the meantime, a country should take measures to prevent itself from relying on imported goods and to export more nationally-produced food for more economic interests.

范文翻译

作为经济全球化的直接结果，近年来世界各地的食物进口稳步上升。食物供应的日益全球化为一个国家的农产品带来了更广泛的选择，使得人们在营养方面的选择更加丰富。

进口食品在确保消费者的选择和营养标准方面都极其重要。在某些水果和蔬菜难以生长或不合时令的国家，进口这些货物保证了一年四季的饮食均衡。相反，如果没有食品进口，可供消费者选择的食品范围和质量将会大大降低。此外，对于国内很少生产的物品，进口也可以作为对一个国家食物系统的补充。例如，一个内陆国家可能必须要从海外购买海鲜，以确保市场的供应。

然而，另一方面，一些人声称，为了一个国家全民的健康，应当将食品进口减少到最低程度。他们认为，进口食品都是经过特殊冷冻和包装处理的，由于增加的运输和存储时间，食品的新鲜度降低。更重要的是，与其他国家进行食品贸易有可能带来人类或动物的疾病。

在我看来，仔细考虑过两方面的因素之后，我要说的是利大于弊。食品加工行业的技术进步使得在长途飞行中保存新鲜食物变得更加容易。只要国家实施了食品进口的详细管制措施，公众可以消除对食品安全的担心。因此我认为对进口食品应当采取积极的态度，这表明了政府对国际贸易所采取的立场。同时，国家应当采取措施避免依赖进口食品，并且出口更多的国产食品以获取更多的经济回报。

闪光词汇

★ **in terms of** 在……方面

He thought of everything **in terms of** money. 他是从钱的角度来看每一件事。

★ **nutritional** [nju:'triʃənəl] *adj*. 营养的

A diet lacking in **nutritional** value will not keep a person healthy. 缺乏营养价值的饮食不能维持人的健康。

★ **guarantee** [ˌgærən'ti:] *vt*. 保证

We can't **guarantee** our workers' regular employment. 我们不能保证我们的工人定期受雇。

★ **when it comes to** 当提到……

When it comes to learning, diligence is indispensable. 说到学习，勤奋是必不可少的。

★ **supplement** ['sʌplimənt] *v*. 补充

She **supplements** her diet with eggs and fruit. 她以鸡蛋和水果来补充饮食。

★ **availability** [əˌveilə'biliti] *n*. 可用性

The **availability** of public transport is also part of the equation. 公共交通的便利也是部分考虑因素。

★ **implement** ['implimənt] *vt*. 贯彻，实现

We need money to **implement** the program. 我们需要钱来实行这个计划。

实用句型

1. **As a direct result of economic globalization, there has been a steady rise in... throughout the world in recent years**. 作为经济全球化的直接结果，近年来世界各地的……稳步上升。这种句型一般用于第一段，介绍背景，同时引出话题。

请看范文中的这句话：

As a direct result of economic globalization, there has been a steady rise in the import of food **throughout the world in recent years**. 作为经济全球化的直接结果，近年来世界各地的食物进口稳步上升。

2. **From my point of view, after considering these two sides more carefully, I would say that the merits outweigh the harm**. 在我看来，仔细考虑过两方面的因素之后，我要说的是利大于弊。这种句型一般用于第一段或最后一段，表明作者的观点。

类似考题

2007 年 6 月 16 日

In many countries, traditional foods are being replaced by international fast foods. This is having a negative effect on both families and societies. To what extent do you agree or disagree?

2008 年 2 月 23 日

People can buy a wide variety of foods transported from other countries. To what extent do benefits outweigh drawbacks?

2010 年 2 月 20 日考题回顾

经济发展和社会价值观念的缺失

WRITING TASK 2

You should spend about 40 minutes on this task.

Write about the following topic：

> ***Many countries aim to improve living standard by economic development，but some important social values are lost as a result. Do you think the advantages of economic development outweigh the disadvantages?***

Give reasons for your answer and include any relevant examples from your own knowledge or experience.

Write at least 250 words.

题目解释

很多国家致力于通过经济发展来提高生活水平，结果却遗失了一些重要的社会价值观念。你认为经济发展利大于弊吗？

高分范文

It is definitely true that economic development would lead to some by-products, including the loss of social values, but these problems cannot cover the outstanding achievements. I think the advantages and disadvantages of economic development will coexist for a long time.

Economic progress is the basis of all the nations in the world. For example, the United States is the most advanced country and the living standard of the people in that country is very high. The citizens have high level of social welfare and they enjoy free medical care and free education. Even the poorest people in the United States can get the social insurance, which ensures their impossibility to get starved.

But one thing we could not ignore is that the social values are losing day by day. Especially in some developing countries, some severe situations occur. For example, in some Asian countries, more and more illegal prostitutes appear, which would cater for the needs of some businessmen, who would use sex as a means of negotiation. In some developed countries, the same thing also exists. Tiger Woods is a typical example. He is a wealthy guy, but he is not loyal to his wife and he had affairs with lots of women. So we could get the idea that economic development would lead to the result that some important social values are lost. Step by step, the values would collapse. Other social values have been lost as well. For instance, in the business world, the colleagues are not cooperative as before; instead the competition makes them to be enemies. As a result, the relationship of the people in the society is much worse than that in the past. Money-oriented society is a formidable thing. And the consequence of that is more than the loss of social values.

The trend of economic development cannot be reversed and most people welcome it much. And as for the disadvantages of economic development, I would say they are almost understandable. More work should be done to solve the problem.

范文翻译

毫无疑问经济发展会带来一些副产品，包括社会价值观念的缺失。但是这些问题不能掩盖显著的成绩。我认为经济发展的优缺点将会长期共存。

经济发展是世界上所有国家的基础。例如，美国是最发达的国家，这个国家人民的生活水平非常高。公民们可以享有高水平的社会福利，并且享有免费医疗和免费教育。即使是美国最穷苦的人也可以获得社会保险，这使得他们不可能挨饿。

但是我们不能忽略的一件事是社会价值观念正在一天天地遗失。特别是在一些发展中国家，出现了一些严重的情况。例如，在一些亚洲国家，出现了越来越多的非法娼妓，这迎合了那些想要把性作为谈判手段的商人的需求。在一些发达国家，同样的事情也一样存在。老虎伍兹是一个典型的例子。他是一个非常富有的人，但是却对妻子不忠，和很多女人有着风流韵事。因此我们可以知道经济的发展可能导致一些重要的社会价值的遗失。日积月累，价值观念可能会崩溃。其他社会价值观也已遗失。例如，在商界，同事们不再像过去那么互相合作，相反，竞争使得他们成了敌人。结果，社会中人们的关系比过去差了很多。以金钱为导向的社会是很可怕的。它的后果不只是社会价值观念的缺失。

经济发展的趋势是不能被逆转的，并且大多数人们也很欢迎它。而经济发展的弊端，我认为它们基本上是可以理解的。应该投入更多的工作来解决这个问题。

闪光词汇

★ **outstanding** [aut'stændiŋ] *adj.* 突出的

The girl who won the scholarship was quite **outstanding**. 得奖学金的女孩相当优秀。

★ **coexist** [kəuig'zist] *vi.* 共存

Our foreign policy is to **coexist** with other countries peacefully. 我们的外交政策是和其他国家和平共处。

★ **cater for** 迎合，满足需要

I expect they will be able to **cater for** your particular food needs. 我预计他们能满足你的特殊饮食需要。

★ **collapse** [kə'læps] *vi.* 倒塌，崩溃

His health **collapsed** from undernourishment. 他的身体因营养不良而垮了。

★ **cooperative** [kəu'ɔpərətiv] *adj.* 合作的

The workmen are very **cooperative**, so the work goes on smoothly. 工人们十分合作，所以工作进展顺利。

★ **formidable** ['fɔːmidəbl] *adj.* 可怕的

This is a **formidable** move. 这是一种很厉害的手段。

★ **reverse** [ri'vəːs] *vt.* 倒转

Please **reverse** the positions of the two pictures. 请把两张图片的位置倒转过来。

实用句型

1. **I think advantages of**…**and disadvantages of that will coexist for a long time**. 我认为……的优缺点将会长期共存。这种句型一般用于第一段，表明作者的观点。

请看范文中的这句话：

I think the advantages and disadvantages of economic development **will coexist for a long time**. 我认为经济发展的优缺点将会长期共存。

类似考题

2008年10月25日

Economic progress is a way to measure the success of one country. What other factors should be considered? Within these factors, do you think anyone is more important than the others?

2006 年 12 月 16 日

Some people believe that personal happiness is directly related to economic success，other people argue that happiness depends completely on other factors. Discuss both viewpoints and give your own opinion.

2010 年 10 月 23 日考题回顾

经济发展与环境保护

WRITING TASK 2

You should spend about 40 minutes on this task.

Write about the following topic:

> ***Pollution and other environmental problems are resulting from a country's developing and becoming richer, some people think this cannot be avoided. To what extent do you agree or disagree?***

Give reasons for your answer and include any relevant examples from your own knowledge or experience.

Write at least 250 words.

题目解释

污染和其他的环境问题是由于一个国家的发展和越来越富有造成的，有些人认为这是不能避免的。你在多大程度上同意或不同意？

高分范文

A question central to today's environmental debate is how economic development and environmental protection interrelate with each other. It seems to be an irreversible trend that no economic target can be attained without some sacrifice made to the environment. As for me, however, countries can pursue sustainable advancement while focusing on environmental issues.

For governments all over the world, encouraging or even impelling large industries and manufacturers to adopt clean technology is a productive approach. Eco-friendly equipment is capable of making optimal use of resources and dispose wastes properly, thereby minimizing pollution and decelerating the depreciation rate of machinery. Moreover, businesses, large or small, can make their production less environment-damaging through technological innovations. The initial operational costs incurred are temporary and can be paid off by forthcoming profits. By this I mean, an environmentally conscious business would win more market shares in the long term, since customers are all keen on pollutant-free products.

On the other hand, it has to be admitted that economic progress is actually accompanied by deterioration of environment, which is particularly true in some underdeveloped countries. Nonetheless, when countries become more economically-developed, they will show more willingness to invest money back into environmental protection. Also, as rich countries rely less on natural resources and their industries have become service-oriented, more funds can be raised for revamping the environment.

My view is that, when nations try to develop their economies and become increasingly flourishing in the process, there is still a lot they can do to create a more livable environment. Economic progress with little environmental impact is possible, as long as actions are taken to promote both sides simultaneously.

范文翻译

当今环境争议的一个核心问题是经济发展和环境保护是怎样相互关联的。没有对环境的一些破换就无法达到经济目标，这看起来是一种不可逆转的趋势。然而对于我来说，国家可以在追求可持续发展的同时仍然关注环境问题。

对于全世界的政府来说，鼓励甚至敦促大型工厂和制造商采用清洁技术是很有效的方法。对生态环境有利的设备对于最佳利用资源和恰当处理废物是很有用的，因此能使污染最小化，减缓机器折旧速率。此外，无论大小企业，都可以通过技术革新使它们的生产减少对环境的危害。引起的初期运作费用是暂时的，可以由随后的收益抵消。我认为通过这样的方式，一个有环保意识的企业在长期会赢得更大的市场份额，因为消费者们都渴望无污染的产品。

另一方面，需要承认的是经济发展确实伴随着环境的退化，在一些不发达国家尤其如此。然而，当国家变得经济更加发达，将会更愿意对环境保护投入资金。并且，由于富有国家对于自然资源的依赖较少，同时其产业已经变为以服务为导向，因此可以投入更多的资金来治理环境。

我的观点是，当国家试图发展经济，并且在这一过程中变得更加繁荣时，仍然可以做很多来创造一个更加宜居的环境。只要在这两方面同时采取行动，经济发展的同时少影响环境是可能的。

闪光词汇

★ **interrelate** [ˌintə(:)riˈleit] *v.* （使）相互关联

All things are **interrelated** and interact on each other. 一切事物都是互相联系又互相作用的。

★ **irreversible** [ˌiriˈvə:səbl; sib-] *adj.* 不能改变的

Technology has had an **irreversible** impact on society. 技术已对社会产生不可逆转的影响。

★ **sacrifice** [ˈsækrifais] *n.* 牺牲

His parents made a lot of **sacrifices** to make sure he got a good education. 他的父母为确保他得到良好的教育而作了很多牺牲。

★ **depreciation** [diˌpri:ʃiˈeiʃən] *n.* 折旧，贬值

They wrote off $500 for **depreciation** of machinery. 他们注销了 500 美元作为机器折旧费。

★ **temporary** [ˈtempərəri] *adj.* 暂时的，临时的

They just reached a **temporary** agreement. 他们只是达成一项临时协议。

★ **revamp** [ˈri:ˈvæmp] *v.* 修补

The writer **revamped** his manuscript. 作家修改了他的原稿。

★ **simultaneously** [siməlˈteiniəsli; (*US*)saim-] *adv.* 同时地

The radar beam can track a number of targets almost **simultaneously**. 雷达波几乎可以同时跟踪多个目标。

2009 年 4 月 4 日考题回顾

消费品价格便宜的优缺点

WRITING TASK 2

You should spend about 40 minutes on this task.

Write about the following topic:

> ***Nowadays people live in the society where consumer goods are relatively cheaper to buy. Do you think its advantages outweigh its disadvantages?***

Give reasons for your answer and include any relevant examples from your own knowledge or experience.

Write at least 250 words.

题目解释

如今，在人们生活的社会，购买消费品是比较便宜的。你认为这种现象的优点大于缺点吗？

高分范文

Nowadays, with the rapid development of science and technology, the price of consumer goods continues to fall. This situation is pounding at people's traditional consumption habit and life styles, with its advantages gradually affecting peoples' lives. As to whether it is a blessing or a curse, however, people take different attitudes.

There are several benefits for people to enjoy cheaper consumer goods. Most important of all, reducing the price of consumer goods can stimulate requirement and boost economy, which is especially important under the background of financial crisis. Besides, with the price of consumer goods less expensive, more ordinary people can afford to buy cell phones and computers, which help people do jobs more effectively each day. In addition, as far as the merchants concerned, in order to sell more, they often cut down the profit margin, which contributes to enhance the total amount of annual sales and reduce stocks.

However, to this issue, some other people hold a different attitude, arguing that cheap consumer goods also bring harm and even disasters to us. For more businesses are striving for the same customers, the lower price may be the result of unfair competition and will undermine the social order. At the same time, for the sake of profits, some merchants use inferior materials and turn out substandard products, which will ultimately do harm to the consumers.

Admittedly, there are some potential risks in reducing the price of consumer goods, but the law can be executed to supervise and manage dealers strictly. In fact, cheap consumer goods can benefit both the customers and the merchants.

范文翻译

如今，随着科技的快速发展，消费品的价格在不断下降。这种情形正在冲击着人们传统的消费习惯和生活方式，它的优势渐渐影响了人们的生活。然而，至于是好是坏，不同的人有不同的态度。

对于人们来说，享受便宜的消费品有很多好处。最重要的是，消费品价格降低可以刺激需求，促进经济，这一点在金融危机的背景下尤其重要。此外，由于消费品的价格不那么昂贵，更多的普通人能够买得起手机和电脑，它们帮助人们每天更有效率地完成工作。另外，就商家而言，为了销售更多，他们经常降低利润，这有助于他们提高年销售额，减少库存。

然而，对于这个问题，另一些人持有不同的态度，认为便宜的消费品也会给我们带来害处甚至是灾难。由于更多的企业为同样的客户竞争，低价可能是不正当竞争的结果，最后会破坏社会秩序。同时，为了盈利，一些商家偷工减料，结果生产出低质量的产品，这最终对消费者是有害的。

无可否认，降低消费品的价格存在一些潜在的风险，但是能够通过执法手段来严格监督和管理商家。实际上，便宜的消费品对消费者和商家都是有好处的。

闪光词汇

★ **stimulate** ['stimjuleit] *vt.* 刺激，激励

The art course **stimulated** me. 艺术课激发了我的灵感。

★ **boost** [buːst] *n.* 促进，改善，激励

This will be a great **boost** to the economy. 这对于经济发展将是巨大的促进。

★ **merchant** ['məːtʃənt] *n.* 商人

The **merchants** of Arab are doing their things all of the world. 阿拉伯商人在世界各地做生意。

★ **cut down** 减少，降低

We were for **cutting down** the cost of production. 我们赞成降低生产成本。

★ **competition** [kɔmpi'tiʃən] *n.* 竞争，竞赛

There is keen **competition** between the two motorcar firms. 两家汽车公司之间存在着激烈的竞争。

★ **undermine** [ˌʌndə'main] *v.* 暗中破坏；逐渐削弱

Illness **undermined** his strength. 疾病逐渐削弱了他的力气。

★ **substandard** [səb'stændəd] *adj.* 标准以下的，不合规格的

The loss was due to the use of **substandard** bags for which you should be responsible. 该损失是由于包装不合标准所致，所以应由贵公司负责这一损失。

实用句型

1. **Nowadays，with the rapid development of science and technology**，... 如今，随着科技的快速发展，……。这种句型一般用于第一段第一句，介绍背景，同时引出话题。
请看范文中的这句话：
Nowadays，with the rapid development of science and technology，the price of consumer goods continues to fall. 如今，随着科技的快速发展，消费品的价格在不断下降。

2. **There are several benefits for people to**... 对于人们来说，……有很多好处。这种句型一般用做第二段的中心句，表示开始分析有利的方面。
请看范文中的这句话：
There are several benefits for people to enjoy cheaper consumer goods. 对于人们来说，享受便宜的消费品有很多好处。

3. **However，to this issue，some other people hold a different attitude，arguing that**... 然而，对于这个问题。另一些人持有不同的态度，认为……。这种句型一般用于第三段的中心句，表示开始分析与前一段观点不同的另一种观点。

请看范文中的这句话：

However, to this issue, some other people hold a different attitude, arguing that cheap consumer goods also bring harm and even disasters to us. 然而，对于这个问题，另一些人持有不同的态度，认为便宜的消费品也会给我们带来害处甚至是灾难。

类似考题

2005 年 2 月 5 日

Food can be produced much more cheaply today because of improved fertilizers and better machinery. However, some of the methods used to do this may be dangerous to human health and may have negative effects on local communities. To what extent do you agree or disagree?

2009年4月18日考题回顾

好的产品是否需要广告

WRITING TASK 2

You should spend about 40 minutes on this task.

Write about the following topic:

> ***If a product is good or it meets people's needs, people will buy it. So advertising is unnecessary and no more than an entertainment. To what extent do you agree or disagree?***

Give reasons for your answer and include any relevant examples from your own knowledge or experience.

Write at least 250 words.

题目解释

如果一种产品很好或者符合人们的需求，人们就会购买它。因此广告是多余的，只不过是一种娱乐。你在多大程度上同意或不同意？

高分范文

Good products have high prestige and quality, which can gain the love of the customers. It is true that a good product sells itself. So some people assert that advertising is unnecessary and no more than an entertainment. Superficially, the above sounds reasonable. But when carefully weighing in the mind, we find that it goes against the fact. A number of causes account for my point.

To begin with, as far as some companies such as Nintendo, Apple, etc. are concerned, it is important for them to spread their most positive and interesting products information to compete against their rivals. These companies are well-known not only for their great customer service and reliable products, but also their advertisements. Apple is known for its humorous adverts. And Nintendo often has colorful advertising aimed towards the youth. These advertisements make people all over the world more familiar with the companies and more curious about their products.

Then, in fact, advertising has proved to be a means of getting the latest product news to spread out quickly and effectively. The companies would probably find that adverts, even if entertaining, can help new products sale tremendously.

Admittedly, some companies are so popular with the public that advertisements are no more than reminders to the masses that they are ever-present in daily life. Examples would be the corporations like Coca-Cola and McDonald's which are so well-known in most countries that their adverts have stopped describing their products but focused more on the images of the companies themselves. For such companies, advertisement is an unnecessary entertainment. However, they may never have reached that status without advertising. For that reason, advertisement is surely not unnecessary.

范文翻译

好的产品有很高的知名度和质量，这一点能够赢得客户的喜爱。好的产品能够自我推销，这是事实。因此，一些人声称，广告是多余的，只不过是一种娱乐而已。表面上看，以上内容听起来很合理，但经过仔细考虑之后，我们发现它违背事实。大量的理由说明了我的观点。

首先，就一些公司而言，例如任天堂、苹果公司等，对于它们来说，传播它们最好最有意思的产品信息来和对手竞争是很重要的。这些公司出名不仅仅是因为它们强大的客户服务和可靠的产品，而且还有它们的广告。苹果公司因为它幽默的广告而出名。任天堂经常有针对年轻人的多彩的广告。这些广告使全世界的人们更熟悉它们的公司，并且对它们的产品更加感兴趣。

其次，实际上，广告已经证明是使最新的产品信息迅速而有效地向外传播的一种手段。一些公司可能会发现，广告，即使是娱乐的，也能帮助新产品大量销售。

无可否认，一些公司在公众中如此知名，以至于广告只不过是提醒大众它们在日常生活中一直存在。以可口可乐和麦当劳公司为例，它们在绝大多数国家是如此的有知名度，以至于广告已经不再描述它们的产品，而是把焦点放在公司本身的形象上。对于这些公司而言，广告是一种不必要的娱乐。然而，没有广告，它们可能永远不会达到那样的地位。因此，广告确实不是不必要的。

闪光词汇

★ **prestige** [pres'tiːʒ] *n.* 声望，威望

The old universities of Cambridge still have a lot of **prestige**. 剑桥历史悠久的大学仍然享有很高的声望。

★ **reliable** [ri'laiəbl] *adj.* 可靠的，可信赖的

The news is **reliable**. 这消息靠得住。

★ **even if** 即使

We should practice economy **even if** we are rich. 即使我们富裕了，也仍应该厉行节约。

★ **reminder** [ri'maində] *n.* 提醒的人，起提醒作用的物，暗示

I wrote a **reminder** in my daily planner. 我在我的每日记事簿里写了个备忘字条。

实用句型

1. **Superficially, the above sounds reasonable. But when carefully weighing in the mind, we find that it goes against the fact. A number of causes account for my point.** 从表面上看，以上内容听起来很合理，但经过仔细考虑之后，我们发现它违背事实。大量的理由说明了我的观点。雅思写作考试中，有些题目给出的观点在逻辑上或表面上看起来很合理，如本文中的观点，但却往往与实际情况不符。遇到这样的情况，就可以在第一段用这个句型引出作者对题目中的观点的评判，同时引出下文。

2. **To begin with, as far as**...**are concerned, it is important for**...**to do**... 首先，就……而言，对于……来说做……很重要。这个句型一般用做第二段的中心句，阐述作者持有某种观点的第一个原因。

请看范文中的这句话：

To begin with, as far as some companies such as Nintendo, Apple, etc, **are concerned, it is important for** them **to spread** their most positive and interesting products information to compete against their rivals. 首先，就一些公司而言，例如任天堂、苹果公司等，对于它们来说，传播它们最好最有意思的产品信息来和对手竞争是很重要的。

类似考题

2007 年 4 月 14 日

The society would benefit from a ban on all forms of advertising because it serves no useful purpose, and can even be damaging. To what extent do you agree or disagree with this opinion?

2007 年 4 月 21 日

Consumers are faced with increasing numbers of advertisements from competing companies. To what extent do you think consumers are influenced by advertisements? What measures can be taken to protect them?

2008年12月4日考题回顾

从国外长途运输商品的优缺点

WRITING TASK 2

You should spend about 40 minutes on this task.

Write about the following topic:

> ***Because of economic globalization, many goods including what we use as daily necessities produced by other counties have to be transported from a long distance. To what extent do the advantages outweigh the disadvantages?***

Give reasons for your answer and include any relevant examples from your own knowledge or experience.

Write at least 250 words.

题目解释

因为经济全球化，许多商品包括我们使用的其他国家生产的日常基本生活用品都是长途运输而来。在多大程度上优点超过了缺点？

高分范文

The global economy is increasingly integrative. Many goods including what we use as daily necessities produced by other countries have to be transported from a long distance. In my opinion, it is a win-win situation for both producing countries and importing countries. And the advantages are prominent.

First of all, it helps the optimization of resources world-wide. Recent surveys have found that nearly 60% of the countries or regions all over the world have to import goods from other countries with the aim of satisfying people's requirements, and among those things from other countries such agricultural products as fruits and vegetables rank first. Secondly, to purchase goods world-wide can ensure best quality and lowest price. The largest retailer, Wal-Mart, always purchases all the goods across the world so that the items sold in its supermarkets are cheap and fine. Lastly, this pattern also brings boom to transportation industry.

As for the disadvantages, they may lie in the following aspects. The first one is package waste. All the transportation requires that the goods be well wrapped and this extra wrap is a huge waste. The second one is that chemical ingredients may be added to foods. Since long-distance transportation might cause some food decay, some chemical ingredients are added in and these ingredients are often harmful to our health. Thirdly, long-distance transportation causes more pollution to the environment. Ships, locomotives, trucks and planes all emit polluting gas.

In summary, long-distance transport of goods plays a vital and indispensable role in both people' life and a country's economy, and it is my firm conviction that people will really utilize it positively since the trend of global cooperation is inevitable and indispensable.

范文翻译

全球经济越来越一体化。许多商品包括我们使用的日常生活必需品都是由其他国家生产并且长途运输而来。在我看来，这对生产国和进口国来说是一个双赢的局面。优点很明显。

首先，它有利于全世界资源优化配置。最近的调查发现，全世界几乎60%的国家和地区都从其他国家进口商品，目的就是满足人们的需要。从其他国家进口的这些商品中，农产品例如水果和蔬菜居于首位。其次，全世界范围内购买商品，可以保证最好的质量和低廉的价格。最大的零售商沃尔玛，所有的商品一直都是从世界各地采购，目的是使得在它的超市出售的商品物美价廉。最后，这种模式也带来了运输行业的兴旺发展。

至于缺点，可能存在于以下几个方面。第一是包装浪费。所有的运输都需要物品被很好地包装，这种额外的包装是一种很大的浪费。第二是化学成分可能被添加到食品中。由于长途运输可能会导致一些食品腐烂，因此一些化学成分被添加，而这些成分往往对我们的健康有害。第三，长途运输造成更多的环境污染。船舶、火车、卡车和飞机等都排放污浊的气体。

总之，长途运输商品在人们的日常生活和国家的经济中都扮演着重要的、不可或缺的角色。我坚信，既然全球合作的趋势不可避免而且不可缺少，人们将会真正积极地利用长途运输进出口货物。

闪光词汇

★ **integrative** ['intigreitiv] *adj.* 综合的，一体化的
The economy is more **integrative**. 经济更加一体化了。

★ **ingredient** [in'griːdiənt] *n.* 成分，因素
The chief **ingredient** in the making of a criminal is avarice. 造成犯罪的主要因素是贪婪。

类似考题

2005 年 11 月 12 日

As global trade increases between different countries，many daily necessities are produced in other countries. Such goods are usually transported a long distance. Do the benefits of this trend outweigh its drawbacks?

2007 年 4 月 28 日

Air transport is increasingly used to export types of fruits and vegetables to countries where they cannot be grown or are out of season. Some people say it is a good thing，but other people think it can't be justified. Discuss both views and give your own opinion.

Unit 9

Government

政 府

2011 年 2 月 17 日考题回顾

艺术家的资金来源

WRITING TASK 2

You should spend about 40 minutes on this task.

Write about the following topic：

Some people think that creative artists should be supported financially by the government of their country, while others believe that they should find financial support from other sources instead. Discuss both views and give your opinion.

Give reasons for your answer and include any relevant examples from your own knowledge or experience.

Write at least 250 words.

题目解释

一些人认为创造性的艺术家应该得到政府的财政支持，而另一些人则认为他们应该从其他来源获得资助。讨论双方观点并给出你的观点。

高分范文

Artists undoubtedly play an increasingly significant role in modern life. Some people think that creative artists should get the financial support from the government, while other people hold the opinion that they should find other sources of support. Both views have their arguments to back up.

On the one hand, some people suggest that for quite a long time in the history and till now, it is a rule for governments to recruit outstanding artists and support them financially so that those artists can devote their attention to art creation without any worries. At the same time, other artists will take them as their models, since support from government not only means benefits but also honors.

On the other hand, some other people strongly despise the above attitude. In their view, this kind of support does not always lead to the prosperous arts and masterpieces. The first reason is that some of those artists are pretty lazy to make progress. The second one would be most of the artists have to do much reluctant work by orders from officials.

As to other sources of support, those who haven't been supported by the government financially are practitioners of this approach. They try all their best to seek support from others to ensure themselves to achieve the goal they are persisting in. Some of them succeed in getting fund, but others fail. However, all of them do not cease the creation. But the environment is different. The former are much like those supported by the government. They have to create after the sponsor's orders, while the latter could freely expresses their own ideas.

It is quite understandable that people from different backgrounds put different interpretations on the same issue. For my part, I am taking a fresh look at it. After checking the famous artists in the long human history, we could see few masters had been supported by the governments or the wealthy. On the contrary, those who could only make their living by themselves left us most of the masterpieces in the history.

范文翻译

艺术家毫无疑问在现代生活中起到日益重要的作用。一些人认为创造性的艺术家应该得到政府的财政支持，而另一些人认为他们应该从其他来源获得资助。两种观点都有各自的理由。

一方面，一些人说，有史以来，政府招募杰出的艺术家并给予他们财政支持是一个沿袭的制度，因此这些艺术家可以没有任何后顾之忧地投身到艺术创作之中。与此同时，其他的艺术家将会把他们视为楷模，因为政府的支持不仅意味着经济利益，而且意味着荣誉。

另一方面，一些人强烈反对上述观点。他们认为，这种支持并不总是带来艺术的繁荣和杰出的作品。首先是因为这些艺术家当中的一些人非常懒于进步，其次可能是大多数艺术家不得不听从官员的命令做很多不乐意做的工作。

至于其他来源的支持，那些没有得到政府资助的艺术家们就是这种方式的实践者。他们尽力寻求其他方面的支持来达到自己一直坚持追寻的目标。他们中的一些人成功获得了资助，而另一些人没有获得。但是，他们所有人都没有停止创作。然而，环境是不同的。前者更像是那些政府资助的艺术家们，他们需要遵循资助者的意愿来创作，而后者可以自由表达他们自己的想法。

来自不同背景的人对于同样的问题有不同的看法，这是可以理解的。在我看来，我对它有新的认识。纵观人类漫长历史中的著名艺术家们，我们可以发现很少有名家是由政府或权贵资助的。相反，大多数历史上的杰作是那些仅能自我维持生计的艺术家们留给我们的。

闪光词汇

★ **devote one's attention to** 专心于

You must **devote your attention to** your work. 你必须专心于工作。

★ **masterpiece** [ˈmɑːstəpiːs] *n.* 杰作

This book is a real **masterpiece**. 这本书是真正的名著。

★ **reluctant** [riˈlʌktənt] *adj.* 勉强的

I am **reluctant** about asking him to do this. 我极不愿意让他去干此事。

★ **seek** [siːk] *v.* 寻求

The police are still **seeking** the men involved in last week's robbery. 警察仍在寻找跟上星期的抢劫案有牵连的人。

★ **persist in** 坚持

She **persisted in** her opinion. 她固执己见。

★ **sponsor** [ˈspɔnsə] *n.* 赞助者

A wealthy **sponsor** came to our rescue with a generous donation. 有个富有的赞助人慷慨捐赠来解救我们。

实用句型

It is quite understandable that people from different backgrounds put different interpretations on the same issue. For my part, ... 来自不同背景的人对于同样的问题有不同的看法，这是可以理解的。在我看来，……。这种句型一般用于结尾段，表示总结全文，并提出自己的观点。

请看范文中的这句话：

It is quite understandable that people from different backgrounds put different interpretations on the same issue. For my part, I am taking a fresh look at it. 来自不同背景的人对于同样的问题有不同的看法，这是可以理解的。在我看来，我对它有新的认识。

类似考题

2006 年 4 月 29 日

Some people think that national sports team and individual sports men and women who represent their country should be financially supported by the government. However, other people believe they should be funded by non-government organizations (eg. business, scholarship). What is your opinion?

2010 年 1 月 14 日

In today's world，it is private companies rather than government who pay for and carry out most of scientific research. To what extent do you think the advantages outweigh disadvantages?

2011年3月5日考题回顾

政府是否应该出资保护少数人讲的语言

WRITING TASK 2

You should spend about 40 minutes on this task.

Write about the following topic:

> ***Some people believe governments should spend money in saving languages of few speakers from dying out completely. Others think this is a waste of financial resources. Discuss both views and give your opinion.***

Give reasons for your answer and include any relevant examples from your own knowledge or experience.

Write at least 250 words.

题目解释

有些人认为政府应当花钱拯救那些少数人讲的语言，避免这些语言完全消失。另一些人认为这是对财政资源的浪费。讨论这两种观点并给出你自己的意见。

高分范文

As globalization increases, people find it easier to conduct business and communicate with those outside their own culture by speaking more widely used languages, like English, Chinese, or French. While some less-known languages are falling out of use, since they are less spread by their speakers or even not passed on by parents to their children. This triggers public cry for financial support from governments to save these languages from dying out.

Undoubtedly, providing funds to prevent language extinction by governments help maintain cultural and linguistic heritage of a country. Each language grows up with its society and serves as a sophisticated system showing how its speakers live, their unique customs, and their own way of viewing the world. Linguists depend on these valuable data to trace its speakers' culture, art and history and figure out how the human mind works in that society. In addition, indigenous languages in many locations possess a rich source of information about local plants, animal species and their biological habits—much not yet documented by scientists. From the scientific perspective, saving these languages prevents loss of information about wildlife.

One might argue that the preservation of endangered languages would be a huge financial burden on governments, since there are so many languages heading for extinction in the world. However, this view is flawed. A government can even be financially rewarded by investing in minority languages. For example, a country can set up museums to store and display literal documentation as well as high-quality recordings of less-known languages, which will cover costs by attracting tourists and promote local tourism in exchange for extra revenues.

My view is that governments should not hesitate to finance the preservation of endangered languages. Language is the most efficient means of transmitting a culture, and it is the owner of a culture who loses the most when a language dies out.

范文翻译

随着全球化的增强，人们发现通过使用英语、中文或法语等广泛使用的语言更容易与外部开展业务，进行沟通。而一些鲜为人知的语言正在逐渐消亡，因为说这些语言的人很少传播它们，甚至父母也并不传给子女。这就引发了公众的呼吁，要求政府给予财政支持，拯救这些语言，避免其消亡。

毫无疑问，政府提供资金防止语言消亡有利于保护一个国家的文化和语言遗产。每一种语言都是随社会成长起来的，是展示掌握这门语言的人的生活方式、独特的习俗以及看待世界方式的复杂体系。语言学家依靠这些宝贵的数据来追踪持这门语言的人的文化、艺术和历史，并发现人类精神如何在他们的社会中发挥作用。此外，许多地方的本土语言记录了关于当地植物、动物物种以及生物习性的丰富信息——很多是科学家都没有记录下来的。从科学的角度看，拯救这些语言可以防止有关野生生物信息的丢失。

有人可能会认为，保护濒危语言对政府将是一个巨大的财政负担，因为世界上有太多的语言正濒临灭绝。然而，这种观点是站不住脚的。政府投资少数民族语言甚至可以得到经济回报。例如，国家可以建立博物馆，存储和展示文字文献以及高质量的鲜有人知的语言的录音，通过吸引游客解决成本费用问题，并且可以促进当地旅游业的发展，赚取额外收益。

我的看法是，政府应当毫不犹豫地资助和保护濒危语言。语言是传播文化的最有效手段，当一种语言消亡时，最大的损失者是这种文化的拥有者。

闪光词汇

★ **spread** [spred] *v.* 传播

Who **spread** these rumours? 谁散布的这些谣言?

★ **trigger** ['trigə] *vt.* 引发

The incident **triggered** an armed clash. 这起事件触发了一场武装冲突。

★ **linguistic** [liŋ'gwistik] *adj.* 语言上的

She is pursuing her **linguistic** researches. 她在从事语言学的研究。

★ **heritage** ['heritidʒ] *n.* 遗产

The ancient buildings are part of the national **heritage**. 这些古建筑是民族遗产的一部分。

★ **indigenous** [in'didʒinəs] *adj.* 本土的

Kangaroos are **indigenous** to Australia. 袋鼠为澳大利亚本地的动物。

★ **perspective** [pə'spektiv] *n.* 角度

She has a great **perspective** on marriage. 关于婚姻生活，她的观点非常有意义。

★ **endangered** [in'deindʒəd] *adj.* 将要灭绝的

This island is maintained as a sanctuary for **endangered** species. 那个岛继续作为濒危物种的保护区。

★ **literal** ['litərəl] *adj.* 文字的

The **literal** meaning of the word "cat" is an animal. "猫"一词的本义是动物。

★ **hesitate** ['heziteit] *v.* 犹豫

If you **hesitate** too long, you will miss the opportunity. 如果你老是犹豫不决，就会错失良机。

2008年3月8日考题回顾

政府还是车主该为公路系统买单

WRITING TASK 2

You should spend about 40 minutes on this task.

Write about the following topic：

> ***The number of cars keeps increasing，so road systems should be expanded. Some people think the cost of road should be paid by the government，while other people think the car owners should pay it. What is your opinion?***

Give reasons for your answer and include any relevant examples from your own knowledge or experience.

Write at least 250 words.

题目解释

轿车数量逐渐增加，因此，公路系统需要扩建。一些人认为政府应该为此买单，而另一些人认为汽车的拥有者应该为此买单。你的观点是什么？

高分范文

With the number of cars increasing, road systems are in bad need of expansion. That raises a heated debate. Some argue that the government should pay for it while others think the cost should be shouldered by car owners. Personally, I am in favor of the former view. That is to say the bill should be paid by the government.

On one hand, as part of infrastructure facilities, roads have always been constructed and maintained by the government. Needless to say, it is the government's responsibility to allocate adequate capital to build the road systems. The reason is obvious, that is, the authorities are in control of the finance power. Actually, the government has devoted a great amount of fund to expanding the road systems recently. And this practice can also ensure that the road system be well planned.

On the other hand, if the road system expansion were paid by car owners, a lot of problems could not be solved. How is the money raised? What standard should car owners follow to pay the cost? How to punish those car owners who do not pay it? To solve these problems needs too much energy and expense, and it is not worth doing at all.

Having considered all the arguments above, I am convinced that it is reasonable for the government to pay for the expansion of the road system, which is easy to operate and efficient to execute. And it is not realistic for car owners to pay for it.

范文翻译

随着轿车数量的增长，公路系统急需扩建。这也引发了一个热烈争论的话题。一些人认为，政府应该支付公路系统扩建的费用，而另一些人认为，成本应该由车主们负担。个人而言，我赞同前一种观点，那就是说这份账单应由政府支付。

一方面，公路作为基础设施的组成部分，一直都是由政府负责修建和维护的。毋庸赘言，分配足够的资金建设公路系统是政府的责任。原因很明显，那就是，当局掌握着财政大权。实际上，政府最近已经投入了大量的资金扩建公路系统。这种做法能保证公路系统被很好地规划。

另一方面，如果扩建公路系统的费用由车主负担的话，很多问题都无法解决。该如何筹集资金？车主缴纳费用依据什么标准？应当如何惩罚那些不缴费的车主？与政府支付费用的做法相比，解决这些问题需要太多的精力和费用，根本不值得这样做。

考虑到上面所有的讨论，我确信，由政府承担扩建公路系统的费用是合理的，既便于操作，也能有效实施。让车主来支付这些费用是不切实际的。

闪光词汇

★ **expansion** [iks'pænʃən] *n.* 扩充

There are plans for the **expansion** of our school building. 有扩大我们学校建筑的计划。

★ **infrastructure** ['infrəˌstrʌktʃə] *n.* 基础结构，基础设施

We should strengthen the **infrastructure** for science and technology. 我们必须加强科技基础设施建设。

★ **execute** ['eksikju:t] *vt.* 执行，实行

Deliberate before you begin，then **execute** with vigour. 着手前要深思熟虑，执行时要果断有力。

实用句型

Having considered all the arguments above，I am convinced that... 考虑到上面所有的讨论，我确信……

这种句型结构用于最后一段，总结全文，强调作者的观点。

请看范文中的这句话：

Having considered all the arguments above，I am convinced that it is reasonable for the government to pay for the expansion of the road system，which is easy to operate and efficient to execute. 考虑到上面所有的讨论，我确信，由政府承担扩建公路系统的费用是合理的，既便于操作，也能有效实施。

2008 年 8 月 9 日考题回顾

企业从大城市迁入地方的优缺点

WRITING TASK 2

You should spend about 40 minutes on this task.

Write about the following topic：

> ***The government should encourage industries and businesses to move out of big cities and into local areas. To what extent do you think the advantages outweigh the disadvantages?***

Give reasons for your answer and include any relevant examples from your own knowledge or experience.

Write at least 250 words.

题目解释

政府应该鼓励企业迁出大城市，迁入地方。你认为在多大程度上优点超过了缺点？

高分范文

Nowadays, more industries and businesses develop in large cities, which cause plenty of problems like pollution, crowdedness and traffic jams. Some people suggest that these industries and businesses move out of large cities and into local areas. In this essay, I will analyse some possible advantages and disadvantages.

The biggest advantage is that people can enjoy a better living environment. It is obvious that the rapid development of industries produces more and more waste, which goes into the water and the air. And most of the noise in big cities also comes from factories and construction sites. Furthermore, many factories and office blocks in big cities occupy large acreage of ground and space. If they were moved out of big cities, people there may enjoy larger community space and gardens.

However, to some extent, I disagree with the opinion that the government ought to encourage enterprises to move into towns, with the explanation that the factories moved out may occupy fields and woods which are essential to agricultural development and environmental protection. At the same time, those industries and businesses may also strongly oppose to moving out because they are used to the current situation and the environment around them. If they had to move into local towns, they would feel lost or uneasy. In other words, the government would cause another trouble—the complaint by bosses and staff—just because of encouraging them to move into small towns.

After pondering this question, I believe that industries and businesses can decide to develop in large cities or small towns by themselves and the government should supervise and guide them rather than simply encourage them to move into local areas.

范文翻译

如今，很多企业在大城市发展起来，这引起了很多的问题，像污染、拥挤和交通堵塞。一些人建议企业应该从大城市迁入地方。在这篇文章中，我会分析一些可能的利弊。

最大的优点是人们能够享受到更好的居住环境。显而易见，工业的快速发展产生了越来越多的废物，它们被排放到水里和空气里。大城市的噪音也绝大部分来自工厂和建筑工地。此外，许多工厂和办公楼在大城市占据了大面积的土地和空间，如果它们被迁出大城市，那里的人们就会有更大的社区空间和花园。

然而，在某种程度上，我不同意政府应当鼓励企业迁入小城市的观点。理由是迁出去的工厂可能占据对农业发展和环境保护都非常重要的田地和森林。而且，那些企业也可能强烈反对迁出，因为他们已经习惯了当前的位置和周围的环境。如果他们不得不迁入地方性城市，他们会感到迷失和不安。换句话说，政府可能正在造成另一个麻烦，那就是老板以及雇员们的抱怨，而这仅仅是因为鼓励他们迁入小城市。

反复考虑这个问题之后，我认为企业能够自己决定在大城市还是小城市发展，政府应该监督和引导他们而不仅仅是鼓励他们迁入地方。

闪光词汇

★ **office block** 办公大楼

The new **office block** blends in with its surroundings. 新的办公大楼与周围的环境很协调。

★ **to some extent** 某种程度上，(多少) 有一点儿

I agree with you **to some extent**. 我部分地同意你。

★ **occupy** [ˈɔkjupai] *vt.* 占领，占据

He **occupies** an important position in the Ministry of Education. 他在教育部充任要职。

★ **oppose to** 反对

Many residents are **opposed to** the plan of building the motorway. 许多居民反对修建那条高速公路的计划。

实用句型

However，to some extent，I disagree with the opinion that…with the explanation that… 然而，在某种程度上，我不同意……的观点，理由是……

上面的句型结构就是用来表示反对意见的，However，to some extent 主要是为了不让反对的语气显得太绝对，因为作者要反对的观点也不是错的或者全无道理；with the explanation that… 则进一步解释反对的理由。

请看范文中的这句话：

However，to some extent，I disagree with the opinion that the government ought to encourage enterprises to move into towns，**with the explanation that** the factories moved out may occupy fields and woods which are essential to agricultural development and environment protection. 然而，在某种程度上，我不同意政府应当鼓励企业迁入小城市的观点。理由是迁出去的工厂可能占据对农业发展和环境保护都非常重要的田地和森林。

Unit 10

Society

社 会

2011年1月15日考题回顾

如何看待男女员工数量的平等

WRITING TASK 2

You should spend about 40 minutes on this task.

Write about the following topic:

Some workplaces are employing an equal number of men and women. Do you think it is a positive or negative development?

Give reasons for your answer and include any relevant examples from your own knowledge or experience.

Write at least 250 words.

题目解释

一些工作场所目前聘用同等数量的男女员工。你认为这是积极的还是消极的发展趋势?

高分范文

Currently, the issue of gender equity is increasingly prevalent. An equal number of women and men can been found in a variety of public occasions, such as offices, social occasions, business, science and so forth. The controversial phenomenon is often brought into public focus. People from different backgrounds hold different attitudes towards the issue.

Some people are of the opinion that this phenomenon tends to be more negative than positive. The main reason to support their view would be out of the burden of the female. For example, in temporary China, most women still have not shaken off heavy burden of housework. Females go to work everyday and do the same jobs as males do. But after work, women have to prepare dinner, take care of children and old people, and do other housework, while men just sit in the living room, watching TV, reading newspapers. Back in the long human history, women were deprived of right of working. In this case, women seem to have possessed the equal right of working in modern times. But this leads to another problem. Many females are forced not to consider having babies, for they are afraid of being taken place by other candidates at the workplace. Some women leave their babies to babysitters or their retired parents. And this incurs a series of serious social problems such as the reduction of overall population, insufficient workforce and children's familial education.

However, the other side of the coin voices its strong opposition, saying that taking the human development as a whole, the exact equal number of the two genders at every workplace is wise. Man and woman have the physical and mental difference, which no one can deny. Thus, some kinds of jobs are more suitable for man and others for woman. If we do not take these factors into consideration, work efficiency could not be improved.

It is quite understandable that people from different backgrounds put different interpretations on the same issue. For my part, I do not think only the equity of number displays the fair status of women and men. It is not proper to define the phenomena as a positive or negative development. That is to say, to seek equal status of different genders, the number of employees is not the only factor to be valued.

范文翻译

目前，男女平等问题变得日益普遍。许多公共场所都有同等数量的男女员工，比如，办公室、社交场合、商业领域和科学领域等等。这个有争议的现象经常引起公众的关注。来自不同背景的人对这个问题有不同的态度。

一些人认为这种现象弊大于利。他们的观点的主要依据是基于女性的负担。例如，目前在中国，大多数的女性仍没有摆脱沉重的家务负担。女性每天和男性一样去上班并且做同样的工作。但在下班后，妇女还要准备晚餐，照顾孩子和老人，以及做其他的家务，而男人下班后只是坐在家里看电视，读报纸。早在人类漫长的历史中，女性被剥夺了工作的权利。在这种情况下，现代女性似乎有了平等工作的权利。但这却又导致了另一个问题。许多女性被迫考虑不要孩子，因为她们担心在单位的工作会被其他人取代。一些妇女将孩子留给保姆或是她们退休的父母照看。这就引发了一系列严重的社会问题，比如，总体人口的减少、劳动力短缺和孩子的家族式教育等。

然而，另外一些人发出反对的声音，他们说，如果将人类发展作为一个整体来看，每个工作场合男女人数平等是明智的。男性和女性在生理和心理上都有差异，没有人可以否定这个事实。因此，有些工作比较适合男性，而有些工作比较适合女性。如果我们不将这些因素考虑在内，那么工作效率就无法提高。

来自不同背景的人对于同样的问题有不同的看法，这是可以理解的。在我看来，只是数量的平衡并不表示男女地位的平等。将这种现象定义为正面的或是负面的发展趋势都是不合适的。也就是说，寻求不同性别地位的平等，雇员的人数并不是唯一需要考量的因素。

闪光词汇

★ **equity** ['ekwiti] *n.* 平等

They shared the work of the house with **equity**. 他们公平地分担家务。

★ **shake off** 摆脱

We managed to **shake off** our pursuers in the crowd. 我们设法在人群中摆脱了跟踪者。

★ **familial** [fə'miljəl] *adj.* 家族的，家庭的

A familial disease can be inherited from generation to generation. 家族疾病可以从一代遗传到下一代。

★ **take into consideration** 考虑

Your teacher will **take** your recent illness **into consideration** when judging your examination results. 老师评考分时会考虑你最近生病的情况的。

★ **interpretation** [inˌtə:pri'teiʃən] *n.* 解释

This passage is open to a variety of **interpretations**. 这篇文章可以有各种不同的解释。

★ **status** ['steitəs] *n.* 身份，地位

Age has **status** in the villages. 在乡村里年长者受人尊敬。

实用句型

1. **The controversial phenomenon is often brought into public focus. People from different backgrounds hold different attitudes towards the issue.** 这个有争议的现象经常引起公众的关注。来自不同背景的人对这个问题有不同的态度。这种句型一般用于第一段，介绍背景，同时引出话题。

2. **Some people are of the opinion that this phenomenon tends to be more negative than positive.** 一些人认为这种现象弊大于利。这种句型一般用做第二段的中心句，表示开始分析不利的方面。

3. **However, the other side of the coin voices its strong opposition, saying that...** 然而，另外一些人发出反对的声音，他们说，……。这种句型一般用做第三段的中心句，表示开始分析与前一段相反的观点。

请看范文中的这句话：

However, the other side of the coin voices its strong opposition, saying that taking the human development as a whole, the exact equal number of the opposite genders at every workplace is wise. 然而，另外一些人发出反对的声音，他们说，如果将人类发展作为一个整体来看，每个工作场合男女人数平等是明智的。

4. **It is quite understandable that people from different backgrounds put different interpretations on the same issue. For my part,** ... 来自不同背景的人对于同样的问题

有不同的看法，这是可以理解的。在我看来，……。这种句型一般用于结尾段，表示总结全文，并提出自己的观点。

请看范文中的这句话：

It is quite understandable that people from different backgrounds put different interpretations on the same issue. **For my part**，I do not think only the equity of number display the fair status of women and men. 来自不同背景的人对于同样的问题有不同的看法，这是可以理解的。在我看来，只是数量的平衡并不表示男女地位的平等。

2011 年 2 月 19 日考题回顾

妇女在警察和军队中的作用

WRITING TASK 2

You should spend about 40 minutes on this task.

Write about the following topic：

> ***Some people think women can play an equal role to men in a country's police force and military force, such as the army. While others think women are not suitable to this kind of work. Do you agree or disagree?***

Give reasons for your answer and include any relevant examples from your own knowledge or experience.

Write at least 250 words.

题目解释

有些人认为女性可以在一个国家的警察队伍和武装力量中发挥平等的作用，比如军队。而另一些人认为女性不适合这种工作。你同意还是不同意?

高分范文

The 21st century has witnessed women's increasing participation in nearly every walk of life. However, the police or military force is still a male-dominated field throughout much of the world. The issue of gender inequality is brought back to the public attention.

Admittedly, serving the army or working for the police seems to be physically demanding for a woman, as both jobs require intensive strength training or even put people at the risk of losing their lives. However, in the information age, academic ability has taken the place of physical strength as a dominant feature in these fields. For example, computerization and automation in the military have made it much easier for women soldiers to operate modern weapons, which overcomes physical limitation and muscle disadvantage. Females can perform military tasks as their male counterparts do, as long as they can be well-educated and well-trained.

More importantly, there are even certain jobs where females in the defense force can make more remarkable contribution than their male counterparts. Since women are accustomed to dealing with matters with accuracy and caution, they are less likely to commit faults. This qualifies them in daily maintenance of the office, clerical jobs, medical services and logistics departments. Other inborn merits, such as the ability to empathize and understand, make females excel in positions involving interaction and communication with human personnel.

My view is that females should be viewed as equals to males in the defense force and their presence should be encouraged. Nature has given different attributes to both men and women, which is supposed to optimize the productivity and efficiency of an organization, rather than to cause gender discrimination.

范文翻译

21世纪见证了女性越来越多地参与到几乎所有的行业中。然而，世界许多地方，警察或武装部队仍然是以男性为主的领域。性别不平等的问题再次引起了公众的关注。

诚然，服兵役或从事警察工作似乎对女性的体质有些苛求，因为这两项工作都需要高强度的体能训练，甚至人们要冒着生命的危险。然而，在信息时代，技能取代体能成为这些领域的主要特征。例如，计算机化和自动化使女性士兵在军队中可以更容易地操作现代化的武器，这克服了身体的局限和体力的弱势。女性可以像男性一样执行军事任务，只要这些女性受过良好的教育和培训。

更重要的是，部队中的女性在一些特定工作中甚至比男性能做出更杰出的贡献。由于女性习惯准确和谨慎地处理问题，她们不太可能出错。这使得她们适合从事办公室的日常维护、文职、医疗服务和后勤部门的工作。其他先天优势，例如同情和理解能力，使女性擅长在与人员互动和沟通的岗位上工作。

我的观点是，在军队中，女性应当与男性的地位平等并且应当鼓励她们的存在。大自然赋予男性和女性不同的特质，这意味着应当以此来优化一个组织的生产力和效率，而不是造成性别歧视。

闪光词汇

★ **military** ['militəri] *adj.* 军事的

My sister works in a **military** hospital. 我姐姐在一家部队医院工作。

★ **inequality** [ˌini(:)'kwɔliti] *n.* 不平等

Inequality and poverty breed class conflict. 不平等和贫困滋长阶级对抗。

★ **at the risk of** 冒着……的危险

He was determined to do it even **at the risk of** being ridiculed. 他决定即使冒着被人嘲笑的危险也要完成它。

★ **academic** [ˌækə'demik] *adj.* 理论的，学术的

That is merely an **academic** discussion. 那只是理论性的讨论。

★ **accuracy** ['ækjurəsi] *n.* 精确性

He aims at great **accuracy**. 他力求十分准确。

★ **logistics** [lə'dʒistiks] *n.* 后勤

He is an officer responsible for **logistics**. 他是负责后勤工作的官员。

★ **empathize** ['empəθaiz] *v.* 同情

If I love you, I can **empathize** with you and see the world through your eyes. 假如我爱你，我会与你产生情感共鸣并能通过你的眼睛看世界。

★ **excel in** 在……方面胜过

They each **excel in** their respective fields. 他们在各自的领域里都是出类拔萃的。

★ **attribute** [ə'tribju(:)t] *n.* 品质，特征

Kindness is one of his best **attributes**. 仁慈是他的好品性之一。

★ **optimize** ['ɔptimaiz] *vt.* 使最优化

You should **optimize** it now. 你应该对它进行优化升级了。

★ **discrimination** [disˌkrimi'neiʃən] *n.* 歧视

He spoke out against racial **discrimination**. 他声言反对种族歧视。

类似考题

2010 年 4 月 15 日

Some people think that men and women have different qualities and some certain jobs are suitable for men and some are suitable for women. To what extent do you agree or disagree?

2010 年 1 月 9 日考题回顾

慈善机构应该帮助哪些人

WRITING TASK 2

You should spend about 40 minutes on this task.

Write about the following topic：

Some people hold the view that charity organizations should help people in greatest need of help，wherever they live. Others think they should help people in their own country. Discuss the two arguments and give your own opinion.

Give reasons for your answer and include any relevant examples from your own knowledge or experience.

Write at least 250 words.

题目解释

一些人认为慈善机构应该帮助那些最需要帮助的人，无论他们居住在何处。还有一些人认为慈善机构应该帮助本国居民。请讨论这两种观点并给出你的观点。

高分范文

With the rapid development of world economy, people's donation to charity organizations is at an unprecedented level, which has brought attention to an ongoing debate concerning whether charity organizations should only assist people in their own countries.

In the proponents' mind, charity organizations should keep the majority of their aid in the country. Initially, it is domestic donations that compose the major proportion of the income of the charity organizations; therefore, the money should be spent mostly on poor people within the country. In addition, the assistance from other countries may spark off unnecessary tensions and misunderstandings due to the political, social and cultural differences. It is commonly held that volunteers without sufficient preparation may violate customs of local communities.

Opponents of charity organizations giving only aid domestically, however, contend that the assistance be open to the people in need no matter where they are from. To start with, it is the functionality of charity organizations to render help to those who are in great need, regardless of their nationalities. Otherwise, it may be considered to go breach of the purpose they are established for. What's more, not only can international charity assistance enhance the friendship of two nations, but also help eliminate the conflicts and misunderstanding, thereby stimulating the cultural exchanges between countries. In the last place, a surplus of resources, including food, cloth and medicine, are produced in developed countries every year. Donating them to the impoverished people in developing countries is more reasonable than just throwing them away.

Overall, I tend to believe that charity should not be constrained in one's own country. It is highly recommended that charity organizations help people alleviate poverty, disease and illiteracy at an international level.

范文翻译

随着世界经济的快速发展，人们对慈善机构的捐助达到了前所未有的水平，这也引起了人们对于慈善机构是否应该只帮助本国居民的持续争论的关注。

支持只帮助本国居民的人认为慈善机构应该将帮助重点放在国内。首先，慈善机构的主要收入来自于国内捐款，因此，这些钱应该主要花费在本国贫民身上。此外，由于政治、社会及文化的差异，来自其他国家的援助可能会引发不必要的紧张和误解。一般来说，没做充分准备的志愿者可能会触犯当地的一些风俗。

然而，反对慈善机构只在国内提供帮助的人认为帮助应该给予那些有需要的人们，无论他们来自何处。首先，不分疆界地帮助那些迫切需要帮助的人是慈善机构的职责。否则，就违背了慈善机构建立的目的。而且，国际慈善救助不仅能够增加两国的友谊，而且还能消除两国之间的冲突和误解，从而促进两国间的文化交流。最后，发达国家每年都会产生许多剩余资源，包括食物、服装和医药。将这些剩余资源捐赠给发展中国家生活贫困的人比扔掉它们更合理。

总之，我倾向于认为慈善机构不应该只拘泥于帮助本国公民。我强烈建议慈善机构从国际范围内帮助人们减少贫困、疾病和文盲。

闪光词汇

★ **donation** [dəu'neiʃən] *n.* 捐款，捐赠品

The hospital receives a good deal of money in **donations**. 这家医院收到捐赠来的大笔款项。

★ **unprecedented** [ʌn'presidəntid] *adj.* 空前的

The air crash caused an **unprecedented** number of deaths. 这次空难的死亡人数是空前的。

★ **domestic** [də'mestik] *adj.* 国内的

This is **domestic** news. 这是国内新闻。

★ **spark off** 导致

His speech seems to have **sparked off** a real argument. 他的发言看来引起了严肃的争论。

★ **violate** ['vaiəleit] *vt.* 冒犯，违反

The bus driver **violated** the traffic regulation. 这位公共汽车司机违反了交通规则。

★ **functionality** [ˌfʌŋkəʃə'næliti] *n.* 功能性

What can we expect with the **functionality** of PS3? 我们能期待 PS3 的什么功能？

★ **render** ['rendə] *vt.* 实施，提供

They will call on you to **render** assistance. 他们将到你那里去帮助你。

★ **eliminate** [i'limineit] *vt.* 消除

You must **eliminate** an unknown quantity. 你必须消去一个未知数。

★ **stimulate** ['stimjuleit] *vt.* 刺激，激励

The art course **stimulated** me. 艺术课激发了我的灵感。

★ **impoverished** [im'pɔvəriʃt] *adj.* 穷困的

He is an **impoverished** writer. 他是一位穷困潦倒的作家。

★ **constrain** [kən'strein] *vt.* 拘泥，约束

Cold weather **constrained** the plant's growth. 寒冷的天气抑制了植物的生长。

★ **alleviate** [ə'li:vieit] *vt.* 减轻

The doctor gave her an injection to **alleviate** the pain. 医生给她注射以减轻疼痛。

实用句型

1. **With the rapid development of world economy**，...，**which has brought attention to an ongoing debate concerning whether**... 随着世界经济的快速发展，……，这也引起了人们对于是否……的持续争论。这种句型一般用于第一段，介绍背景，同时引出话题。

请看范文中的这句话：

With the rapid development of world economy，people's donation to charity organizations is at an unprecedented level，**which has brought attention to an ongoing debate concerning whether** charity organizations should only assist people in their own countries. 随着世界经济的快速发展，人们对慈善机构的捐助达到了前所未有的水平，这也引起了人们对于慈善机构是否应该只帮助本国居民的持续争论的关注。

2. **In the proponents' mind**，... 支持……的人认为……。这种句型一般用做第二段的中心句，表示开始分析支持者的观点。

请看范文中的这句话：

In the proponents' mind，charity organizations should keep the majority of their aid in the country. 支持只帮助本国居民的人认为慈善机构应该将帮助重点放在国内。

3. **Opponents of**...，**however**，**contend that**... 然而，反对……的人认为……。这种句型一般用做第三段的中心句，表示开始分析反对者的观点。

请看范文中的这句话：

Opponents of charity organizations giving only aid domestically，**however**，**contend that** the assistance be open to the people in need no matter where they are from. 然而，反对慈善机构只在国内提供帮助的人认为帮助应该给予那些有需要的人们，无论他们来自何处。

4. **Overall**，**I tend to believe that**... 总之，我倾向于认为……。这种句型一般用于结尾

段，表示总结全文，并提出自己的观点。

请看范文中的这句话：

Overall, I tend to believe that charity should not be constrained in one's own country. 总之，我倾向于认为慈善机构不应该只拘泥于帮助本国公民。

类似考题

2006 年 6 月 10 日

Some people prefer to provide help and support to those people who need it in local communities directly. However, other people prefer to give money to national and international charitable organizations. Discuss both sides and give your reasons.

2009 年 11 月 21 日

Individuals and countries can not help everyone who need help in the world, so we should be only concerned about our own communities and countries. To what extent do you agree or disagree?

2010 年 9 月 16 日考题回顾

遵守法律规则与行为自由

WRITING TASK 2

You should spend about 40 minutes on this task.

Write about the following topic：

> ***Society is based on rules and laws. If individuals were free to do whatever they want to, it could not function. To what extent do you agree or disagree?***

Give reasons for your answer and include any relevant examples from your own knowledge or experience.

Write at least 250 words.

题目解释

社会是建立在规则和法律基础上的。如果人们都可以为所欲为，不受约束，社会就无法正常运转。你同意还是不同意？

高分范文

The condition of massive chaos would happen in our society if all individuals were free to do whatever they want to. I give all my support to this view. Society is based on rules and laws. Otherwise, the society could not function well.

Firstly, only in accordance with rules and laws, can people's action be permitted and protected. For criminals like thieves, robbers, rapists or even murderers, it is proper not to let them out of jails, because they do not obey rules and laws and pose threat to our society. Thus it can be seen that without powerful rule of laws, the root of crimes would remain and society would not function smoothly.

Secondly, social order needs to be maintained by rules and laws. People drive cars on the right side; they cross the streets when green lights are on. Why? Everybody abides by the rules and laws. Imagine what a mess our society would be in if there were no rules and laws.

But on the other hand, rules and laws should not impose restriction on everything. On the contrary, people's creativity should be encouraged. If all actions were monitored strictly, individuals could not appreciate so colorful lives and the world would become monotonous, too. In fact, only when the government encourages people to express their own ideas and take some actions freely, can the country make progress and prosper.

In conclusion, rules and laws are the results of social development, and vice versa, they play an active role in social development. Without rules and laws, the society would not function any longer.

范文翻译

如果我们每个人都可以自由地想做什么就做什么，那么我们的社会将会产生巨大的混乱。我完全支持这种观点。社会是基于各种规则和法律之上的，否则，社会将无法正常运行。

首先，只有遵守规则和法律，人们的行为才能被允许并受到保护。像小偷、抢劫犯、强奸犯甚至杀人犯，把他们关在监狱里是正确的，因为他们没有遵守规则和法律，对社会构成了危害。由此可见，没有强有力的法治，犯罪的根源就会存在，社会就无法正常运转。

其次，社会秩序需要由规则和法律来维持。人们开车靠右走；绿灯亮时过马路。为什么？每个人都在遵守规则和法律。想象一下，如果没有这些规则和法律，社会将会混乱成什么样。

但是另一方面，规则和法律不应该对一切都加以限制。相反，人们的创造能力就应该受到鼓励。如果所有的行为都被严格监管，人们就不会享受如此多彩的生活，世界也会变得很乏味。实际上，只有政府鼓励人们自由地表达他们的想法并实施一些行为时，国家才能进步繁荣。

总之，规则和法律是社会发展的结果，反之亦然，规则和法律在社会发展中发挥着积极的作用。如果没有规则和法律，社会将无法继续运行。

闪光词汇

★ **massive** ['mæsiv] *adj*. 巨大的

We must make **massive** efforts to improve things. 我们必须作出极大的努力去改善一切。

★ **be based on** 以……为基础

The progress of society **is based on** harmony. 社会的进步是以和谐为基础的。

★ **maintain** [men'tein] *vt*. 维持，保持

We must **maintain** keen vigilance at all times. 任何时候我们都要保持高度的警惕。

★ **vice versa** 反之亦然

We support them and **vice versa**. 我们支持他们，他们也支持我们。

★ **play a role** 扮演……角色

The state and the government **play a** crucial **role** on this issue. 在这一点上，国家和政府的作用将是决定性的。

★ **function** ['fʌŋkʃən] *n*. 功能，作用 *vi*. 运行，行使职责

The old machine won't **function** properly if you don't oil it regularly. 那台旧机器如果不经常加油是不能正常运转的。

实用句型

I give all my support to… 我全力支持……

在这种句型结构前面，作者先做出一种假设或引用别人的观点，紧接着用这句表示我全力支持上述观点或假设情形的存在，实际是引出自己的观点。

请看范文中的这句话：

The condition of massive chaos would happen in our society if all individuals were free to do whatever they want to. **I give all my support to** this view.

如果我们每个人都可以为所欲为，不受约束，那么我们的社会将会产生巨大的混乱。我完全支持这种观点。

类似考题

2008年10月11日

Society is based on rules and laws. If individuals were free to do whatever they want to, it could not function. To what extent do you agree or disagree?

2009 年 1 月 10 日考题回顾

科技进步与贫富差距

WRITING TASK 2

You should spend about 40 minutes on this task.

Write about the following topic：

Some people believe the range of technology available to individuals today is widening the gap between poor people and rich people. Others think it is having an opposite effect. Discuss these points of view. What is your opinion?

Give reasons for your answer and include any relevant examples from your own knowledge or experience.

Write at least 250 words.

题目解释

一些人认为，当今，人们可以更广泛地利用科技，这增大了穷人和富人之间的差距。另一些人认为，它有一个相反的作用。讨论这些观点。你的观点是什么？

高分范文

Presently, many people believe the thriving of modern technology is widening the gap between the rich and the poor. But some others would dispute this view. What lies between such arguments is the definition of the word "gap", and the pros and the cons would argue from their points of view as follows:

The pros for such an idea come up with many examples, ranging from the Internet stock exchange to mobile communication, they believe such methods of technology have broadened the gap between the well-off and the poor because they can add much more to the wealthy people's fortune and less to the poor people's wallets. Examples of millionaires are various from Bill Gates to some famous website owners, who are mostly related to the development of the Internet or communication. In this sense, the gap between them and the rest is widening.

The cons stand still to their definition of "gap". The gap in living standards between the poor and the rich is actually decreasing with the improvement of technology. In the past, car owners liked very much showing off their status and wealth, quite similar to the first generation of mobile phone owners. But when technology has filled up such a gap, we can see how common cars and mobile phones are. And they are no longer any symbols of status.

In conclusion, I would say that such a dispute can achieve no result due to the vagueness of the topic. Compared with ancient feudal society, the gap between the poor and the rich is pretty small nowadays, which is partially due to the development of technology. Wealth imbalance is not the result of technological development, but the disparity of information. And technology is just the remedy for that disparity.

范文翻译

目前，许多人相信，蓬勃发展的现代技术增大了贫富之间的差距。但是另一些人则不同意这种观点。这种争议实际是对“差距”的定义不同。从他们的观点来看，利弊如下：

赞成这种想法的人举出许多例子，从互联网证券交易到移动通信，他们相信这些技术方法已经增大了境况较好的人和较贫穷的人之间的差距，因为它们可以更快地增加富人的财富，而对穷人的钱包增加很少。以各种富翁为例，从比尔·盖茨到一些著名的网站拥有者，这些人几乎都跟互联网或通信的发展有关。从这个意义上讲，他们和其他人之间的差距正在增加。

反对者仍然坚持他们对“差距”的定义。因为技术的改进，穷人和富人之间生活水平的差距实际上正在下降。过去，有车的人非常喜欢炫耀他们的地位和财富，这个例子跟第一代的手机拥有者十分相似。但是，当技术已经弥补了这种差距的时候，我们可以看到小汽车和手机是多么的普及。它们不再是地位的象征。

最后，我要说的是，这种争议由于主题的含糊是不会有任何结果的。与古代封建社会相比，如今的穷人和富人之间的差距是相当小的，部分原因是技术的发展。财富失衡不是技术发展的结果，而是信息的不对称。而技术正好是对这种不对称的弥补。

闪光词汇

★ **thrive** [θraiv] *vi.* 兴旺，繁荣

Some types of pines will **thrive** even in the sandhill areas. 有些松树甚至在沙丘地区也长得很茂盛。

★ **gap** [gæp] *n.* 差距

The **gap** is still wider in the newer industries. 新兴工业的差距就更大了。

★ **dispute** [dis'pjuːt] *v.* 争论，辩论；反对，辩驳

It is ridiculous to **dispute** about such a thing. 为这样的事情而争论简直荒谬可笑。

★ **come up with** 提出，拿出

Have you **come up with** a more practical idea? 你有没有想出一个更实际的办法？

★ **broaden** ['brɔːdn] *vt.* 放宽，加宽

You should **broaden** your experience by travelling more. 你应该多到各地走走以增加见识。

★ **decrease** [di'kriːs] *vi.* 减少

It is necessary to **decrease** the amount of coal used. 有必要减少煤的使用量。

★ **disparity** [dis'pæriti] *n.* 不同，不对等

The rich and the poor live side by side but in conditions of extraordinary **disparity**. 富人和穷人居住在一起，但居住条件极为悬殊。

★ **remedy** ['remidi] *n.* 补救，赔偿 *vt.* 补救，修补

Your only **remedy** is to go to law. 你唯一的补救办法是诉诸法律。

类似考题

2010 年 1 月 23 日

The gap between the rich and the poor is becoming wider. The rich is growing richer and the poor is growing poorer. What are the causes of this? What measures can be taken to reduce this problem?

第二篇

历年高频话题

Unit 1

Education and Learning

教育与学习

Test 1
学生评价老师

WRITING TASK 2

You should spend about 40 minutes on this task.

Write about the following topic:

Some people think students should be allowed to evaluate their teachers' job performance. Others believe that will lead to loss of respect and discipline. Discuss both views and give your own opinion.

Give reasons for your answer and include any relevant examples from your own knowledge and experience.

Write at least 250 words.

题目解释

一些人认为学生应该被允许评价他们老师的工作。另一些人认为那样将会导致对老师的不尊重和无纪律，讨论这两种观点并给出你的观点。

高分范文

In this day and age, it is a standard practice for business executives to fill out performance-evaluation forms to give their assessment of their subordinates' work. But when it comes to the evaluation of school teachers' job performance by their students, people hold divergent views. Some argue that students should be allowed to do so. Others contend that disrespect and indiscipline will ensue if students evaluate their teachers' work. Personally, I believe both views have some merits.

Admittedly, there could be some possible drawbacks of students evaluating their teachers' work. First, if not well-managed, evaluation by the students may be completely worthless or even misleading. It is manifest that not all students would give their evaluation responsibly and some students may make mean comments. Secondly, some students criticize their teachers not because their teachers have an irresponsible attitude toward their job but because these students dislike or even despise schooling.

However, encouraging students to evaluate their teachers can also bring about numerous boons. In the first place, it is an effective means of motivating the teachers to improve their teaching. Teachers have to keep adjusting their teaching to measure up to the expectations of the students. In the second place, regular input affords the teachers objective and balanced ideas about their own performance. Without such feedback, it would be hard for the teacher to have accurate assessment of their own teaching. In the third place, a measure of students' autonomy can make the students better prepared for their adult life. The students become better at decision-making and critical thinking.

In the final analysis, I concede that enabling the students to evaluate their teachers' performance might have some potential drawbacks. However, by averaging out students' appraisal and encourage them to evaluate responsibly can eliminate the downside of this practice. On balance, I am convinced that allowing students to evaluate their teachers is in the best interests of students, teachers, school administrators, and society as a whole.

范文翻译

如今，填评估表格评价下属的工作是企业行政管理人员的常用做法。但是，当谈到学生评价老师的工作，人们的观点则有分歧。一些人认为学生应该被允许这样做，而另一些人则主张，如果学生评价老师的工作，就会产生对老师的不尊敬和无纪律。我认为，两种观点都有一定的道理。

诚然，学生评价老师的工作可能会有一些坏处。首先，如果没有很好地组织，学生的评价可能彻底没有价值或者是误导。显然，并不是所有学生都愿意对他们的评价负责任。一些学生可能会做出恶意的评价。其次，一些学生批评他们的老师并不是因为他们老师对待工作的态度不负责任，而是因为这些学生不喜欢乃至是鄙视学校教育。

然而，鼓励学生评价老师也能带来很多的好处。第一，它是促进老师提高教学质量的有效方法，老师不得不持续调整他们的教学以达到学生的期望。第二，经常的评价使老师客观公正地看待他们自己的表现。没有这样的反馈，老师很难准确地评价他们自己的教学。第三，学生的这种自治权利使他们能够更好地为他们的成年生活做好准备。学生在决策和批判思考方面可以变得更好。

总之，我承认，学生评价老师的工作可能有有些潜在的缺点。然而，通过平均学生的评价并且鼓励他们负责任地评价就能消除实践中的缺点。总而言之，我确信，允许学生评价他们的老师符合学生、老师、学校管理者和整个社会的最大利益。

Test 2

体育课程的重要性

WRITING TASK 2

You should spend about 40 minutes on this task.

Write about the following topic：

> ***Because of the pressure of new subjects such as business studies，many schools have dropped sport or physical education（PE）from the curriculum. How important is sport or PE in a young person's education?***

Give reasons for your answer and include any relevant examples from your own knowledge and experience.

Write at least 250 words.

题目解释

因为新学科例如商科学习的压力，许多学校放弃了体育运动或者是体育课程。体育运动或体育课程在年轻人的教育当中有多重要？

高分范文

Nowadays, there is increasing pressure on schools to prepare their students for work in the twenty-first century. As a result, physical education is losing ground on the school curriculum to employment-related subjects like business and some other academic subjects. While many see this shift as inevitable, I would argue that physical education is a vital part of the school program and should be maintained. Sport and PE add variety to the curriculum, broaden the students' experience and teach essential life skills.

Within the school day, students need physical activity to balance the long-hour sitting at the desk. PE provides a break from the mental focus of academic subjects. A good PE program should include a variety of sports plus non-competitive activities like dance and aerobics so that students can experience exercise both challenging and fun.

There is a growing concern among parents and educators about obesity in children. Many students have a sedentary lifestyle that revolves around TV, computers or cars. Physical education ensures that all students get some form of regular exercise during the school day. In addition they can learn about the importance of keeping fit.

In conclusion, physical education programs in schools are not only worth maintaining but should also be developed. The result will be that students are happier, healthier and more productive in class. They will grow into adults who value fitness and enjoy participation in sports. These are lessons for a lifetime, as important as any subject on the school curriculum.

范文翻译

当今，学校帮助学生准备好在 21 世纪工作的压力越来越大。结果是，体育课在学校准备的与工作有关的课程像商业和学术科目当中就失去了存在的基础。尽管一些人认为这种转变不可避免，我认为，体育是学校教育中很重要的一部分，应当坚持。运动和体育课程可增加课程的种类，拓宽学生的经历，教会他们实际的生活技能。

在学校的日子，学生需要体育活动来调剂长时间的伏案工作。体育使学生从对学术科目的专注中获得休息。一个好的体育课程应该包括各种各样的体育活动和一些非竞争的活动，像跳舞和有氧运动，使学生参加的体育活动既具有挑战性又充满乐趣。

对于孩子们的肥胖问题，父母和教育者越来越关注。许多学生有久坐的生活习惯，他们围着电视、电脑转，动辄坐车。体育锻炼能确保所有的学生在学校里有规律地运动。另外，他们还能够学习保持健康的重要性。

总之，学校里的体育课不仅值得保留，而且应该被发展。结果就是学生更开心、更健康而且在课堂上效率高。他们会成长为重视健康并且乐意参加体育运动的大人。这是一生的课程，和学校的任何课程同等重要。

Test 3

英语发展的利弊

WRITING TASK 2

You should spend about 40 minutes on this task.

Write about the following topic:

> ***English is spreading very fast in today's world. To what extent do you think the advantages of this situation outweigh its disadvantages?***

Give reasons for your answer and include any relevant examples from your own knowledge and experience.

Write at least 250 words.

题目解释

英语在当今世界迅速传播。你认为这种情况优点在多大程度上超过了缺点?

高分范文

In the contemporary world，English is prevalent on the international scenes of politics，economy and culture. Moreover，it has been consolidating its status as the most-studied tool of communication in hundreds of thousands of educational institutions. Yet in the meantime，the dominant role of English has long been a hotbed of spirited debates，not just within the linguistic academia，but also in the press as well as the general public. As I see it，the boons brought about by the spread of English far outweigh the banes.

Admittedly，the proliferation of English does not come without drawbacks. First，it renders a host of indigenous languages obsolete. According to a recent study conducted by UNESCO，over 200 ethnic languages went extinct in 2005，chiefly due to the linguistic assimilation of ethnic minorities into the English language. Secondly，the expansion of English erodes the cultural identity of other races. Specifically，the prevalence of English has a chilling effect on the purity of other languages，which in turn，aggravates the sense of cultural inferiority among the non-native speakers of English.

Nevertheless，the proliferation of English can create even greater benefits. To begin with，English as a global lingua franca makes for cross-cultural communication. To illustrate，today eight in ten international conferences designate English as their chief working language；and ninety-eight percent leading scientific journals in the world are published in English or have English versions. Lastly，the expansion of English also enables people whose native tongue is not English to appreciate the English-speaking cultures more efficiently and more fully.

In the final analysis，I concede that the linguistic dominance of English has created some adverse effects on the world cultures. Nonetheless，its spread has produced even more blessings to our lives. I am convinced that we should sustain the extensive use of English as a global language，while at the same time do our utmost to honor and preserve other languages and cultures.

范文翻译

当代世界，英语在国际政治、经济和文化领域很流行。而且，在几十万的教育机构里，英语作为一种研究最多的交流工具，它的地位一直很巩固。然而同时，英语的主导地位一直是语言学界、媒体和公众热议的话题。在我看来，英语繁荣带来的好处远远超过了它的害处。

诚然，英语的发展并不是没有缺点。首先，它导致许多本土语言荒废。根据联合国教科文组织最近的一份研究显示，超过 200 个种族的语言在 2005 年消失，主要是由于英语同化了小语种。其次，英语的发展削弱了其他种族的文化特征。尤其是，英语的流行对其他语言的纯洁性产生了可怕的影响，反过来，这也增大了母语非英语的人的文化自卑感。

然而，英语的发展能产生更大的利益。首先，英语作为一种全球通用语有助于跨文化的交流。例如，如今，每十场国际会议就有八场把英语作为首要的工作语言。世界上 98%的主要科学杂志用英语出版或者有英语译文。最后，英语的发展使母语不是英语的人能够更有效、更充分地欣赏英语国家的文化。

总之，我承认英语在语言上的统治在世界文化领域已经产生了一些负面的影响。然而，它的普及对我们人类产生了更多的好处。我深信我们应该坚持把英语作为一种国际语言广泛使用，同时尽最大努力尊重和保护其他的语言和文化。

Test 4

单独学习还是一起学习

WRITING TASK 2

You should spend about 40 minutes on this task.

Write about the following topic：

Some people hold that students should study by themselves instead of in a group. What is your opinion?

Give reasons for your answer and include any relevant examples from your own knowledge and experience.

Write at least 250 words.

题目解释

一些人认为，学生应该自己单独学习而不是在一起学习，你的观点是什么？

高分范文

In most countries in the world, governments require children to attend schools where professional teachers are responsible for educating the children using approved curricula. However a significant number of parents believe that it is much better for their children to be educated at home. This essay will examine the question of home schooling and discuss which is the best option for the children.

Most of the parents who choose home schooling are unhappy with the quality or depth of education offered by schools. One social factor that influences their decision is that the parents worry their children will suffer from being bullied or will be forced into antisocial behavior by pressures from peers. They believe that the good behavior they have taught the child will be lost in school. Another reason is concern over the quality of schooling available. Schools frequently have large classes. They are often under-funded, and staffed by teachers without sufficient knowledge of the subjects. Other parents may disagree with the aims of the school curricula. Finally, some children with special needs may need particular parental care.

However, there are many arguments in favor of sending children to conventional schools and receive education together with other students. The first reason is that group education can increase children's communication skills. In school, children will interact with each other and develop social skills eventually. At the same time, children will learn to function outside the family. They will not be dependent on their parents for their educational, emotional and social needs. In addition to that, children will find it easier to integrate when they finish school, as they will, when they start work or college.

Overall, while many parents work hard to teach their children at home, conventional schools are still the right choice for most children. Group education is not perfect, but it seems to be a proven way of preparing our children for the real world.

范文翻译

世界上的大多数国家的政府都要求该国的孩子们上学，在学校里专业的老师负责对孩子们教授经过批准的课程。但是，相当多的家长都认为让他们的孩子在家学习更好。本文将探讨家庭教育的问题并且讨论对于孩子哪一种是最好的选择。

大多数选择家庭教育的家长都对学校提供的教育质量和深度感到不满。一个影响他们决定的社会因素是：家长们担心他们的孩子在学校会受到别人的欺负或者在同辈的压力下被迫做出反社会的行为。他们认为孩子在学校里会丢掉在家里学会的好行为。另外一个原因是关注教学质量。学校里总是大课堂，而且经常资金不足，配备的老师也缺乏足够的相应学科知识。其他一些家长可能反对的是学校的课程目标。最后，一些有特殊要求的孩子需要特定的家庭照顾。

然而，也有很多人反驳，认为应该把孩子送到传统的学校，和其他孩子一起接受教育。首要原因是集体教育可以增强孩子的沟通技巧。在学校，孩子互相交流，最终提高了社交能力。同时，孩子们会学习在外面发挥作用。他们不会在教育、情绪和社会需求上依赖父母。另外，完成学业后，不管他们参加工作还是进入大学学习，他们都会按照自己的意愿很容易地融入新环境中。

总之，当许多父母辛苦地在家里教育他们的子女的同时，传统学校还是大多数孩子的正确选择。集体教育虽然并不完美，但是看来它还是一条经过证明的使我们的孩子能够适应这个现实社会的道路。

Unit 2

Government and Society

政府与社会

Test 5

政府资金分配

WRITING TASK 2

You should spend about 40 minutes on this task.

Write about the following topic：

Some people think the government should invest more in weapons and national defense. Others think this money should be invested in arts and sports facilities such as stadiums. Discuss both views and give your opinion.

Give reasons for your answer and include any relevant examples from your own knowledge or experience.

Write at least 250 words.

题目解释

一些人认为，政府应该在军备和国防方面投入更多。另一些人认为，应该在艺术和体育设施如体育馆方面投入更多。讨论这两种观点并给出你的观点。

高分范文

How to strike a proper balance between different sectors of the country has been a major concern of the government and a topical subject in the media. Some people argue that more investment should be devoted to the national defense-related sector, while others claim arts and sports departments deserve more funds. Views on the issue vary from person to person.

On one hand, the power of national defense is crucial because it can safeguard the country from potential threat. With the wide application of information technology, the military expenditure has been greatly increased. True, constant negotiations have been held by UN and joint efforts have been conducted among different countries to reach agreements on such issues as nuclear nonproliferation, disarmament and cutting down on military expenses, but until a substantial progress is made, to slash necessary defense investment would pose risks and undermine the security of the country.

On the other hand, arts and sports facilities better the living standard of the people, which is conducive to the stability, prosperity and harmony of the society. Galleries, sculptures, museums and stadiums provide places of entertainment and sports for citizens to enjoy their leisure time and build up their physical health; and for the society to preserve cultural, historical and artistic heritage.

In conclusion, it is preferable to keep a balance between patronizing arts, sports facilities and subsidizing national defense according to the specific circumstances and different developing stages of the country. What needs to be kept in mind is that priority should be given to national security as it is the primary matter in the hierarchy of a country's needs.

范文翻译

在国家的不同部门之间如何努力达到适当的平衡一直是政府部门和媒体关注的主要课题。一些人认为，更多的投资应该分配给与国防有关的部门，而另一些人认为艺术和体育部门应该得到更多的资金。人们在这个问题上的观点各不相同。

一方面，国防力量很关键，因为它能保卫国家不受潜在的威胁。随着信息技术的广泛应用，军费支出一直大幅增长。事实上，联合国召开了很多的会谈，国家之间也在努力合作，就一些问题达成了一些协议，如防止核扩散、裁军和削减军费。但是除非取得实质性的进步，削减必要的国防投入将会带来危险并且破坏国家的安全。

另一方面，艺术和体育设施提高人们的生活水平，有助于社会的稳定、繁荣和和谐。美术馆、雕塑馆、博物馆和体育馆为市民提供娱乐和体育活动的场所，丰富他们的业余生活，强健他们的身体，也为社会保存文化、历史和艺术遗产。

总之，最好是根据特定的环境和国家的不同发展阶段在艺术、体育设施和国防经费之间平衡分配资金。应该牢记在心的是应该给国家安全以优先权，因为它是国家最基本的需要。

Test 6

由政府还是学生来决定学习科目

WRITING TASK 2

You should spend about 40 minutes on this task.

Write about the following topic：

Some people think that the government should decide the subject for students to study in university. Others believe that students should be allowed to apply for the subject they prefer. Discuss both views and give your opinion.

Give reasons for your answer and include any relevant examples from your own knowledge or experience.

Write at least 250 words.

题目解释

有些人认为政府应该为大学生确定他们所应学习的科目，而另一些人认为应该允许学生申请学习自己喜欢的科目，讨论双方的观点并提出你自己的看法。

高分范文

With the current emphasis on individuality in education, many people are against the traditional practice of compulsory courses. They believe the subjects one chooses to study should be left for individuals to decide rather than the government. I will discuss this subject from two sides.

On one hand, being the biggest supporter of educational system, the government should have the right to decide what contents student should learn. Franklin once said that educated people were easy to govern and hard to enslave, which clearly reveals the aim of education of a country is to cultivate its labor force to be better citizens so as to improve the national strength. Consequently, it is wise for the government to list the necessary courses for students to upgrade the population quality.

On the other hand, besides the compulsory courses that are decided by government, students are entitled to choose whatever subjects which appeal to them. Different subjects have different impact on one's life. Histories make men wise; poems witty; mathematics subtle; natural philosophy deep; moral grave; logic and rhetoric able to contend.

Generally speaking, people study for different reasons and various intentions. Some people study because they believe certificates, diplomas, and degrees are symbols of social status, and a passport to a private club of money and power. Others study because they are interested in certain subjects. But above all, we should always study for our country and the subjects chosen by the government will benefit not only our life but also the future of our nation.

范文翻译

随着人们目前对个性化教育的重视，许多人开始反对传统的必修课课程形式，他们相信让学生们自主选择想要学习的课程比让政府选择要好得多。在这篇文章里，我将从两方面讨论这个问题。

一方面，政府作为教育系统的最大支持者有权决定学生应该学习什么内容。弗兰克林曾经说过，受过教育的人易被统治，但难于被奴役。这表明一个国家教育的目的就是把劳动力培养成更好的公民，以提高民族实力。因此，政府为学生选择必修课程，提高人口质量的这种做法是明智的。

另一方面，除了政府决定的必修课之外，人们有权选择任何他们感兴趣的科目。不同科目对人的生活有不同影响。历史使人明智；诗词使人灵秀；数学使人周密；自然哲学使人深刻；伦理使人庄重；逻辑修辞学使人善辩。

一般来说，人们出于不同的原因和各种各样的目的学习。一些人学习因为他们相信证书、文凭和学位是社会地位的象征，是通往金钱和权力的私人俱乐部的通行证。另外一些人学习出于他们对某些学科的兴趣。但是综上所述，我们更应该为国家学习，政府选定的科目不仅有利于我们的生活，而且有利于整个民族的未来。

Test 7
移民的挑战

WRITING TASK 2

You should spend about 40 minutes on this task.

Write about the following topic:

People today move to new cities and new countries more than ever before. What challenges do they experience? What strategies are there to meet these challenges?

Give reasons for your answer and include any relevant examples from your own knowledge or experience.

Write at least 250 words.

题目解释

人们比以前更多地移民到新城市和新国家。他们经历的挑战有哪些？有什么策略去迎接这些挑战？

高分范文

People today are clearly more mobile than in the past. This is largely due to modern technology which makes traveling and communicating easier and quicker. Why do people move? Often people re-locate to large cities for employment; and some move to study overseas. Whatever the reason, moving away from home may confront many challenges.

Firstly there are practical problems such as finding accommodation, managing finances, shopping and so on. These might present challenges to someone who has not lived independently before. In addition, adapting to a new city environment includes understanding the public transport system, possibly in another language, while trying not to get lost. The best strategy for minimizing such anxious moments is to prepare in advance as much as possible, for it might be helpful to get advice from someone familiar with the local area. Ideally, sharing accommodation with someone who is familiar with the city, or staying in a "homestay" on arrival in a new country may overcome many of these problems. Homestay families or "sharemates" will provide company and be able to explain aspects of the new city or culture that may seem strange at first.

There are also emotional issues to deal with, like loneliness or language problems. Moreover, starting a new job or course may be stressful at first. Generally, however, there are organizations such as overseas students' associations in an educational institution, or other sports or hobby clubs where it is possible to meet people and make friends.

In conclusion, although there are many challenges when leaving home for a new city or country, planning in advance can transform an ordeal into an interesting adventure.

范文翻译

显然，当今人们比过去移民的更多。这主要是由于现代技术使迁移和沟通更容易更快速。为什么人们移民呢？人们经常为了工作到大城市重新定居，一些人到海外学习。无论什么原因，离开家很远都可能遇到很多挑战。

首先，有很多实际问题，例如，找住宿、管理钱财、购物等。这对于以前没有独立居住过的人来说可能有很多挑战。另外，适应新的城市环境包括了解公共交通系统，可能还包括另一种语言，同时还要不迷失自己。尽量减少这种焦虑时刻的最好策略是尽可能提前做好准备，从熟悉当地情况的人那里获取建议可能很有帮助。实际上，和熟悉城市的人合住，或者一到新的国家就待在当地人家里可能会克服很多的问题。当地的家庭或者是室友将会陪伴你并且向你解释新城市和文化的很多方面，这些最初在你看来可能会很陌生。

也有感情的问题需要处理，像孤独或者是语言问题。而且，开始一份新的工作或者是课程最初可能会很有压力。然而，一般来说，有一些组织，例如在教育机构里的海外学生联合会，或者其他的运动或爱好俱乐部，那里可能遇到一些人并且交朋友。

总之，尽管离开家到新的城市或者国家会有很多挑战，提前计划就会把考验变成有趣的探险。

Test 8
青少年犯罪

WRITING TASK 2

You should spend about 40 minutes on this task.

Write about the following topic:

There are an increasing number of juvenile delinquents. What are the causes of this phenomenon?

Give reasons for your answer and include any relevant examples from your own knowledge and experience.

Write at least 250 words.

题目解释

有越来越多的青少年犯罪，这种现象的原因是什么？

高分范文

In this day and age，the incidence of juvenile offenses has been growing at an alarming rate；and the severity of youth offenses has been staggering to adults. A recent survey conducted by the Chinese Ministry of Justice revealed that one out of four crimes today was committed by minors. Hence，it is imperative that we pinpoint the causes of this disturbing phenomenon.

In the first place，many instances of juvenile delinquency have been attributed to the violent or pornographic content of some TV shows and video games. Now we are confronted with a proliferation of blood and nudity on TV，the computer and the Internet. As a consequence，many youngsters，especially boys，get addicted to such scenes. Lacking the ability to distinguish between right and wrong，they develop criminal tendencies.

In the second place，parental neglect and domestic violence play a pivotal role in the increase of youth crimes. Today，there are an ever-growing number of dis-functional families. Generally，the children raised in such families are far more likely to be afflicted with constant fear. In the end，they develop a hatred for society and other individuals.

In the third place，the rise of juvenile crime rate is symbiotically connected with that of adult crime rate in society. In other words，the more adult crimes，the higher the probability of youngsters falling prey to adult offenders. For instance，many youths are tempted by evil adults into committing crimes.

In sum，many factors contribute to the surge of juvenile delinquency. It is crucial that we take stringent measures to tackle these problems and ensure that the future of our nation，that is，the youngsters，have a more promising future ahead of them.

范文翻译

如今，青少年犯罪以惊人的速度增长。青少年犯罪的严重性震惊了成年人。中国司法部最近的调查表明，如今有 1/4 的犯罪是由未成年人实施的。因此，我们必须查明这种纷乱的社会现象的原因。

首先，许多青少年犯罪事例是由于一些电视节目或者是电子游戏的暴力或色情内容引起的。如今，我们面临着电视、电脑和互联网上出现的血腥赤裸的内容，结果，许多年轻人，尤其是男孩儿，对这样的场面很上瘾。由于缺乏辨别是非的能力，他们产生了犯罪的倾向。

其次，父母的忽视和家庭暴力在青少年犯罪增加方面起了关键的作用。如今，有很多不健康的家庭。一般说来，成长在这样家庭里的孩子更容易被不断的恐惧所折磨。最后，他们对社会和他人产生了仇恨。

再次，青少年犯罪率的上升与社会上成年人犯罪率的上升相关。换句话说，成年人犯罪越多，青少年受成年人犯罪影响的可能性就越大。例如，许多年轻人受邪恶的成年人的引诱而实施犯罪。

总之，青少年犯罪的增加是多种因素的结果。至关紧要的是，我们要采取严厉的措施解决这些问题，确保我们的民族，也就是年轻人，在他们的前面有一个更有希望的未来。

Unit 3

Technology and Efficiency

科技与效率

Test 9

科技进步带来的问题

WRITING TASK 2

You should spend about 40 minutes on this task.

Write about the following topic：

> ***Scientific and technological advances have changed our lives. But some scientists in some fields say that they are not able to find solutions to the problems they have created. To what extent do you agree or disagree?***

Give reasons for your answer and include any relevant examples from your own knowledge or experience.

Write at least 250 words.

题目解释

科技进步改变了我们的生活。但是一些领域的科学家说他们不能找到他们所带来的问题的解决方法。你同意还是不同意？

高分范文

We are surely living differently from our parents did decades ago with the help of scientific and technological advances. The changes are wide and profound. At the same time, we are facing challenges and problems which were unknown in the past. Could we find solutions to problems created by scientific development? In my opinion, the answer seems to be no.

Some of the most obvious problems caused by technological advances lie in the IT industry. At a time when we did not have computers and electronic bank services, people took money with them and paid in cash. If they were robbed, only the amount they brought with them was lost. But now as credit cards are more commonly used in shopping malls and other places, crimes against us have become more serious and caused greater losses to people. A thief may tape the code of your credit card and make a copy of it. Then he could safely withdraw all your money from an ATM machine. Crimes like this type are too sticky to solve because there is no witness and the surveillance cameras give little help to the police.

Another example is the issue of information controlled by the media industry including TV networks and the Internet that give easy access to information regardless of people's age. This has created a huge problem for parents and schools because teenage people are particularly vulnerable to adult materials and violent information. In the past, when most information came in the form of print, it was relatively easy to control what children read. When a parent put away a book unsuitable for children, they were cut off from the source of information. With computer parents could use software to filter bad web sites but could not prevent new ones from appearing every day.

In conclusion, developments in many fields of our life have brought us both benefits and problems. People are working very hard to solve such problems that come along with advances in science and technology, but the efforts are not sufficient and not very successful. So it is so ironic that scientists are not able to find solutions to the problems they have created.

范文翻译

科技进步了，我们的确和我们父母几十年前的生活不同了，变化广泛而深远。同时，我们正面临着过去所不知道的挑战和问题。我们能够通过科学的发展找到这些问题的解决方案吗？在我看来，答案似乎是不能。

技术进步引起的最明显的问题在 IT 领域。在我们没有计算机和电子银行服务的时候，人们随身携带并且用现金支付。如果他们被盗了，也仅仅是他们随时携带的数额丢失了。但是现在信用卡在商场和其他的地方被越来越多地使用，针对我们的犯罪也变得更严重，并且造成人们更大的损失。小偷可以录下信用卡的密码并且制作一个副本。然后他就能安全地从自动存取款机上取出你所有的钱。这样的犯罪很难侦破，因为没有证据，而监控摄像头对警察也没有多大帮助。

另外一个例子就是信息问题，被媒体系统包括电视广播网络和互联网控制的信息使无论什么年龄的人们都容易有机会接触他们。这就给父母和学校带来了巨大的问题，因为青少年特别容易受成人资料和暴力信息的影响。过去，当大多数信息以打印的形式出现的时候，控制孩子们读什么相对容易。当父母把不适合孩子读的书收藏起来的时候，他们就切断了信息的来源。对于计算机，父母可以用软件过滤掉不好的网站，但是不能每天都阻止新的出现。

总之，我们生活中很多领域的发展既给我们带来了利益，也给我们带来了问题。人们努力解决科技进步带来的问题，但是成就很少、很不成功。因此，科学家不能找到他们所带来的难题的解决办法，这真是个讽刺。

Test 10

技术改变生活

WRITING TASK 2

You should spend about 40 minutes on this task.

Write about the following topic:

> ***Some people think that the earlier technology has changed our life more than recent technology. Do you agree or disagree?***

Give reasons for your answer and include any relevant examples from your own knowledge or experience.

Write at least 250 words.

题目解释

一些人认为，早期的技术比最近的技术更大地改变了我们的生活。你是否同意这种观点？

高分范文

The history of human society has been connected with the development of technologies, compass, paper making, steam engine, lighting bulb and telephone, to name but a few. Some people assume that the earlier technology has changed our life more than recent technology. From my perspective, the latest technological breakthroughs take a more active part in the dramatic changes of society.

To start with, modern transportation technology symbolized by the invention of motorized aircraft facilitates international trade and contributes to the flourishing of tourism industry. Never before in history have people enjoyed such a high speed and comfort of traveling. It is by no means an exaggeration to say the plane, one of the greatest innovations, is the foundation for contemporary transportation, tourism, economic and cultural integration, contributing massively to the prosperity of the earth.

Furthermore, Information technology represented by the computer and the Internet triggers a series of unprecedented economic and social transformations. As the most sophisticated working instrument, learning tool and communicative medium, computers have brought about economic growth, better quality of life, and a peaceful and stable international community. It is not a perfect renovation given the fact that the Internet still has some adverse effects on society, but it has become an indispensable part of modern life.

Admittedly, traditional technological development laid a solid foundation for following inventions, making massive impacts on our life, but the more up-to-date breakthrough, the more powerful the influence it tends to exert over the world, which seems to be one of the laws of life.

范文翻译

人类社会的历史是和指南针、造纸术、蒸汽机、灯泡和电话等不胜枚举的技术发展紧密相连的。一些人认为，早期的技术比最近的技术更大地改变了我们的生活。在我看来，最近的技术突破在我们的社会变革中起的作用更积极。

首先，以机动航空器的发明为标志的现代交通技术促进了国际贸易的发展和旅游业的繁荣。以前历史上的人们从来没有享受到这样高速舒适的旅行。说飞机是最伟大的发明之一，是现代运输、旅游、经济和文化融合的基础，这一点都不夸张，它极大地促进了世界的繁荣。

而且，以计算机和互联网为代表的信息技术引起了一系列空前的经济和社会变革。作为最尖端的工作手段，学习工具和交流媒体，计算机带来了经济的飞速发展、生活水平的提高和国际社会的和平和稳定。由于互联网仍然对社会有一些负面的影响，它并不是一个完美的革新，但是，它已经是现代生活不可缺少的一部分。

不可否认，传统技术的发展为后来的发明奠定了坚实的基础，对我们的现代生活有很大的影响。但是，越是近期的突破，对世界的影响越大，这似乎是生活的定律。

Test 11

信息时代的人际关系

WRITING TASK 2

You should spend about 40 minutes on this task.

Write about the following topic:

> ***We live today in an electronic information age. It is easier to be connected by technology yet many people seem no closer to feeling happy in their lives. Do you agree or disagree?***

Give reasons for your answer and include any relevant examples from your own knowledge or experience.

Write at least 250 words.

题目解释

如今我们生活在电子信息时代，人们很容易通过技术手段来联系。但是许多人在生活中不是变得更开心了。你是否同意这种观点？

高分范文

The electronic information age that we live in today certainly makes communication very quick and easy. It is simple for many people to contact dozens of others every day via the computer，but does this make them feel happier? Whether modern communication has increased people's feeling of happiness is，however，debatable.

There are many advantages of being connected electronically. In the first place，instead of local phone and distant mail，we can stay in touch via email with our family or friends around the world. In this way isolation by distance can be overcome. For example，information that would only be available to the local people living in Finland，a distant northern European country is now at our fingertips and has been acknowledged by the dwellers in Australia. In the second place，thousands of people from all over the world use chat rooms and Internet dating sites every day. It is not only convenient but also economical for people to communicate in this way.

On the other hand，there is concern that people are in fact becoming more isolated only communicating on-line. On this evidence they seem unhappier today. Thus it seems to be the case that depression and suicide rates are high and the divorce rate is increasing. Employees complain about longer working hours and increasing stress levels.

Perhaps，there is more awareness of current problems because so much information is available through technology and media. Even so，it seems that the quality of our relationships and therefore our level of happiness are unrelated to modern technology，which is，after all，only a tool.

范文翻译

毫无疑问，我们如今生活的电子信息时代使交流更快、更容易。人们每天通过计算机就可以与许多其他的人联系，但是，这使他们感到更开心吗？现代信息技术是否提高了人们的幸福感仍然存在争议。

用电子技术联系有很多的优点。首先，无须电话和长途邮件，我们可以通过电子邮件与家人和世界各地的朋友保持联系。通过这种途径，长距离产生的孤独被克服了。例如，仅仅由居住在一个遥远的北欧国家——芬兰本地的人能够获得的信息，现在就在我们的指尖，已经被居住在澳大利亚的居民获得。其次，来自世界的很多人每天用聊天室和网络聊天。用这种方式交流不仅方便而且经济。

另一方面，仅仅通过网上交流，人们实际上变得更加孤独了。显然，如今他们看起来更不开心。因此，忧郁和自杀率很高，离婚率也正在上升。雇员抱怨工作时间长、压力大。

或许更多的人已经意识到了当前的问题，因为通过技术和媒体有如此多的信息可以获得。即使这样，似乎我们的关系的质量以及由此导致的幸福的水平都与现代技术无关，毕竟，它只是一个工具。

Unit 4
Media and Advertising
媒体与广告

Test 12
媒体影响生活

WRITING TASK 2

You should spend about 40 minutes on this task.

Write about the following topic:

> ***People think that news media have influenced people's lives nowadays. They are therefore a negative development. To what extent do you agree or disagree?***

Give reasons for your answer and include any relevant examples from your own knowledge or experience.

Write at least 250 words.

题目解释

人们认为，如今新闻媒体影响了人们的生活。因此它是一个负面的发展。你同意还是不同意？

高分范文

The impact that news media have had on our daily life and society in general is undeniable. No doubt they offer more convenient and effective ways to our information acquirement and social supervision. Although I support that we should be aware of the existence of some negative aspects which are not easy to be resolved, such as bothering personal lives of famous people and reporting inaccurately, it is only a small part.

News media render people many advantages. First and foremost, they broadcast information instantly. They tell us what has happened in the world right away with very impressive vivid pictures. During the 18th World Cup, many people watched the games on TV or the Internet live. Additionally, they can also tell us the world events, latest development of science and technology, and even the fashion trend nowadays, which can keep us abreast with the world.

Furthermore, news media exercise active social supervision function in addition to their role in publicity and dissemination. Many newspapers, TV stations, radio stations and other media have columns or programs devoted specifically to the anti-graft issues and have in fact exposed quite a lot of problems covering abuse of power, neglect of responsibility, corruption in administrative affairs committed by governmental departments or officials. Consequently, the government can get over information failure caused by false statistical data and get known about the reality, which is the ground of sound policy.

Nevertheless, as we are all aware, owning to their business-orientation, news media sometimes publish inaccurate reports which may mislead the masses and stories about the privacy of famous people. Confronted with these problems, we should realize that sociologists have been seeking prompt and feasible solutions to reduce their negative effects to the minimum, and already scored some achievements. Consequently, I believe that news media will be more beneficial than harmful.

范文翻译

新闻媒体给我们的日常生活和社会所带来的影响是不可否认的，无疑它们使我们在获得信息和社会监督方面更方便、更快捷。尽管我承认我们应意识到媒体给我们带来一些负面影响，并且这些负面影响很难消除，比如打扰名人的私人生活，报道不实；然而，这只是一小部分。

新闻媒体有许多优点。首先，最重要的是新闻媒体能够快速报道信息，及时告诉我们世界上所发生的事情并有生动的图片。在第十八届世界杯中，许多人通过电视或上网观看现场直播。而且，媒体报道发生在世界的大事，科学技术的最新发展甚至当今流行趋势，使我们与世界保持联系。

而且，除了传播信息，新闻媒体还在社会监督中发挥着积极作用。许多报纸、电视台、广播台和其他媒体开辟了专栏或节目，并且披露了许多问题如政府部门和官员滥用权力、渎职、腐败。因此，政府能避免由统计数据造成的信息不准，从而更好地制定政策。

尽管如此，我们都意识到，由于经济利益的驱使，新闻媒体有时会发布不实报道，这些报道可能误导大众，还会有名人私生活的报道。面临这些问题，我们应意识到社会学家一直在寻找可行的措施将其负面影响降低到最小，并且已取得一些成绩。因此，我相信新闻媒体将会更有利而不是有害。

Test 13
政府控制媒体

WRITING TASK 2

You should spend about 40 minutes on this task.

Write about the following topic：

International media such as TV and the Internet are influencing our lives. Some people think the government should control the violence in international media. Do you agree or disagree?

Give reasons for your answer and include any relevant examples from your own knowledge or experience.

Write at least 250 words.

题目解释

国际媒体例如电视和网络正在影响我们的生活。一些人认为政府应该控制国际媒体上的暴力。你同意还是不同意？

高分范文

In the contemporary world, the media have become one of the most popular industries and exerted a profound impact on our lives. However, with the crime rate hovering at a high level, both the print media and the electronic media are inundated with violent contents. Some people claim that showing violence is beneficial to boost television and Internet ratings, whereas many others assert that the government should control violence in international media. Personally, I think their view has both merits and demerits.

Admittedly, the scenes full of excitements will boost television and Internet ratings, especially violent contents. It is apparent that more and more violent TV programs and Internet websites are mushrooming to meet the audience's needs. Therefore, the violence on the media cannot be strictly prohibited because both the media and audience will partly profit from it.

Nevertheless, the disadvantages of showing violence on the media outweigh the advantages. In the first place, excessive violent contents generate baneful influence upon the youngsters. Many youngsters get addicted to such scenes because they still do not have the ability to distinguish between right and wrong. Even some of them may have criminal tendencies. In the second place, violence showed by the media affords the potential criminals pragmatic crime skills. To some extent, it helps those who are in the process of planning some violent acts to perfect their plans.

In the final analysis, I concede that showing violence on the media helps to boost television and Internet ratings. However, there are even much more drawbacks. The government should take measures to control the violence in international media, thereby preventing children from falling prey to violent contents and reducing the potential violent acts.

范文翻译

当今世界，媒体成了最流行的产业之一，对我们的生活有很深远的影响。但是，随着犯罪率的急速上升，一些纸质媒体和电子媒体充斥着犯罪的内容。一些人主张表现暴力内容对提高电视的收视率和网络的点击率有利，而另一些人认为，政府应该控制国际媒体的暴力内容。个人而言，我认为他们的观点各有优点和缺点。

诚然，激动人心的场面会提高电视的收视率和网络的点击率，尤其是暴力内容。显然，越来越多的充满暴力的电视节目和网站激增，以满足观众的需要。因此，媒体上的暴力不能被严格禁止，因为媒体和观众都将在一定程度上受益。

然而，媒体表现暴力内容，弊大于利。首先，过多的暴力内容对年轻人产生有害的影响。许多年轻人沉溺于这样的场景，因为他们仍然没有能力辨别是非。甚至他们当中的一些人会有犯罪的倾向。其次，媒体表现暴力内容给潜在的犯罪分子提供了非常实用的犯罪技巧。在某种程度上，媒体帮助那些在准备实施犯罪行为的人完善了他们的犯罪计划。

总之，我承认，表现暴力内容对提高电视收视率和网络点击率有利，然而，缺点更多。政府应该采取措施控制国际媒体中的暴力内容，从而保护儿童不受暴力内容的侵害，减少潜在的犯罪行为。

Unit 5

Travel, Development and Globalization

旅游、发展与全球化

Test 14

国际旅游的利弊

WRITING TASK 2

You should spend about 40 minutes on this task.

Write about the following topic：

International tourism creates tension rather than understanding between people from different cultures. To what extent do you agree or disagree?

Give reasons for your answer and include any relevant examples from your own knowledge or experience.

Write at least 250 words.

题目解释

国际旅游使不同文化的人们之间关系紧张而不是理解。你是否同意这种观点？

高分范文

When it comes to international tourism, there is always a heated discussion among people. Some people claim that tourism enhances understanding between the local people and tourists. While others argue that tourism causes tension. As far as I am concerned, the former is more persuasive than the latter.

There is no denying that international tourism brings some disadvantages to us. For the lack of knowledge of local customs, the tourists often offend the local people. Too many tourists can crowd public places that are also enjoyed by the native inhabitants, which may lead to the resentment of the local people. Nevertheless, compared with the problems, the advantages of tourism are more striking.

Firstly, there is no exaggeration to say that tourism helps maintain world peace. Cross-cultural contacts with indigenous people promote friendship and goodwill, removing prejudice and hostility. If people travel to other countries, they can not be misled by hearsay or films and television. For instance, with the development of China's tourism, more and more foreigners recognize that Chinese men no longer wear long braids and Chinese women's feet are not bound any longer, and Chinese people are able to communicate with them in English. As the old saying goes: "Seeing is believing."

Secondly, tourist industry plays a positive role in economic development. For instance, tourism provides jobs for many people and helps ease or solve the social problem of unemployment, accelerating urban construction and embellishment.

In sum, instead of causing tension, international tourism promotes mutual understanding of the people from different countries.

范文翻译

在国际旅游这个问题上，人们一直存在激烈的争议。有人认为旅游业加强当地人与游客之间的相互理解。而另一些人认为旅游业造成关系紧张。我认为，前者的观点比后者更有说服力。

不可否认，国际旅游有很多弊端。由于缺乏对当地风俗的了解，游客经常冒犯当地人。太多的游客挤占了当地居民的空间引起他们的怨恨。尽管如此，与这些问题比起来，旅游的好处还是显而易见的。

首先，可以不夸张地说旅游业有利于保持世界和平。与当地居民接触有利于加强友谊，消除偏见和对立。如果到其他国家旅游，就不会被传言或者电影和电视所误导。例如，随着中国旅游业的发展，越来越多的外国人认识到中国男人不再留长辫子，而女人也不再裹小脚了，并且中国人能用英语与他们交流。如谚语所说："眼见为实。"

其次，旅游业有利于经济发展。比如旅游业为很多人提供了就业机会，有助于解决或缓解社会失业问题并加快城市建设。

总之，国际旅游进一步加强了各国人民之间的相互理解而不是造成关系紧张。

Test 15

改善交通状况

WRITING TASK 2

You should spend about 40 minutes on this task.

Write about the following topic:

> ***The only way to improve safety on the road is to give driving offenders stricter punishment. To what extent do you agree or disagree?***

Give reasons for your answer and include any relevant examples from your own knowledge or experience.

Write at least 250 words.

题目解释

有人认为对违法司机重罚是改善交通状况的唯一方法，对此你在多大程度上赞成或反对。

高分范文

Road accidents are responsible for the casualties of an ever-increasing number of people. Some people claim stricter punishment against driving offenders is the best choice. In my opinion, before solutions to this problem can be found, it is necessary to examine the main causes of accidents: vehicle roadworthiness, road conditions and human error.

Many accidents are caused by inadequate vehicle maintenance, such as driving with defective brakes or bald tyres which add to the stopping time. Regular mechanical inspections would help reduce the number of unworthy vehicles on the road.

Bad road conditions also lead to accidents. Heavy rain, fog or snow can make roads slippery and accidents can occur. In addition, narrow, winding roads and road surfaces which are in a state of disrepair contribute to the number of road fatalities. A greater proportion of money needs to be allocated to improve roads and provide clear road signs.

The third cause of accidents is drivers' errors. Drunken driving and speeding are frequently the cause of drivers misjudging distance and losing control of their vehicles. Other examples are drivers failing to signal a turn and overtaking other vehicles without due care. Although these problems of human error are the most difficult to resolve, advertising campaigns have proved effective in educating drivers about road hazards.

In conclusion, although it is inevitable that some accidents will occur, there are ways to reduce their frequency. Governments need to put in place stricter vehicle tests and penalize careless drivers more severely. It is also necessary to allocate more money to maintaining and upgrading roads and educating drivers. By implementing these measures, the roads will be safer for everyone.

范文翻译

对于目前持续增长的伤亡人数，交通事故负有不可推卸的责任。一些人主张，对违章司机采取更严厉的惩罚是最好的选择。在我看来，在找到解决这个问题的办法之前，有必要审视造成交通事故的原因：车辆的性能、道路状况以及人为的过失。

许多事故都因汽车缺乏维护造成，例如驾驶刹车不灵或轮胎磨平了的汽车上路，致使遇到紧急情况不能及时刹车。经常对汽车做检查可以减少道路上行使的问题车辆的数目。

道路状况不好也会引发事故。大雨、雾天或雪天会使路面变滑，从而造成事故发生。另外，狭窄、弯曲以及路面破损的道路都会造成车祸。政府应把大量的资金用于改善路况和提供清晰的路标。

第三种引起事故的原因是驾驶错误。酒后驾车和超速行驶经常能够使驾驶员错误地判断车距以致汽车失控。又比如驾驶员转弯没有示意，盲目超车。尽管人的失误最难解决，但广告攻势被证实对驾驶人员在道路安全问题上的教育起到了一定作用。

总之，尽管某些事故的发生不可避免，还是有办法可以减少事故的发生率。政府应该采取更严格的车辆检查制度，对违规驾驶员实行更严厉的惩罚。划拨更多的资金来维护、升级道路以及教育驾驶人员也是必要的。实施了这些措施之后，道路就会变得对每个人都更加安全。

Unit 6

Environment and Pollution

环境与污染

Test 16

科技与环境和能源

WRITING TASK 2

You should spend about 40 minutes on this task.

Write about the following topic:

Some people hold that the development of modern science and technology leads to environmental pollution and energy shortage. What do you think?

Give reasons for your answer and include any relevant examples from your own knowledge or experience.

You should write at least 250 words.

题目解释

一些人认为现代科技的发展导致环境污染和能源短缺，你怎样认为？

高分范文

Science and technology have been developing rapidly during the past ten years. Their development has brought lots of benefits to mankind. Science has greatly changed today's world. Due to science, we now live safer, more comfortable and convenient lives. However, some people argue that while progress has brought us many time-saving machines, it has also brought us environmental pollution and energy shortage. I totally agree with the opinion.

Science has been responsible for pollution. Modern industry, as well as modern traffic conveniences, has created a serious problem of air pollution. The "green house effect" is now threatening the existence of mankind. The population of the earth is increasing very fast. Humans must make the earth support the increasing population. This has made it necessary for agriculture and industry to develop rapidly. Such rapid developments are results of modern science, which produces more and more waste. And all the pollutants go into the water, the soil and the air. Some of the poisonous waste may do great harm to the people around them.

With the development of technology and the increase of population, the amount and range of materials used has increased. It is estimated that this trend will continue in the years to come. However, natural resources are not inexhaustible. Some resources have been nearly used up. For example, the end of the world's fuel is already within sight. Such an essential daily item as water is in short supply in many parts of the world. With the expansion of industrialization, requirement for energy all over the world is on the rise. We have a great need for energy because of all kinds of scientific and technological inventions.

From what I have mentioned above, I believe that it is the development of science and technology that leads to the pollution of environment and shortage of energy.

范文翻译

科学技术在过去十年中迅速地发展。科技的发展给人们带来了很多好处。科学已经很大程度地改变了当今世界。因为科学，我们现在过着更安全、更舒适、更方便的生活。然而一些人认为，虽然科技进步带给我们很多省时的机器，它同时也带来了环境污染和能源短缺。我完全同意这一观点。

科学造成污染。现代工业和现代交通便利已经造成了严重的空气污染问题。“温室效应”正威胁着人类的生存。地球人口增长非常迅速。人类必须使地球能承受人口的增加。这使得农业和工业必须迅速发展。这样的快速发展是现代科技的成果，随之产生了越来越多的废物，所有的废物都被排进了水、土壤和空气中。一些有毒废物有可能对周围的人产生极大的危害。

随着技术的发展和人口的增加，使用材料的数量和种类都有所增加。据估计这种趋势在未来还会继续下去。然而，自然资源不是无限的。有些资源已接近用罄。例如，世界燃料的尽头已经可以预见。在世界的很多地方，水这一日常生活必需品非常紧缺。随着工业化的扩大，世界各地对能源的需求日益增多。因为各种科技发明，我们对能源的需求很大。

综上所述，我认为是科学技术的发展导致了环境污染和能源短缺。

Test 17
环境方面的国际合作

WRITING TASK 2

You should spend about 40 minutes on this task.

Write about the following topic：

> ***Environmental problems are too big for countries or persons to address. In other words, we have reached the stage that environmental problems must be solved by concerted international efforts. To what extent do you agree or disagree?***

Give reasons for your answer and include any relevant examples from your own knowledge or experience.

Write at least 250 words.

题目解释

环境问题绝非一个国家和个人所能解决。换句话说，我们已经到了一个应该由国际社会共同解决环境问题的阶段。对此你在多大程度上赞成或反对。

高分范文

To improve and beautify the environment is the theme of today's world. Coordinate operation at the international level is highly desirable. I fully agree with the claim that international joint efforts are the best way to protect the environment.

Obviously, most of the environmental problems, ranging from deforestation in a small area to global warming, are not the results of any individual country. In fact, a growing number of problems are no longer confined to a certain region or country. Massive oil spills can threaten international waters and submarine animals; the depletion of the ozone layer will increase the amount of UV radiation that reaches the Earth's surface and may even affect the global climate. Both cases, of course, go far beyond individual countries. It is in such cases that international cooperation is not only integrant, but also obligatory. International committees should be set up and international standards established, so that individual efforts can be coordinated and resources used to their fullest potential.

Next to that, efforts of any individual country or people should not be ignored. Manufacturers can conduct a pollution prevention inspection of facilities and organize employee work groups to brainstorm process improvement to reduce pollution. At the same time, communities can facilitate bicycle riding by providing safe bike lanes. The government should encourage park managers and individuals to use less pesticide on lawns.

Therefore, it is not difficult for us to come to the conclusion that the best way, if there is one, is that we should deal with environmental problems at both individual and international levels.

范文翻译

改善环境和美化我们的世界是当今全球的共同主题，世界范围内的统一协调是人们共同期待的。我非常赞同全球携手努力是最好的解决方案。

很明显，全球的很多环境问题，从乱砍滥伐到全球变暖不是单个国家的问题。实际上，很多问题如今已经不是某个区域或国家的问题。如石油泄漏可能威胁全球的水源和海洋生物；臭氧层的破坏会增加到达地表的紫外线，甚至影响全球气候。这两个事例当然都非单个国家可以解决的。正是在这种情况下，国际合作不单单是必须的，甚至是每个国家的义务。国际组织和标准应该建立起来，这样个体努力能够得到协调，资源也会被充分利用。

此外，单个国家和个人的努力也不容忽视。工厂主可以对设备进行防污染检测，并组织员工集思广益提出减污措施，与此同时，社区可以通过修建安全自行车道，以方便自行车的使用。政府应当鼓励公园的管理者和个人减少杀虫剂的使用。

因此，我们不难得出结论，如果有一条最好的办法来解决环境问题，那就是应该由个体和全球共同努力。

Unit 7
Woman and Family
妇女与家庭

Test 18
家庭成员关系

WRITING TASK 2

You should spend about 40 minutes on this task.

Write about the following topic：

It is generally acknowledged that families are now not as close as they used to be. Give possible reasons and your recommendations.

Give reasons for your answer and include any relevant examples from your own knowledge or experience.

Write at least 250 words.

题目解释

人们普遍认为家庭成员之间的关系不像过去那么紧密，分析可能的原因并给出一些建议。

高分范文

It is a widely acknowledged fact that families are not as close as they used to be. Parents and their kids hardly communicate with each other in most of the families. Young people may talk to Mom three times a day, but they are talking to friends all day long. Mom is the least of their contacts. In this essay, I will explore the possible reasons for and solutions to this problem.

There are several reasons for this tendency. First of all, the crowded modern life makes solitude a luxury. When working hard under pressure every day, people want to be alone in their scarce spare time, and they are becoming increasingly sick of discussion and argument. Moreover, there are more choices of entertainment and amusement, which can be enjoyed on one's own, and conversation seems unnecessary at home. Thirdly, generation gap also contributes to this trend.

How can family members create a better common topic? First of all, to improve communication skill is one of the solutions. We should be supportive, but not overbearing; incisive, but not judgmental towards our family members. Besides that parents should try to talk about the same topic with their children. Most importantly, people in the same family should always temper their criticism. Parents should not offer too much unsolicited advice to adult children. A parent's voice, even when whispered, is louder than anyone else's voice in their grown-up kids' ears.

Home is a place where we can rest and a close family relationship can surely be maintained as long as we realize the significant role it plays in our lives.

范文翻译

如今人们普遍认为家庭成员之间的关系不像过去那样紧密。大多数家庭的父母与孩子之间甚少交流。年轻人之间可能一天到晚都在交谈，可跟他们的母亲说不到三次话。妈妈成了跟他们联系最少的人。在本文中，我将探讨这个问题可能的原因及解决办法。

这种趋势有很多原因。首先，繁忙的现代生活使独处变成了一种奢侈的享受。当人们每日在压力之下忙碌的时候，越来越少有时间独处，人们越来越讨厌讨论和争辩。其次，如今人们有更多可以自娱自乐的方式，似乎在家里聊天变得无足轻重。再次，代沟也加大了这种趋势的发展。

那么家庭成员之间如何创建一种共同的话题呢？首先，改善交流技巧是一种解决之道，对待家庭成员，我们应该是支持的，而不是给太多压力；敏锐的，而不做太多评判。其次，父母应该学会用孩子的语言跟他们沟通。更为重要的是，家庭成员之间应该注意批评的方式，对于成年子女，父母不要主动给予太多的建议。对于成年子女而言，父母的建议，即使是再微弱的声音，也比其他人的声音响亮百倍。

家是一个我们可以休憩之地，如果我们意识到它在我们的生活中起到一个多么举足轻重的作用，维系亲情就比什么都来得重要。

Test 19

妇女参军

WRITING TASK 2

You should spend about 40 minutes on this task.

Write about the following topic:

> ***Some people think women should be allowed to join the army, the navy and the air force just like men. Do you agree or disagree?***

Give reasons for your answer and include any relevant examples from your own knowledge and experience.

Write at least 250 words.

题目解释

一些人认为妇女应该被允许参加陆军、海军和空军。你同意还是不同意?

高分范文

In the contemporary world, in any truly enlightened and progressive countries, women play essential roles in the political, economic and cultural arenas as do men. Yet whether ladies should be entitled to serve in the military has triggered spirited debate. Some assert that the status quo should be changed and ladies should be enabled to join the armed forces. Speaking for myself, I fundamentally agree with their assertion for three reasons.

In the first place, history has shown that women are fully capable of performing well in the military. Historically, there were a host of valiant women soldiers whose achievements really put their male counterparts to shame. In my observation, their determination, courage and dignity, to this day, are still being admired by male soldiers and civilians alike throughout the world.

In the second place, now, women can learn and teach, work and supervise, vote and get voted in most countries just like men. Given this sweeping progress in gender equality, there is really no sense in denying them the right to defend their home country when a war breaks out.

Lastly, common sense and our experiences as humans inform us that would-be service women largely possess the capacity to operate modern weapons. It is true that physically women are, on average, not as strong as men ; nevertheless, it is an indisputable fact that most of them have the mental ability and the psychological well-being to operate the highly-automated arms that do not really require big biceps.

In sum, keeping military service out of bounds of women in the information age is unwarranted. And I am convinced that it is in the best interest of a nation if ladies are also granted equal rights in this respect.

范文翻译

当今世界，在任何一个文明和进步的国家，妇女在政治、经济和文化的舞台上都和男人一样扮演着很重要的角色。然而，关于妇女是否有资格参军引起了热烈的争论。一些人认为应该改变现状，使妇女能够参军。就我而言，我基本同意他们的观点，理由有以下三个。

首先，历史表明妇女完全有能力在军队中表现很好。在历史上，有很多勇敢的女兵，她们的功绩真的使她们的男同胞们汗颜。据我观察，直到今天，她们的决断、勇敢和尊严仍然被男士兵和全世界的人们尊敬。

其次，现在，在绝大多数国家，妇女能够像男人一样学习和教学，工作和管理，选举和被选举。由于这种性别平等方面的彻底进步，否认她们在战争爆发的时候行使保卫国家的权利真的没有意义。

最后，人类的常识和经验告诉我们将来服役的妇女大部分拥有操作现代武器的能力。诚然，身体方面，总的看来，妇女不如男人强壮，然而，不可争议的事实是她们当中的大多数有智力能力和良好的心理素质来操纵这些高度自动化的武器，这些武器真的不需要强大的肩膀。

总之，在信息时代不让妇女参军是无根据的。我深信，如果女人在这方面有平等的权利对国家是很有利的。

Unit 8
Animal
动　物

Test 20

养宠物的利弊

WRITING TASK 2

You should spend about 40 minutes on this task.

Write about the following topic:

> ***Many people keep dogs and cats as companions. Discuss the advantages and disadvantages of pet ownership for the animals involved and for the community as a whole.***

Give reasons for your answer and include any relevant examples from your own knowledge or experience.

Write at least 250 words.

题目解释

许多人养猫和狗作为陪伴。讨论拥有宠物的优缺点以及对整个社区的利弊。

高分范文

Dogs and cats can be wonderful companions but there are also a number of problems associated with pet ownership，both for the animals and for the community.

In the best situation，pets are fed，cared for and loved as part of a family. It is easy to see how much attention is given to pets，by the range of products available in the pet section of supermarkets. In return，cats and dogs contribute to the well-being of the community in many ways. Dogs are useful for protection and serve as guides for the disabled. People with pets are not only happier and healthier，but may even live longer. Thus the animals benefit individuals and the community as well.

There are，however，also negative aspects for the pets and for the community. The freedoms of both dogs and cats are increasingly restricted. In Australia there is community pressure to force owners to keep cats inside at night to protect native birds and animals. Dogs can no longer run free in parks and at the beach but must be kept on leashes. These restrictions have been imposed by the community to protect the public. The community also has to pick up the costs of dogs and cats that have been abandoned by irresponsible owners.

So the relationship between pets and the community is a complex one. More and more communities are intervening to force pet owners to restrict the activities and freedom of their pets. Some responsible owners also prepare to give adequate time and attention to their cats and dogs.

范文翻译

猫和狗可能是很好的陪伴，但是拥有宠物也会有很多的问题，既包括动物方面也包括社区方面。

最好的情况是宠物像家庭成员一样被喂养、照料和宠爱。显而易见，看看超市里有多少宠物的产品就知道有多少关心给了宠物。反过来，猫和狗通过多种途径回报社区的人们。狗在保护残疾人和给残疾人当向导方面很有帮助。拥有宠物的人们不仅活得开心健康，甚至活得更长。因此，动物对社区和个人都有好处。

然而，饲养宠物对宠物和社区也有负面的影响。猫和狗的自由越来越受到限制。在澳大利亚，社区迫使宠物所有者晚上把猫关起来以保护当地的小鸟和动物。狗不能在公园和海滩自由跑动而必须拴起来。社区实施这些措施保护人们。社区不得不负担被不负责任的主人抛弃的猫和狗的开销。

因此，宠物和社区的关系是很复杂的。越来越多的社区干预并要求宠物所有者限制宠物的行为和自由。一些负责任的主人也准备给他们的猫和狗足够的时间和关注。

第三篇

图表作文

Unit 1

Table

表　格

Test 1

居民对社区的评价

WRITING TASK 1

You should spend about 20 minutes on this task.

The table shows the results of a survey in 2007 which asked men and women whether they were satisfied with the facilities in the community.

Write a report for a university lecturer describing the information shown below.

You should write at least 150 words.

Area	People	Very satisfied	Quite satisfied	Not at all satisfied
Sport facilities	Women	58%	32%	10%
	Men	59%	31%	10%
Community bar	Women	47%	27%	26%
	Men	70%	22%	8%
Supermarket	Women	80%	14%	6%
	Men	50%	30%	20%

高分范文

The table displays people's different attitudes towards facilities of a community in 2007.

As is shown in the table, while being questioned about the contentment of sport facilities, both men and women in the community seemed to hold the same point of view, where approximately 90% of individuals expressed their satisfaction, leaving only 10% of individuals feeling in an opposite way.

However, divergence emerged among men and women when it came to questions about the community bar and supermarket. The majority of men favored the community bar, whereas 26% of women, 18% higher than men, were critical of the bar. On the contrary, men appeared to be more complaining about supermarket, with 20% of men announcing their dissatisfaction, which exceeded the proportion of criticism within women by 14%.

Generally speaking, most of the individuals had a favorable comment on the community facilities, yet women seemed to be a little harsher than men.

范文翻译

此表格显示了2007年人们对某社区的设施的不同态度。

如表格所示，当被问到是否对体育设施满意时，社区的男人和女人似乎有同样的观点，大约90%的男人和女人表示他们很满意，只有10%的人感到不满意。

然而，当被问到关于社区酒吧和超市，男人和女人的观点出现了分歧。大部分男人对社区的酒吧满意，然而有26%的妇女，比男人高18%，对酒吧不满。相反，男人似乎对超市有更多的抱怨，有20%的男人表达了他们的不满，比妇女对超市的批评比例高了14%。

总的说来，大多数人对社区的设施表示满意，然而女人似乎比男人更苛刻。

闪光词汇

★ **display** [di'splei] *vt.* 陈列，显示

The children's work was **displayed** on the wall. 孩子们的作品在墙上展出来了。

★ **point of view** 观点

Everybody explains his own **point of view**. 每个人都说明了自己的观点。

★ **divergence** [dai'vɜːdʒəns] *n.* 分歧

The **divergence** between the United States and China is partly because of a lack of mutual understanding. 美国与我们的分歧部分原因是缺乏了解造成的。

★ **be critical of** 不满

He **is critical of** the report. 他对报告表示不满。

★ **generally speaking** 一般而言，总的说来

Generally speaking，he is an honest young man. 总的说来，他是一个诚实的年轻人。

实用句型

Generally speaking 总的说来

这种结构用于结尾，总结概括全文的观点。

例如范文结尾的这句话：

Generally speaking，most of the individuals had a favorable comment on the community facilities，yet women seemed to be a little harsher than men.

总的说来，大多数人对社区的设施表示满意，然而女人似乎比男人更苛刻。

Test 2
人们的休闲活动

WRITING TASK 1

You should spend about 20 minutes on this task.

The table below shows the results of a survey of the leisure pursuits of 100 old people and 100 young people.

Write a report for a university lecturer describing the information shown below.

You should write at least 150 words.

Leisure pursuits	Number of young people	Number of old people
Reading	41	91
Listening to music	28	84
Chess	0	69
Surfing the Internet	98	95
Basketball	85	8
Football	83	5
Golf	59	0

高分范文

The table compares the difference in seven types of leisure pursuits of youngsters and the elderly. The leisure pursuits can be generally classified into two broad types: physically demanding and intellectual.

In general, more young individuals than old folks engage in physically demanding sports such as basketball, football and golf, while a greater number of senior citizens participate in intellectual leisure pursuits. For instance, 85 young people play basketball whereas only 8 old people do so. It is quite interesting to note that no old folks take up golf as their leisure pursuit. While the number of the elderly who listen to music is three times as many as that of youngsters. It is even more interesting to note that the numbers of young people and old people surfing the Internet are similar. A striking difference lies in chess, where there are 69 old people but no youngsters.

In conclusion, it is evident that the elderly and youngsters have different preferences as to leisure pursuits. Basically, youngsters like sports that require physical strength while old folks are fond of intellectual pursuits.

范文翻译

这个表格比较了年轻人和老年人七种不同的休闲方式。休闲活动大体上可以分为两大类：体力型和脑力型。

一般来说，年轻人比老年人更愿意参加体力型运动，例如篮球、足球和高尔夫球，而更多的老年人愿意参加智力休闲活动。例如，有 85 个年轻人打篮球，而仅仅有 8 个老年人做这件事。有趣的是，没有老年人把高尔夫球当作休闲活动。而老年人听音乐的人数是年轻人的 3 倍。更有趣的是，年轻人和老年人上网的数字相似。最大的差别是象棋，有 69 个老年人参加而没有年轻人。

总之，很明显，老年人和年轻人在休闲活动方面有不同的偏好。基本上说，年轻人喜欢要求体力的体育运动，而老年人喜欢脑力活动。

闪光词汇

★ **in general** 通常，大体上，一般而言

In general, youngsters are fond of taking an active part in sports. 一般来说，年轻人喜欢积极参加体育运动。

★ **engage in** 从事于，参加

The man announced his readiness to **engage in** the contest. 那个人宣布对于比赛他已准备就绪。

★ **participate in** 参加，参与，分享

He will **participate in** the conference next week. 他下周要参加大会。

★ **take up** 开始从事

He **took up** art while at school. 他在学校时开始从事艺术。

★ **preference** [ˈprefərəns] *n.* 偏爱，优先选择

He has a **preference** for poem. 他特别喜爱诗。

实用句型

It is quite interesting to note that … 很有趣需要指出的是……

这种句型结构一般用来描述图表中现实的比较特别或有特殊特点的现象或趋势。

请看范文中的这句话：

It is quite interesting to note that no old folks take up golf as their leisure pursuit. 有趣的是没有老年人把高尔夫球当作休闲活动。

Test 3

中国的经济状况

WRITING TASK 1

You should spend about 20 minutes on this task.

The table below presents information about Chinese economy in the late 1990s. Write a report describing the trends in profits shown in the table.

Write a report for a university lecturer describing the information shown below.

You should write at least 150 words.

COMPANY PROFITS BEFORE TAX，BY INDUSTRY（$ million）

Period	Mining	Retail Trade	Manufacturing	Other
1996—1997	2 989	598	3 990	1 198
1997—1998	2 970	798	6 877	1 598
1998—1999	2 659	1 299	8 756	1 706
1999—2000	4 771	1 459	6 999	405

高分范文

The table shows Chinese company profits before tax by industry such as mining, retail trade, manufacturing and others in the late 1990s.

As we can see from the table, every industry had a different trend in gaining profits during that period. Firstly, manufacturing's profits had a great jump between 1996 and 1999 from 3,990 to 8,756 million. However, at the end of late 1990s, its profits fell to 6,999 million. Secondly, mining's profits dropped slightly from 1996 to 1999. Even then, the profits still had a dramatic increase in 2000 to 4,771 million. Thirdly, as far as retail trade was concerned, it increased steadily in gaining profits in the late 1990s. The same as manufacturing, other industries also had a great jump from 1996 to 1998 and then fell suddenly at the end of the late 1990s.

To sum up, the manufacturing industry always had the most profits, mining the second and retail trade the third among the whole industry during the given four-year period.

范文翻译

这个表格展示了 1996 年至 2000 年中国工业如矿业、零售业、制造业以及其他行业的税前利润。

我们从表格中可以看出，每种工业在那段时间都有不同的获利趋势。首先，制造业的利润从 1996 年到 1999 年有很大的上升，从 39.9 亿上升到 87.56 亿。然而，在 2000 年制造业的利润下降到 69.99 亿。其次，矿业的利润在 1996 年到 1999 年期间有轻微的下降。即使如此，利润在 2000 年仍有一个急剧的上升，达到了 47.71 亿。第三，至于零售业，从 1996 年到 2000 年期间在获取利润方面稳步上升。和制造业相同，其他工业的利润从 1996 年到 1998 年也有大幅度的上升，然后到 2000 年突然下降。

总之，在过去的四年期间，制造业一直是最盈利的，矿业排第二，零售业在那段时间在整个工业企业中排第三。

闪光词汇

★ **trend** [trend] *n.* 倾向，趋势

This **trend** will continue. 这个趋势将继续下去。

★ **sum up** 计算……的总数，概括，总结

Please **sum up** what you said just now. 请把你刚才说的总结一下。

实用句型

As we can see from the table 从表格可以看出

这种句型结构一般用于主体段的开头，表示接下来要开始描述表格所显示的细节或趋势。

请看范文中的这句话：

As we can see from the table，every industry had a different trend in gaining profits during that period. 从表格可以看出，每种工业在那段时间都有不同的获利趋势。

...**had a great jump**... ……有很大的上升

图表作文中，经常要表示上升或下降，本文也多次涉及这方面的表达。

例如范文中的这句话：

Firstly，manufacturing's profits **had a great jump** between 1996 and 1999 from 3,990 to 8,756 million. 首先，制造业的利润从 1996 年到 1999 年有很大的上升，从 39.9 亿上升到 87.56 亿。

Unit 2

Bar Chart

柱形图

Test 4

中国人的婚姻状况

WRITING TASK 1

You should spend about 20 minutes on this task.

The chart below gives information about marriage and divorce rates between 1977 and 2007 and the marital status of Chinese adults in two of the years. Summarize the information by selecting and reporting the main features, and make comparisons where relevant.

You should write at least 150 words.

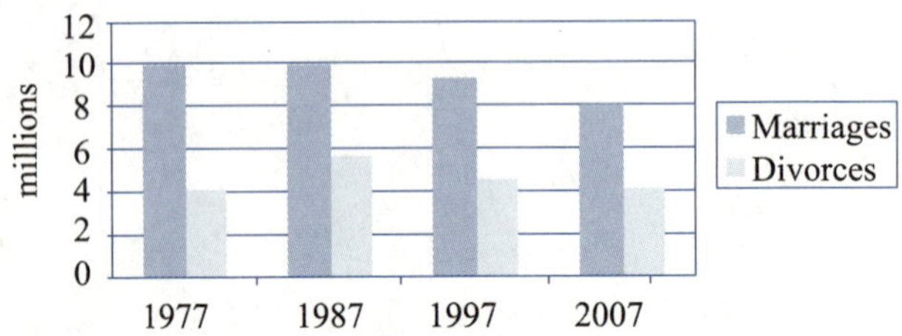

Number of marriages and divorces in CHINA 1977—2007

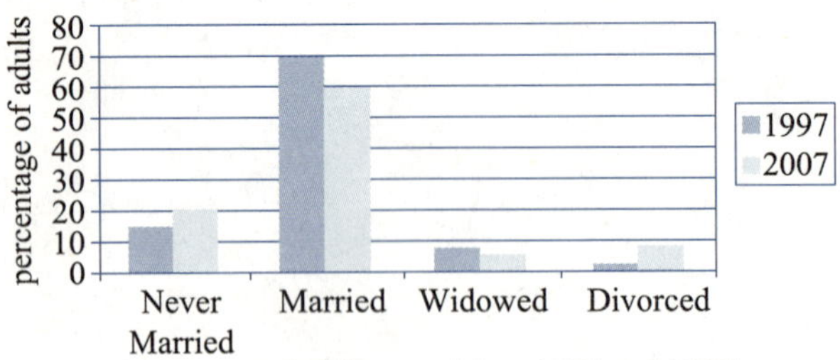

Marital status of Chinese adults, 1977 and 2007

高分范文

The two bar charts compare the number of marriages and divorces in China from 1977 to 2007 and the general marital status of Chinese adults in 1977 and 2007.

As is shown in the first chart, over the past thirty years, the number of marriages falls steadily, but on the other hand the number of divorce waves. The second chart shows that as compared with the situation in 1977, the adults' marital status in 2007 changed greatly.

Moreover, as we research into the second chart, we find that the percentages of those who were determined not to be in a marriage and of those who chose to end their marriages by divorce in 2007 were both higher than the figures in 1977. The two groups of figures are 20% : 14% and 9% : 3% respectively.

According to the other two categories, namely, married and widowed, the figures for 1977 were higher than those for 2007 and they are 70% : 60% and 8% : 6% respectively.

From the comparison and contrast made above, we can gain an insight into the attitudes of Chinese towards marriage and their multifaceted marital status in the past three decades.

范文翻译

这两个柱形图对比了 1977 年至 2007 年里中国人结婚与离婚的人数以及 1977 年和 2007 年中国成年人的整体婚姻状况。

从图 1 可以看出，在过去的 30 年里，结婚的人数逐步下跌，但是另一方面，离婚人数呈现波动。图 2 显示，2007 年成年人的婚姻状况较之 1977 年发生了巨大的变化。

此外，根据图 2 所示的成年人婚姻状况，我们看到，决意不结婚者和离婚者在 2007 年的百分比都要高于 1977 年，两组数据的对比分别是 20% : 14%，9% : 3%。在结婚和丧偶两项上，1977 年的数据高于 2007 年，数据对比分别是 70% : 60%，8% : 6%。

通过以上的比较与对比，我们可以了解到过去的 30 年里中国人对待婚姻的态度以及他们多方面的婚姻状况。

闪光词汇

★ **marital** ['mæritl] *adj*. 婚姻的

What's your **marital** status? 请问你的婚姻状况?

★ **insight into** 洞察……

She have given me an **insight into** American literature. 她使我对美国文学有了深入的了解。

Test 5
男女休闲时光

WRITING TASK 1

You should spend about 20 minutes on this task.

The chart below shows the amount of leisure time enjoyed by men and women of different employment status.

Write a report for a university lecturer describing the information shown below.

You should write at least 150 words.

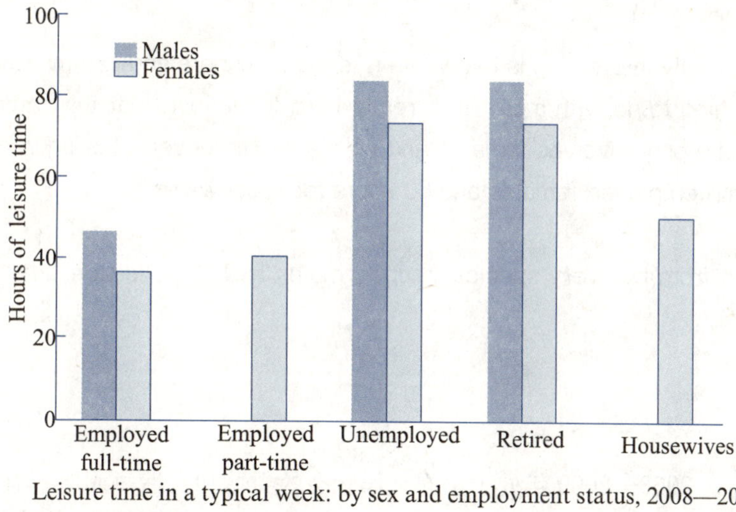

Leisure time in a typical week: by sex and employment status, 2008—2009

高分范文

The bar chart indicates the amount of leisure time per week that males and females of various employment statuses enjoyed over a one-year period of time from 2008 to 2009. The employment statuses referred to here are grouped into five categories：employed full-time，part-time，unemployed，retired and housewives.

As is indicated in the chart，under the backgrounds of being employed full-time，unemployed and retired，males had more leisure time to enjoy than females did. But with the other two statuses，namely，being employed part-time and being pure housewives，males had nothing to compare with females.

Firstly，unemployed and retired males and females enjoyed the greatest amount of leisure time. The average weekly leisure time enjoyed by males and females were 85 hours and 70 hours respectively. Among those who were retired，men had 84 hours while women had 69 hours. Generally speaking，males and females under these two statuses of employment showed very slight difference in terms of the amount of leisure time being enjoyed.

Secondly，for those who worked full-time，males also had more leisure time than females and the chart shows that males had 45 hours while women 37 hours.

Thirdly，what is really interesting is that while it is totally understandable that the housewives category had nothing to do with men，it is really hard to believe that the category of being employed part-time only involves females and no males. Moreover，the figure we see is 40 hours for part-time employed females and 50 hours for housewives.

In general，apart from two very special groups，males had more leisure time to enjoy than females.

范文翻译

该柱状图显示的是2008—2009年处于不同工作状态的男性和女性每周所享有的闲暇时光。这里所指的不同工作状态细分为全职、兼职、失业、退休和家庭主妇五大类。

如图所示，在全职、失业和退休状态下，男性的休闲时间要比女性多，而在另外两个类别，即：兼职和作为纯家庭主妇的状态下，女性与男性毫无可比性，呈一枝独秀状况。

首先，我们看到失业与退休的男性与女性享受到的休闲时间最多。处于失业状态的两性群体分别有每周 85 小时和 70 小时的空余时光；而退休群体中，男性有 84 小时闲暇时间，女性有 69 小时。可以说在这两种状态下，男性与女性的闲暇时光相差甚微。

其次，对于全职工作者来讲，男性也比女性享有更多的闲暇时间，两者分别为 45 小时和 37 小时。

再者，很有趣的一点是：家庭主妇类与男性无缘完全可以理解，但兼职状态下却只有女性，没有男性，这就难以令人理解了。此外，我们看到的数据是兼职的女性每周有 40 小时的休闲时间，家庭主妇有 50 小时。

总体而言，除了非常特别的两个群体外，男性比女性的休闲时间要多。

闪光词汇

★ **apart from** 除……之外

Apart from a few scratches，the car was undamaged. 除了几处刮痕外，汽车没有什么损坏。

实用句型

…**refer to**… 是指……

这个句型结构是用来解释图表中的词组的具体含义范围的。

请看范文中的这句话：

The employment statuses **referred to** here are grouped into five categories：employed full-time，part-time，unemployed，retired and housewives. 这里所指的不同工作状态细分为全职、兼职、失业、退休和家庭主妇五大类。

Test 6
美国人出游

WRITING TASK 1

You should spend about 20 minutes on this task.

The chart below shows the number of American tourists traveling abroad between 1995 and 2005 and the graph reveals U. K.'s share of the American tourist market.
Write a report for a university lecturer describing the information shown below.

You should write at least 150 words.

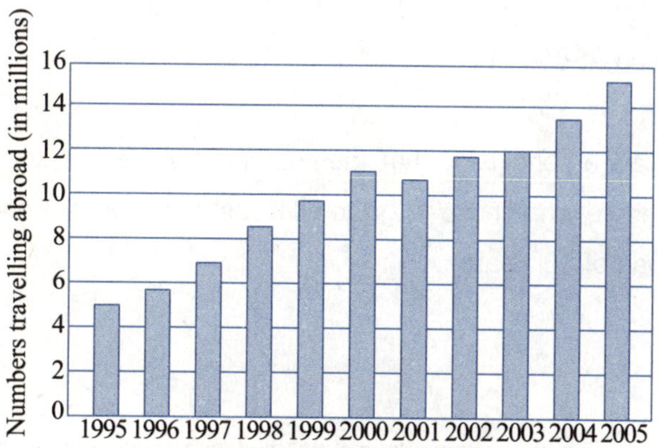

American tourists travelling abroad

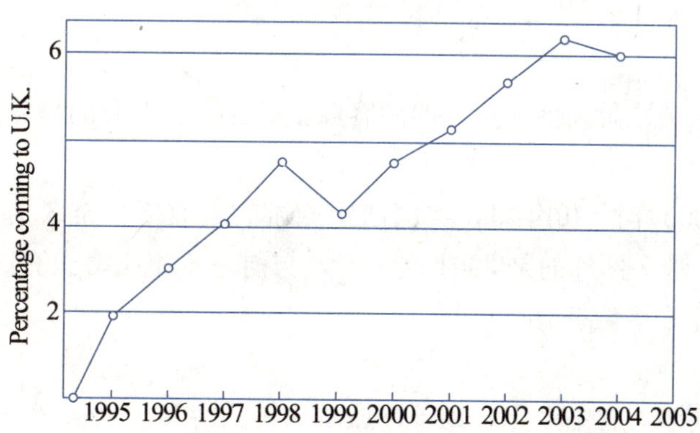

U.K.'s share of American tourist market

高分范文

The chart and the graph respectively show the number of American tourists traveling abroad and the number of American tourists to U. K. from 1995 to 2005.

As is shown in the chart and graph, there was a steady increase both in the number of American tourists traveling abroad and in U. K.'s share of America's tourist market.

In the first place, from 1995 to 2005, the number of American tourists traveling abroad was tripled, growing from just about 5 million to more than 15 million. The only exception was the year of 2001, when there was a slight decline as compared with the previous year. By contrast, all the other years witnessed a gradual increase.

In the second place, the graph displays that during the first three years, the percentage of American tourists to U. K. rocketed from 2% to 4. 8%. This is an increase by 2. 8%. Nonetheless, in the following year, we see a slight drop. Surprisingly, between 1999 and 2003, there appeared a significant rise from 4. 2% to 6. 2%, which was the peak in the designated decade, and it ended up at 6% in 2004.

To sum up, we can draw a conclusion that the number of American tourists traveling abroad and those American people who chose to go to U. K. as their destination both show an overall trend of rise over a span of 10 years.

范文翻译

这两个图分别显示了从 1995 到 2005 年的 10 年间美国人出国旅游的游客数量以及到英国旅游的游客数量。

如图所示，美国人出国旅游和前往英国的游客数量都呈稳步上升的趋势。

首先，从 1995 到 2005 年的 10 年里，美国出国旅游的人数增长至 3 倍，从仅 500 万左右增长到 1 500 多万。唯一例外的是 2001 这一年，与前一年相比略微有所降低。与此相反，其他年份都呈现出逐步增长态势。

其次，按第二个图所示，在前 3 年，到英国旅游的美国游客比例从 2% 快速上升至 4. 8%，增长了 2. 8%。然而，在接下去的一年，我们看到了略微的下降。令人惊讶的是，从 1999

年到 2003 年，我们又看到了令人瞩目的快速增长，从 4.2%大幅增长到 6.2%，这也是这 10 年间出现的最高点，最终在 2004 年以 6%收尾。

综上所述，美国出国旅游的人数以及选择英国作为目的地的人数在 10 年间均显示出全面上升的趋势。

闪光词汇

★ **triple** ['tripl] *n.* 三倍数　*adj.* 三倍的　*v.* 增至三倍，三倍于

His income was **tripled**. 他的收入增至三倍。

★ **designated** ['designeitid] *adj.* 指定的，派定的

The area has been **designated** as a natural reserve. 该地区已被指定为一个自然保护区。

Unit 3

Pie Chart

饼　图

Test 7

水的使用

WRITING TASK 1

You should spend about 20 minutes on this task.

The charts below show the result of a survey of water use in a certain city in 2008.

Write a report for a university lecturer，describing the information shown below：

You should write at least 150 words.

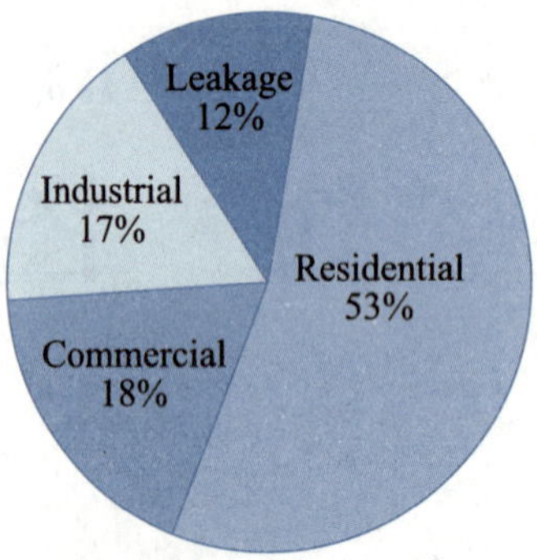

Municipal water use by sectors, 2008

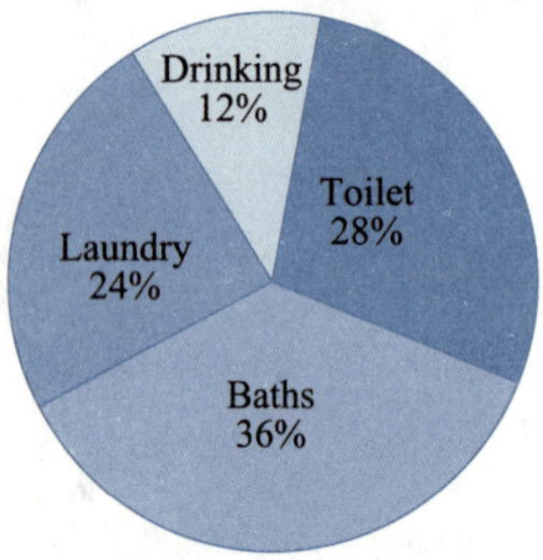

Water use in the home

高分范文

Presented in the two pie charts are the outcomes of a survey of water consumption in a city in 2008. One chart depicts a sectoral analysis of water use，the other analyses domestic use.

As is shown in the first pie chart，overall use was dominated by residential consumption，which accounted for over half（53%），whilst commercial，industrial and leakage each only amounted to about one-third as much（18%，17% and 12% respectively）.

As for water used in the home，bathroom use（36%），and toilet flushing（28%），together took up as much as two-third（64%）of the total. The water used for cleaning clothes（laundry）accounted for 24%. Among the remaining categories of domestic use，drinking（12%）took up only half as much as laundry，this was the lowest amount recorded.

范文翻译

两个饼图显示了2008年某个城市对水的消费的调查结果。一个图显示了水在各部门的使用分析，另一个图分析了家庭用水。

如第一个饼图所示，全部用水中居民消费占主导地位，超过了一半，是53%，而商业、工业和渗漏每项用水仅仅占剩余用水的1/3，分别是18%，17%和12%。

至于家庭用水，浴室用了36%，冲厕所用了28%，这两项一共占总用水量的2/3（64%）。洗衣服用水占24%。在家庭的其他用水中，饮用水仅仅是洗衣用水的一半，占12%，这是用水最少的纪录。

闪光词汇

★ **present** [pri'zent] *vt.* 提出，呈现

He **presents** an important suggestion. 他提出了一项重要的建议。

★ **dominate** ['dɔmineit] *vt.* 支配，占优势

A great man can **dominate** others by force of character. 伟人能以人格的力量支配他人。

Test 8

交流方式的变化

WRITING TASK 1

You should spend about 20 minutes on this task.

The two pie charts show the types of communication used in 1982 and in 2002.

Write a report to describe the information shown in the graph.

You should write at least 150 words.

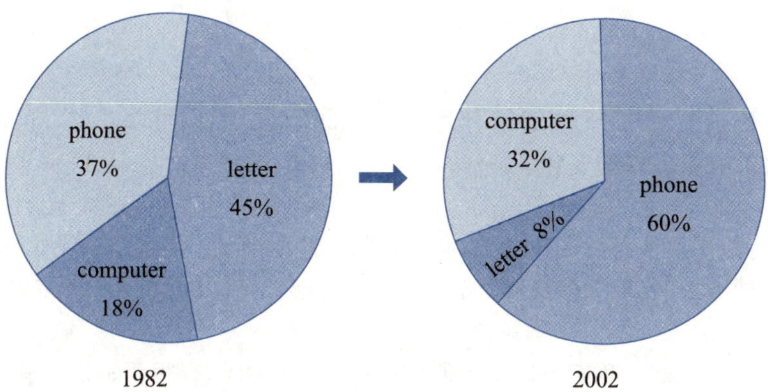

高分范文

The two pie charts compare different ways of communication used in 1982 and 2002. We can see that for the three media surveyed, there are significant changes for each.

In 1982, letter writing was the most popular form of communication, taking up 45% of the total. However, its use decreased dramatically after that. By 2002, this figure dropped to only 8%, the smallest of that year's figures.

On the other hand, during this same period, we can see that the use of the phone and computers both increased significantly. In 1982, the use of telephone just occupied 37% and the computer was the least used form of the three methods (18%). In 2002, the telephone, at 65%, became the most used form of communication. Similarly, the use of computers increased to 32%.

Overall, we can see some important changes in the forms of communication used during the two decades. More and more people appreciate the convenience brought about by the phone and the computer.

范文翻译

这两个饼状图比较了 1982 年和 2002 年通讯方法的不同。我们可以看出，被调查的这三种方式中每一种都有很重要的变化。

在 1982 年，写信是最流行的通讯方式，占到了全部的 45%。然而，从此以后这种方式的使用开始剧烈地减少。到了 2002 年，这个数字下降到了仅仅占 8%，是该年份中最少的。

另一方面，在同一时期，我们可以看到使用电话和计算机都有很明显的增长。在 1982 年，使用电话的仅仅占 37%。在三种方法中，使用电脑的最少（18%）。在 2002 年，使用电话的占 65%，成为最常用的通讯方式。同样的，使用计算机的也快速增长到了 32%。

总之，在这 20 年里我们看到通讯方式有了很多重要的变化。越来越多的人喜欢电话和电脑所带来的方便。

闪光词汇

★ **dramatically** [drəˈmætikəli] *adv.* 引人注目地
The international situation changed **dramatically** in 2001. 2001 年，国际形势发生了巨大的变化。

★ **convenience** [kənˈviːniəns] *n.* 便利，方便
Busy people are always eating **convenience** food. 忙碌的人常吃速食。

Test 9

留学生的日常花费

WRITING TASK 1

You should spend about 20 minutes on this task.

The pie chart below shows the average way in which foreign students learning in America spend their money over the course of a week.

Write a report for a university lecturer describing the information in the chart below.

You should write at least 150 words.

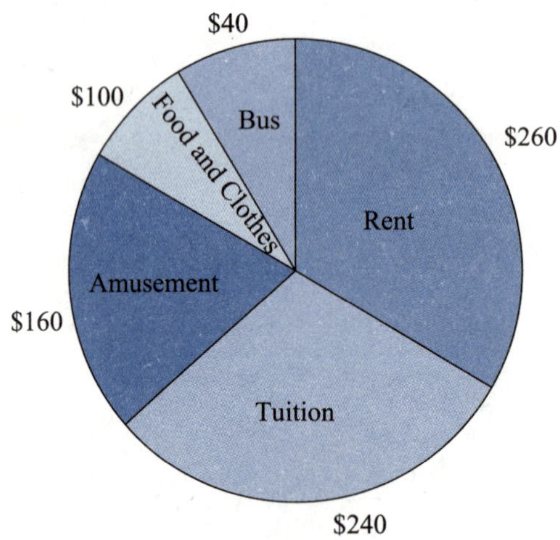

Student spending

高分范文

The pie chart reveals typical spending patterns for foreign students taking English language courses in schools in America. The average spend can be divided very roughly into five parts. The first and largest part is spent on rent, the total amount being $260. The second part is on tuition and the others are divided among amusement, food and clothes and bus. The total spend for international students is shown to be $800 per week.

According to the information in the pie chart, it can be seen that rent accounts for approximately a third of the total amount spent by students, amounting to $260 per week. This is the biggest single expense for students in America. The second greatest expense is tuition, the average being $240 per week. Entertainment accounts for a fifth of the total spend for students in America, and the remaining money ($140) is used to travel on the bus and buy clothes and food.

范文翻译

这个饼图揭示了在美国学习英语课程的外国学生的典型的消费模式。一般的消费大致可以分成五个部分。第一也是最重要的部分花在房租方面，总数是 260 美元。第二部分花在学费方面，其他的花在了娱乐、食物、衣服和公共汽车方面。图中显示，国际学生一周的总花费是 800 美元。

根据饼图提供的信息，我们可以看出，房租大约占了学生全部花费的 1/3，每周是 260 美元。这是外国学生在美国最大的一笔花费。第二大支出是学费，平均每周是 240 美元。娱乐占了外国学生在美国花费的 1/5。其他剩余的 140 美元用在了公共汽车交通以及买衣服和食品方面。

闪光词汇

★ **typical** ['tipikəl] *adj*. 典型的，象征性的

It is **typical** of him to take hard jobs. 他的典型特征是勇挑重担。

★ **approximately** [ə'prɔksimətli] *adv*. 近似地，大约

This exercise takes **approximately** 10 minutes. 这个练习花费大约 10 分钟的时间。

实用句型

It can be seen that ...**accounts for** ... 可见……占……

account for 是表示所占比例的词组，这种句型结构在饼状图中最常使用。

请看范文中的这句话：

According to the information in the pie chart，**it can be seen that** rent **accounts for** approximately a third of the total amount spent by students，amounting to $260 per week. 如图所示，我们可以看出，房租大约占了学生全部花费的 1/3，每周是 260 美元。

Unit 4
Line Chart
折线图

Test 10

加拿大和英国的失业率

WRITING TASK 1

You should spend about 20 minutes on this task.

> *The chart below shows the unemployment rates in the U. K. and Canada between May 2003 and May 2009.*
>
> *Write a report for a university lecturer describing the information shown below.*

You should write at least 150 words.

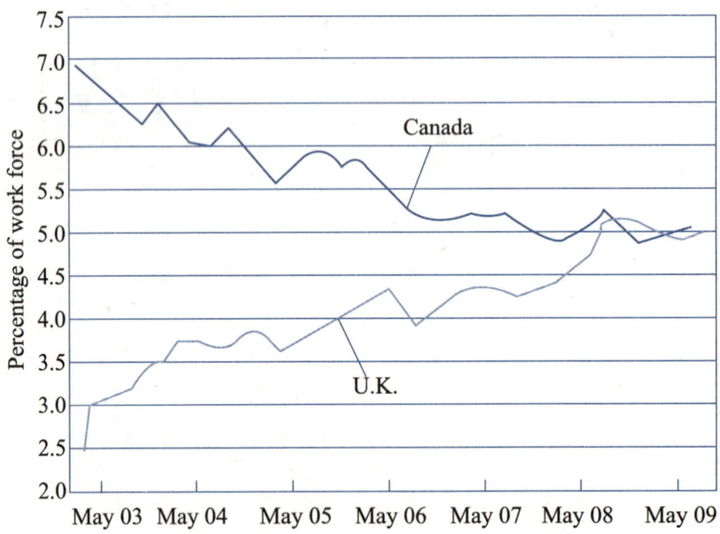

Unemployment Rates: Canada and U.K.

高分范文

The graph compares the unemployment rates in Canada and in the U. K over a span of 6 years from May 2003 to May 2009.

As can be seen from the graph, during this period of time, the unemployment rate in Canada revealed a trend of gradual decline, whereas that in the U. K. witnessed an opposite tendency, namely, a steady rise.

Obviously, there was a dramatic increase in the unemployment rate in the U. K. between 2003 and 2004, rising from about 2. 5% to 3. 85%. Nevertheless, the following year experienced a slight fluctuation. From May 2005 to the middle of 2008, there was a stable growth accompanied by occasional fluctuations. Particularly in 2008, it peaked at approximately 5. 4% and afterwards began to show minor drop before finally ending up at 5%.

On the other hand, the unemployment rate in Canada was totally different from that in the U. K. As is shown from the graph, Canada's unemployment rate fell significantly from the original 7. 0% to the final 5. 2%. The lowest rate, which appeared in 2008, reached about 4. 8%, almost being level with the highest rate in the U. K.

Thus, we have acquired some information about the unemployment rates in Canada and the U. K. between 2003 and 2009.

范文翻译

本图对比的是加拿大和英国从 2003 年 5 月到 2009 年 5 月 6 年间的失业率情况。

从图中可以看出，在这期间，加拿大的失业率呈现出逐渐下降的趋势，而英国的失业率却显现出截然相反的趋势，即节节攀升。

很明显，从 2003 年到 2004 年，英国的失业率从约 2. 5%快速地上升到 3. 85%。然而，接下来的一年经历了轻微的震荡。从 2005 年 5 月到 2008 年中期，伴随着偶尔的波动，失业率继续呈现出稳定的增加趋势。尤其在 2008 年，失业率曾一度达到了约 5. 4%的最高值，然后才开始再次转入微弱的下跌，最终以 5%收尾。

另一方面，加拿大的失业率走向与英国完全不一样。从图表上看，加拿大失业率从最初的 7. 0%下降到了最后的 5. 2%。特别是在 2008 年，一度达到了 4. 8%的最低点，几乎与英国的最高点持平。

由此，我们了解了加拿大和英国在 2003 到 2009 年间失业率的一些情况。

闪光词汇

★ **gradual** ['grædjuəl] *adj*. 逐渐的，逐步的

His health showed **gradual** improvement. 他的健康逐渐恢复。

★ **occasional** [ə'keiʒnəl] *adj*. 偶然的

His work involves **occasional** journey. 他的工作需要偶尔出差。

★ **original** [ə'ridʒənəl] *adj*. 最初的，原始的

This is the **original** painting，and these others are copies. 这幅画是原作，其他的是复制品。

实用句型

There was a dramatic increase in ... ……急剧上升

这种表示“上升”的句型结构在曲线图中经常用到。

请看范文中的这个句子：

Obviously，**there was a dramatic increase in** the unemployment rate in the U. K. between 2003 and 2004，rising from about 2. 5% to 3. 85%. 很明显，从2003年到2004年，英国的失业率从约2. 5%快速地上升到3. 85%。

Test 11

癌症的治疗效果

WRITING TASK 1

You should spend about 20 minutes on this task.

> ***The graphs below indicate the effect of treatment in two types of cancer in females. Using the information in the graphs, describe and compare the situation with and without treatment for the two types of cancer.***

You should write at least 150 words.

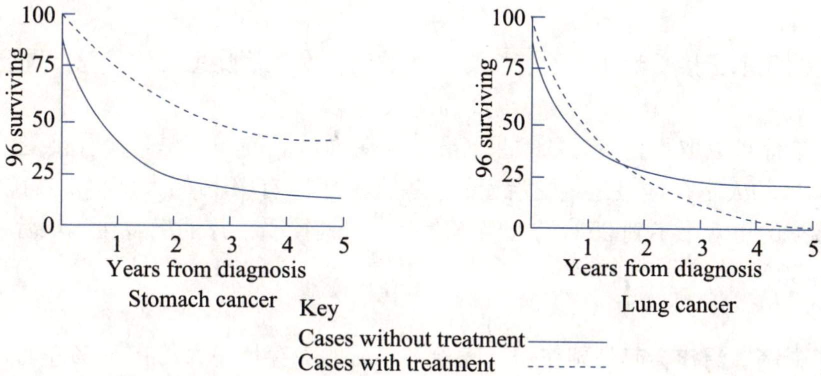

高分范文

The two graphs show the situation with and without treatment for two types of cancer in women：stomach cancer and lung cancer.

For stomach cancer，treatment can be reasonably effective. Only 30% of the patients survive one year after diagnosis without treatment，but when treatment is applied about 75% of the patients survive one year. Without treatment，fewer than 25% of the patients survive for five years after diagnosis，but with treatment the survival rate after five years increases to nearly 50%.

For lung cancer，however，treatment can have a negative effect. The survival rate one year after diagnosis is around 30%，whether treatment is applied or not. But survival rate with treatment is lower than that without treatment beyond one year. After five years，25% of untreated patients are still alive，whereas none of the cases studied who have received treatment survive for five years after diagnosis.

In conclusion，we should suit the remedy to the case. It is the most essential to the patients.

范文翻译

这两个曲线图显示了接受治疗和没有接受治疗的两类女性癌症患者的状况：胃癌和肺癌。

对于胃癌，治疗可以取得比较好的效果。虽然，在确诊后的一年里，没有接受治疗的患者中仅仅有30%的人幸存，但是接受治疗的患者在一年后有75%的人幸存。在确诊5年后，没有接受治疗的患者中不到25%的人能够幸存，但是接受治疗的患者在5年后幸存的比率增长到接近50%。

然而，对于肺癌，治疗会起到副作用。确诊一年后的幸存比率大约在30%左右，不管是否接受了治疗。但是一年后接受治疗的人要比没有接受治疗的人的幸存比率低。5年后，没有接受治疗的患者有25%的人还活着，然而确诊5年后，在接受治疗的人中没有存活的案例。

总之，我们应该对症下药，这对病人来说是最关键的。

闪光词汇

★ **situation** [ˌsitjuˈeiʃən] *n.* 情形，境遇

The **situation** was complicated. 形势非常复杂。

★ **reasonably** [ˈriːzənəbli] *adv.* 适度地，相当地

The first one is **reasonably** good. 第一个相当地好。

★ **survive** [səˈvaiv] *v.* 幸存，生还

This patient will not **survive** without treatment. 没有治疗这个病人是不会活下去的。

★ **diagnosis** [ˌdaiəgˈnəusis] *n.* 诊断

The engineer made a complete **diagnosis** of the bridge's collapse. 工程师对桥的倒塌做一次彻底的诊断分析。

★ **suit the remedy to the case** 对症下药

Test 12

食品的消费

WRITING TASK 1

You should spend about 20 minutes on this task.

The line graph below shows changes in the amount and types of fast food consumed by American teenagers from 1980 to 2005.

Describe the information shown in the graph.

You should write at least 150 words.

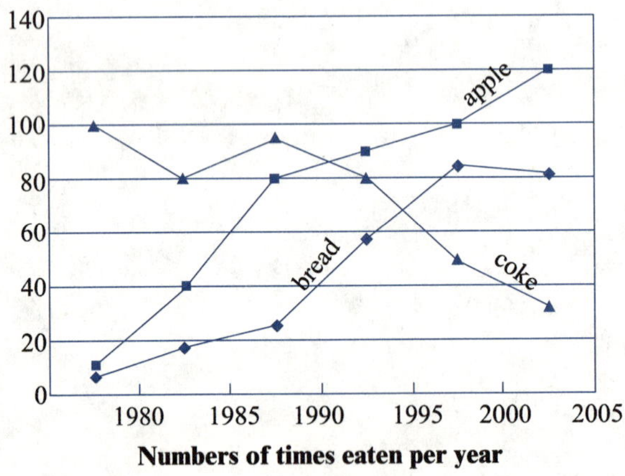

高分范文

The line graph reveals the amount of fast food consumed by American teenagers over a 25-year period between 1980 and 2005. The figures reveal that apple is the most popular fast food，bread coming a close second and coke being the least popular.

The graph shows that teenagers in America ate 10 times as many apples in 1998 as they did in 1980. Coke was consumed by this age group 100 times before 1980，or roughly twice a week. In 1980，bread was eaten approximately 10 times a year. This number rose sharply and by 2000，American teenagers ate bread over 80 times a year. The figure remained stable at this level. In contrast，figures for the consumption of coke fluctuated slightly and then fell over the same period. Although coke was approximately 10 times more popular than the other two types of fast food in 1980，it was eaten fewer than 40 times a year in 2003.

范文翻译

这个曲线图揭示了从 1980 年到 2005 年的 25 年间美国青少年消费快速食品的数量。数字表明，苹果是最受欢迎的快速食品，面包第二，紧随其后，可乐最不受欢迎。

曲线图显示，美国青少年在 1998 年吃苹果的数量是 1980 年的 10 倍。这个年龄段的人群在 1980 年之前每年喝 100 次可乐，或者大概每周两次。在 1980 年，面包每年大约被吃 10 次。这个数字急剧上升，到 2000 年他们每年吃面包超过 80 次，数字就一直保持在这个稳定的水平。比较而言，可乐的消费数字轻微波动然后在同期出现下降。尽管可乐在 1980 年比其他两种快速食品受欢迎 10 倍，但它在 2003 年每年被消费少于 40 次。

闪光词汇

★ **fast food** 速食

What do you usually have for **fast food**? 你一般吃什么快餐?

★ **fluctuate** [ˈflʌktjueit] *vi.* 变动，波动 *vt.* 使动摇，使波动

Prices **fluctuate** from year to year. 物价年年波动。

Unit 5

Diagram

图 画

Test 13

塑料瓶制作

WRITING TASK 1

You should spend about 20 minutes on this task.

As a class assignment you have been asked to write a description of how plastic bottles are produced and then broken down.
Using the information in the diagram, write a description of the cycle. You may use your own knowledge and experience in addition to the diagram.

You should write at least 150 words.

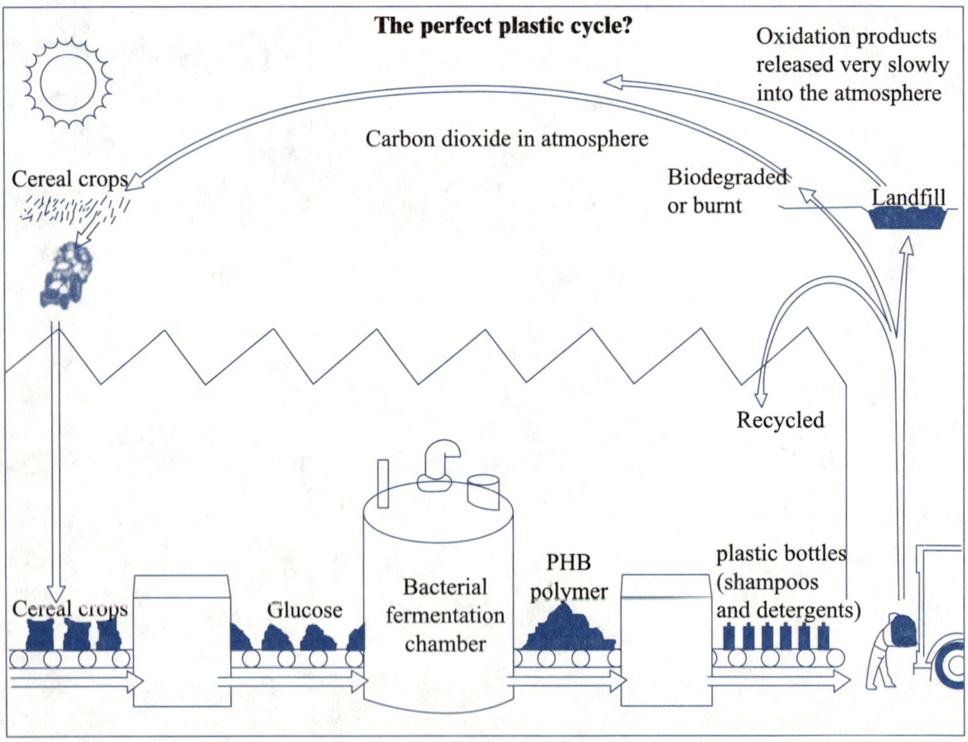

高分范文

As can be seen from the picture, the process of making, using and reclaiming plastic bottles is a circle.

First, cereal crops are harvested and taken to a factory, and glucose is extracted from them. Then the glucose passes into a bacterial fermentation chamber, where the process of fermentation produces a type of plastic called PHB polymer. This can be used to make plastic bottles to hold shampoos, detergents and so on.

When these plastic bottles are thrown away, they may be recycled by dustmen and delivered to the factories. In other words, they are used again in the same form. However, they may also be buried in a landfill. In this case, they are digested by bacteria in the soil and broken down. The oxidation products from the landfill sites are released slowly into the atmosphere. At the same time, other discarded bottles are burnt or biodegraded and send out carbon dioxide into the atmosphere. Cereal crops require carbon dioxide in order to grow, and then these crops are used in the manufacture of new plastic which may be used to make bottles again.

范文翻译

从这幅图画可以看出，塑料瓶从制作到利用再到回收是一个不断循环的过程。

首先，谷物收获以后会被送到工厂去，从中萃取出葡萄糖。然后把葡萄糖放入细菌发酵室里，在这里通过发酵过程产生一种塑料，叫做 PHB 聚合体。这种塑料可以被制作成用来装洗发水或清洁剂的瓶子。

当这种塑料瓶子被丢弃以后，它们可能被回收。换句话说，就是它们还可以以同样的形式再次被使用。然而，它们也有可能被掩埋在垃圾填埋场。在这种情况下，它们被土地里的细菌消化和分解。垃圾填埋场的氧化产物缓慢地释放到大气中。同时，其他被丢弃的瓶子会被燃烧或被生物降解，并且会向大气中释放二氧化碳。在这种情况下，谷物为了生长需要二氧化碳，然后这些谷物又会被用来制作成新的塑料，然后这种塑料再次被制成瓶子。

闪光词汇

★ **cereal** ['siəriəl] *n.* 谷类食品，谷类

Sam eats **cereal** for breakfast every day. 山姆每天早餐吃谷类食品。

★ **glucose** ['gluːkəus] *n.* 葡萄糖

We injected the **glucose** into the patient's vein. 我们给病人的静脉里注射了葡萄糖。

★ **extract** [iks'trækt] *vt.* 榨取

We can **extract** oil from olive. 我们可以从橄榄中榨油。

★ **bacterial fermentation** 细菌发酵（作用）

★ **polymer** ['pɔlimə] *n.* 聚合体

★ **detergent** [di'təːdʒənt] *n.* 清洁剂，去垢剂

This **detergent** will whiten your laundry. 洗洁剂会使你的衣服变白的。

★ **oxidation** [ˌɔksi'deiʃən] *n.* [化] 氧化

★ **biodegrade** [ˌbaiəudi'greid] *vt.* 生物递降分解

★ **carbon dioxide** [化] 二氧化碳

Carbon is an element, while **carbon dioxide** is a compound. 碳是元素，而二氧化碳是化合物。

Test 14
玻璃制作

WRITING TASK 1

You should spend about 20 minutes on this task.

The diagram below shows the process of glass recycling.

Using the information in the picture, write a description of the process. You may use your own knowledge and experience in addition to the diagram.

You should write at least 150 words.

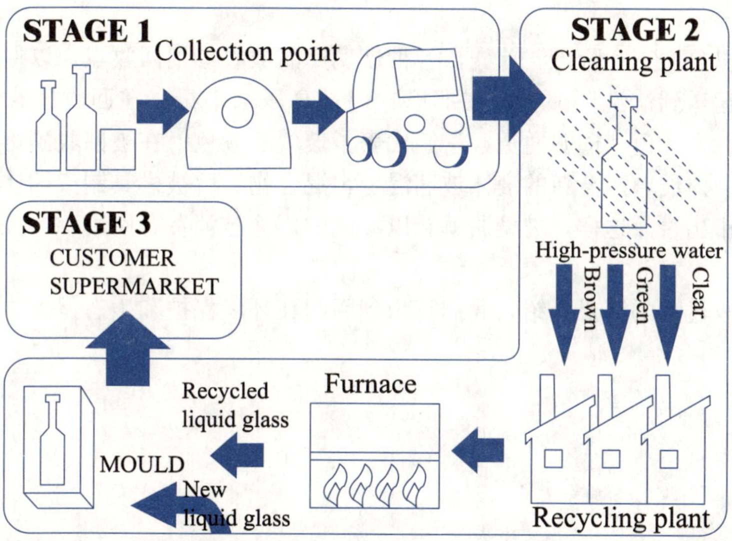

高分范文

The flow chart displays the recycling process of glass. As is shown in the picture，it is really a complex one.

The overall process can be categorized into three stages. First，glass products in various forms are gathered in the collection point，so that they are easily transported by special trucks or vans to the cleaning plant，where they get sterilization by high-pressure water. There are three different channels in the recycling plant，namely brown，green and clear，which represent the colors of glass. After recycled in the furnace，glass products are melted into recycled liquid glass. Mixed with new liquid glass，the compound is finally moulded into solid glass，which，afterwards，will be sent to various customer supermarkets for selling. Thus，the glass will go to the customers for different purposes.

Through a brief introduction of the circle of glass recycling，we realize that recycling plays a vital role in environmental protection and ecological preservation.

范文翻译

这个流程图展示了玻璃的回收过程。如图所示，这个过程是很复杂的。

全部的过程可以分为三个阶段。首先，各种玻璃产品被收集到回收点，以便被特殊的卡车或者有篷货车运送到清洗厂那里，在那里它们被高压水消毒。在回收厂有三个不同的通道，也就是棕色、绿色和透明通道，它们代表了玻璃的颜色。在被回收到熔炉以后，玻璃制品被融化成液体玻璃。与新的液体玻璃混合，混合物最后被模具制成固体玻璃瓶，然后被送到各种超市出售。这样，玻璃瓶就会以不同的用途被消费者使用。

通过对玻璃回收过程的简要介绍，我们意识到回收在环境保护和生态保护方面起着关键的作用。

闪光词汇

★ **flow chart** 流程图，生产过程图解

★ **categorize** [ˈkætigəraiz] *vt.* 将……归类，分类
We **categorize** information. 我们对信息进行分类。

★ **vital** [ˈvaitl] *adj.* 重大的，至关重要的
Perseverance is **vital** to success. 毅力对于成功是不可或缺的。

实用句型

Through a brief introduction of…，**we realize that** … 通过对……的简要介绍，我们意识到……
这种句型结构用于文章结尾，它要表达的重点不在于图画本身，作者是要升华主题，揭示图画所表达的深层内涵。
请看范文中的这句话：
Through a brief introduction of the circle of glass recycling，**we realize that** recycling plays a vital role in environmental protection and ecological preservation. 通过对玻璃回收过程的简要介绍，我们意识到回收在环境保护和生态保护方面起着关键的作用。

图书在版编目（CIP）数据

剑桥雅思最新真题题源详解．写作．学术类/刘民编著．—2 版．—北京：中国人民大学出版社，2011.8
ISBN 978-7-300-14137-4

Ⅰ．①剑… Ⅱ．①刘… Ⅲ．①IELTS－英语－写作－题解 Ⅳ．①H319.6

中国版本图书馆 CIP 数据核字（2011）第 169507 号

剑桥雅思最新真题题源详解——写作（学术类）（第二版）
刘民　编著
Jianqiao Yasi Zuixin Zhenti Tiyuan Xiangjie——Xizuo（Xueshu Lei）（Di-er Ban）

出版发行	中国人民大学出版社		
社　　址	北京中关村大街 31 号	邮政编码	100080
电　　话	010－62511242（总编室）		010－62511398（质管部）
	010－82501766（邮购部）		010－62514148（门市部）
	010－62515195（发行公司）		010－62515275（盗版举报）
网　　址	http://www.crup.com.cn		
	http://www.1kao.com.cn(中国 1 考网)		
经　　销	新华书店		
印　　刷	北京市易丰印刷有限责任公司	版　　次	2009 年 8 月第 1 版
规　　格	185 mm×260 mm　16 开本		2011 年 9 月第 2 版
印　　张	25	印　　次	2011 年 9 月第 1 次印刷
字　　数	397 000	定　　价	55.00 元